Voices for Children

Voices for Children

Rhetoric and Public Policy

William T. Gormley Jr.

BROOKINGS INSTITUTION PRESS
Washington, D.C.

ABOUT BROOKINGS

The Brookings Institution is a private nonprofit organization devoted to research, education, and publication on important issues of domestic and foreign policy. Its principal purpose is to bring the highest quality independent research and analysis to bear on current and emerging policy problems. Interpretations or conclusions in Brookings publications should be understood to be solely those of the authors.

Library of Congress Cataloging-in-Publication data
Gormley, William T., 1950–
    Voices for children : rhetoric and public policy / William T. Gormley Jr.
        p.   cm.
    Includes bibliographical references and index.
"Focuses on why children's issues and programs have been given less attention and monies compared to those for the elderly with emphasis on how the mass media have covered children's issues and how this has influenced public opinion and, in turn, lawmakers"—Provided by the publisher.
    ISBN 978-0-8157-2402-5 (pbk. : alk. paper)
    1. Child welfare—United States. 2. Children—United States—Social conditions. 3. Children—Services for—United States. I. Title.
    HV741.G645 2012
    362.70973—dc23   2012028178

9 8 7 6 5 4 3 2 1

Printed on acid-free paper

Typeset in Sabon

Composition by Cynthia Stock
Silver Spring, Maryland

Printed by R. R. Donnelley
Harrisonburg, Virginia

To Rosie and Angela

Contents

Acknowledgments

This book originated because I believe that we must improve the quality of public discourse about children and public policy. Based on a growing body of literature, issue frames seem to be particularly important. But we lack hard evidence on which issue frames advocates prefer, how this has changed over time, and which issue frames appeal to the general public and political elites. I sought to obtain that evidence and to weave it into a broader narrative about political persuasion.

My focus on children's issues is not accidental. For two decades I have devoted much of my own research agenda to our youngest citizens, whom we claim to love but who nevertheless often get short shrift when public policy is made. They deserve better public policies and a better future.

While writing this book, I benefited enormously from many people who offered advice, criticism, and support.

I would like to thank my colleagues at Georgetown University and especially the Georgetown Public Policy Institute for many intellectual contributions. I owe a special debt to Jon Ladd for helping me to think through the logistics of some issue-framing experiments, to Shay Bilchik, who helped me to understand child welfare and juvenile justice issues, and to E. J. Dionne, who did not always agree with me but who offered many opportunities to refine my arguments. Two faculty seminars at GPPI helped to sharpen my thinking.

I would like to thank Steve Wayne, Mark Rom, and Victor Cha for opening their classrooms to me for an issue-framing experiment that basically set this project in motion. I am also grateful to Dan Hopkins for very helpful comments and for recommending that I turn to Knowledge Networks for a vital second experiment. Stefan Subias at Knowledge Networks was accessible, resourceful, and responsive.

The Urban Institute kindly offered me an office for a year, so that I could concentrate on writing without interruption. Olivia Golden, Ajay Chaudry, Gina Adams, and others offered helpful criticisms and suggestions. At a critical juncture I also received excellent feedback from several faculty members at the University of Virginia's Batten School of Leadership and Public Policy. My thanks to Eric Patashnik for arranging this visit.

As this book took shape, several excellent research assistants gathered, coded, and analyzed data. Kitt Wolfenden, Mark Hines, Anne Hyslop, Emily Page, Helen Cymrot, Shirley Adelstein, and Kim Dancy did great work and were indispensable to this project. I would like to extend a special thanks to Meg Loftus for converting my text into documents that looked like actual newspaper articles.

I benefited greatly from conversations with people who have thought deeply about child advocacy, issue framing, or the policymaking process, including Susan Bales, Emily Holcombe, Mary Fairchild, Megan Foreman, Beth Fuchs, Sarah Hammond, Ron Haskins, Jack Hoadley, Nina Owcharenko, Tim Smeeding, Kent Weaver, Jim Weill, Amy Wilkins, and of course my long-time coconspirator, Deborah Phillips. Tim Bartik and two anonymous readers gave the penultimate draft a careful reading, which helped me to integrate my arguments better.

I am grateful to fifty children's advocates affiliated with Voices for America's Children who agreed to in-depth interviews on their organization's issue priorities, strategies, and tactics. Their ideas contributed significantly to chapter 3. I also owe a special debt to twenty-seven congressional staff members active in national children's policy debates and twenty-eight public officials and advocates active in state-level children's policy debates in Utah, Pennsylvania, North Carolina, and Connecticut. Without them, chapters 6 and 7 would not have been possible.

From the start, I thought that the Brookings Institution Press would be the perfect home for this book. I would like to thank Bob Faherty, director of the Press, for his early support; Janet Walker, managing editor, who oversaw the editing details with Diane Hammond, a meticulous copyeditor; and Larry Converse and Susan Woollen for their attention to the development of the cover, as well as the typesetting and printing.

Finally, I dedicate this book to the two women in my life: my wife, Rosie, and my daughter, Angela. At playgrounds, libraries, schools, and amusement parks (especially Harry Potter World) we have experienced the exhilarating joys of childhood together. Rosie and I want Angela to live in a world where these joys are within reach of every child.

CHAPTER ONE

Children:
Beloved but
Neglected

It must not for a moment be forgotten that the core of any social plan must be the child.

Franklin Roosevelt, 1935

The condition of children in the United States is marked by a puzzling paradox: we view children very positively, but our public policies do not reflect that positive view. The federal government spends seven times as much on senior citizens as it does on children. Although state and local governments spend much more on children than on the elderly, all governments in the United States, combined, spend 2.4 times as much on the elderly as on children.[1] Not surprisingly, given this considerable disparity, children are more likely than the elderly to be poor.

Poverty among senior citizens has declined dramatically since the 1960s, while poverty among children has not (figure 1-1).[2] In 2010, 22 percent of all children were poor, as opposed to 9 percent of senior citizens. The situation was even grimmer for minority children: more than a third of Hispanic children and 40 percent of African American children live in poverty. Recent statistics, which capture the effects of government safety net programs, are somewhat less alarming: according to the Census Bureau's supplemental poverty measure, the child poverty rate declines to 18 percent once social programs and tax deductions are taken into account.[3] On

1. Isaacs (2009).

2. Child poverty rates declined during the Clinton years, largely in response to a booming economy. Child poverty rates then rose during the George W. Bush years, partly in response to lower taxes and lower social program spending.

3. These same statistics show a higher poverty rate for seniors. However, many seniors have paid off their homes, thus reducing one set of expenses considerably.

Figure 1-1. *Poverty Rates for Children and Seniors, 1960–2010*

Percent

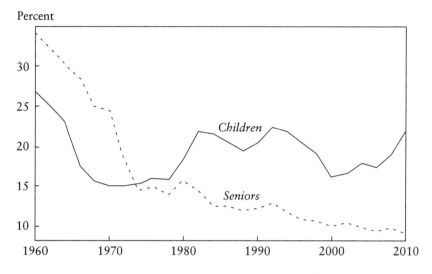

Source: U.S. Census Bureau (2011).

the other hand, these same revised figures suggest that we have underesti-
mated the near poor in our midst, including near-poor children.[4]

If we look beyond income to specific social conditions, the situation
facing many children is distressing. One of every ten children suffers from
asthma, approximately 14 percent of all students have one or more learning disabilities, one in four children lives in a household that runs out of
food, and one in four children is raised by a single parent—the highest rate
of any industrialized country.[5] Furthermore, one in four teen-aged girls
has a sexually transmitted infection, one in three school-aged children
is overweight or obese, and adolescents (aged twelve to nineteen years
old) are much more likely to be victims of violent crime than are adults.[6]
Overall, child well-being deteriorated during the 1980s. It improved during the 1990s, but since then, although community engagement and social
relationships indicators have improved, family economic well-being and

4. See Renwick (2011); Fletcher (2011); Sparks (2011); DeParle, Gebeloff, and
Tavernise (2011).

5. Mak (2011); Dillon (2007); Beckmann (2010); Associated Press (2011).

6. Waxman (2008, p. 1); Hellmich (2011); Child Trends (2010).

health indicators have deteriorated. It is telling that only 25 percent of young people are qualified to serve in the military.[7]

These statistics are worrisome not only because of what they imply for conditions experienced by children today but also because of what they portend when these children become adults. Numerous studies show that, as adults, people's earnings, crime rate, health, and mortality are influenced profoundly by their experiences as children: children who are overweight or obese are more susceptible to type 2 diabetes, asthma, and other diseases; abused and neglected children are more likely to experience depression and suicidal thoughts and more likely to engage in crime and substance abuse; and low-birth-weight children have lower test scores, educational attainment, wages, and probability of being employed as of age thirty-three. Children who grow up poor face a wide variety of adverse effects; specifically, economic deprivation before age five is associated with lower earnings and fewer work hours three decades later.[8]

Children who grow up in poor families are far less likely to complete high school, and children who fail to complete high school earn substantially less ($260,000) over the course of a lifetime than those who graduate from high school. Poor children who do not attend a high-quality preschool are more likely to be arrested and more likely to have substance abuse problems later in life. Family structure also matters: growing up with a divorced or never-married mother leads to worse schooling outcomes and more behavioral and psychological problems as an adult. Adult males are more likely to die early if they were raised by a father and stepmother than if they were raised by both biological parents.[9]

Despite these outcomes, the United States does not invest enough in its children, and this is especially true in comparison with government spending on the elderly. The spending gap between older and younger citizens is greater in the United States than in most other countries (although Greece, Japan, Italy, Spain, and Austria also tilt in that direction).[10] In part, U.S. spending reflects the fact that many programs for the elderly

7. See Szabo (2010); Watson and Dugger (2010, p. 135).
8. See Duncan and Brooks-Gunn (1997); Poppendieck (2010, p. 10); Stagner and Lansing (2009, p. 24); Currie and Hyson (1999); Duncan, Ziol-Guest, and Kalil (2010).
9. See Haveman, Wolfe, and Wilson (1997, p. 442); Rouse (2005, p. 24); Schweinhart and others (2005); Reynolds and others (2011); McLanahan (1997); Hayward and Gorman (2004).
10. Lynch (2006, p. 185).

are insurance programs, to which beneficiaries contributed earlier in life. But it also reflects societal values.

The United States is also less likely than other industrialized nations to adopt policies that assist children and families with children. Of twenty-nine advanced industrialized countries, only South Korea and the United States have no provisions for paid parental leave.[11] According to UNICEF, the United States ranks twentieth of twenty-one rich countries in overall child well-being. Among thirty industrialized countries, the United States ranks twenty-second in preventing low birth weight, twenty-third in neonatal mortality, twenty-seventh in infant mortality, and thirtieth in relative child poverty.[12]

In education, the evidence is similar. Tests of fifteen-year-olds in thirty-four OECD countries by the Program for International Student Assessment show that the United States ranks fourteenth in reading literacy, seventeenth in science, and twenty-fifth in math. U.S. students do about as well as students in Estonia and Poland. The U.S. high school dropout rate, compared to other industrialized nations, is worse than the average. Approximately one-fourth of all U.S. public high school students fail to complete high school on time or at all. The college graduation rate for adults ages twenty-five to thirty-four has slipped to sixteenth place among thirty-six developed nations.[13] Unlike most industrialized countries, the United States has no children's allowance or family allowance.[14]

In addition, America's children face an unprecedented financial challenge when they grow up, due to deficits and national debt levels that threaten the country's economic future. Federal spending in 2010 represented 24 percent of GDP, the highest level since World War II. At the same time, tax levels represented only 15 percent of GDP, the lowest level since 1950. U.S. national debt has increased dramatically, from 33 percent of GDP in 2001 to 62 percent of GDP in 2010. Without draconian reforms, it will escalate even higher. By 2025, if trends continue, federal revenue will be sufficient to cover entitlements and interest payments

11. Australia began a paid parental leave program in 2011.
12. See Kamerman (2004); UNICEF (2007, p. 2); Edelman (2009, p. 15).
13. This statistic reflects the possession of either a two-year or four-year degree. The United States ranks second, behind Norway, in the share of adults aged twenty-five to sixty-four with four-year degrees. See DeParle, Gebeloff, and Tavernise (2011); de Vise (2011). However, many economists believe that two-year degrees with practical utility are more beneficial in today's economy than four-year liberal arts degrees.
14. See Duncan (2010a); Jacobson (2010); Rumberger (2011).

only; everything else will have to be borrowed. As then New Hampshire senator Judd Gregg noted in supporting recommendations from the cochairs of the President's National Commission on Fiscal Responsibility and Reform, "We are putting future generations in a terrible predicament, with few options and even fewer opportunities."[15]

In many ways, it is a Catch-22 situation. If we spend more money on children and fail to raise taxes, then we raise the short-term deficit and the national debt, to the detriment of children today and tomorrow. Yet if we do not spend more money on children and think more creatively about children's needs, then their conditions are likely to worsen. Either way, it seems, children lose out.

Why We Neglect Children

There are several possible explanations for public policy neglect of children in the United States. First, and most obviously, children don't vote. Unlike senior citizens, who vote in record numbers, children cannot demand that politicians attend to their needs. Instead, they must rely on surrogates, including parents and advocacy groups. Many of these surrogates are clever, devoted, and resourceful. Unlike other advocates, however, they cannot mobilize those who stand to benefit the most from public policy reform.[16]

This handicap is less critical in parliamentary systems, which make it easier for governments to enact legislation, but it is a big challenge in the United States, where divided government and polarized political parties make coalition building difficult. Thus while children can't vote in Great Britain or Canada either, this seems to be less of an impediment to the passage of prochild legislation. In contrast to the United States, Canada has a universal child care benefit for all parents with young children, and Great Britain has universal preschool for three-year-olds and four-year-olds. Thanks to a strong commitment by Tony Blair and the New Labour Party, Great Britain's child poverty rate has plummeted to the point where it is now half that of the United States. Differences in political systems help to explain these policy differences.[17]

Second, although the American people have a soft spot for children, children are not unique in being positively constructed. When Shanto

15. See National Commission (2010, p. 10); Bai (2010); Gregg (2010).
16. Franklin (2008); Schattschneider (1960).
17. See Waldfogel (2010, p. 79).

Iyengar exposed randomly assigned subjects to television news clips on poverty, featuring different individuals suffering from poverty, he found that respondents viewed children, elderly widows, and unemployed males in positive terms, attributing their poverty to societal causes; in contrast, respondents viewed single mothers (both adults and teenagers) in negative terms, attributing their poverty to individual failings. When Fay Cook and Edith Barrett asked a cross-section of Americans to assess several demographic groups in terms of deserving financial assistance, they rated the disabled elderly and the poor elderly highest, followed by poor children. Disabled adults, poor female family heads, and poor unemployed men received lower ratings. In short, children are generally viewed as deserving claimants, but so too are other groups in society. When attention and resources are scarce, as they often are, children must compete with other positively constructed constituencies for public support.[18]

Third, the mass media devote a fair amount of attention to children and public policy (education, child health, and, to a lesser extent, child welfare), but mass media coverage has not galvanized the American public to support a strong children's agenda. Trends in *New York Times* coverage help to explain why. As figure 1-2 indicates, this newspaper's attention to children's issues has sometimes been substantial, as in 1997.[19] However, the number of children's stories has declined since 1997.[20] Coverage rebounded again in 2003 but declined after that. More generally, the absolute amount of mass media coverage of children's issues leaves something to be desired, when one considers that most big-city newspapers devote much less attention to children's issues than the *New York Times*.[21] There may also be problems with the kind of coverage children's

18. See Iyengar (1991, pp. 59–61); Cook and Barrett (1992, p. 72).

19. Congressional consideration of the Children's Health Insurance Program (CHIP) bill and widespread coverage of Catholic Church sex scandals in the United States contributed to extensive coverage of children's issues in 1997.

20. A possible explanation for declining news coverage might be the phenomenon of shrinking "news holes" in U.S. newspapers. However, according to a *New York Times* editor, the paper has been largely immune from this trend. See also Pressman (2008).

21. A systematic comparison of *New York Times* stories on children with those of nine other big-city newspapers for a three-month period (January through March 1997) reveals that the *New York Times,* on average, ran about twice as many stories on children's issues as the other newspapers. Presumably, this is because the *Times* has a much bigger news hole. The nine newspapers were *Chicago Sun-Times, Denver Post, Houston Chronicle, Minneapolis Star-Tribune, Philadelphia Inquirer, Pittsburgh Post-Gazette, Richmond Times-Dispatch, St. Louis Post-Dispatch*, and *San Francisco Chronicle*.

Figure 1-2. *Mass Media Coverage of Children's Issues, 1960–2005*

Number of articles

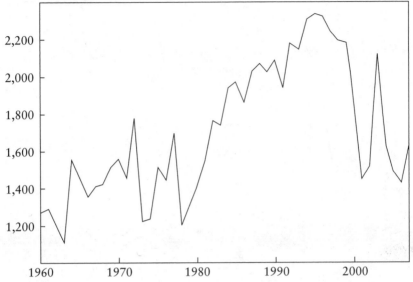

Source: Author's compilation based on ProQuest search of the *New York Times*. Search used these parameters: "child or children or youth w/15 law or policy or program or Congress or legislation or legislative or legislator or government or governor or mayor and not classified ad, display ad, obituary, rebroadcast."

issues receive—for example, too many episodic frames that focus on a single person or event and imply individual responsibility, not enough thematic frames that provide more background information and imply social responsibility.[22] According to Iyengar, episodic frames draw attention to the human interest aspects of a story rather than to the story's policy implications.

Fourth, Congress devotes a good deal of attention to children but frequently fails to act decisively in support of bold new initiatives that are likely to make a substantial difference in children's daily lives. Congress has devoted many hearings to children and public policy, averaging about a hundred per congressional session (figure 1-3). Many of these hearings concern elementary and secondary education, a subject of considerable interest on Capitol Hill and elsewhere. Congress has also enacted a good

22. Iyengar (1991).

Figure 1-3. *Congressional Hearings on Children, 1961–2008*

Number of hearings

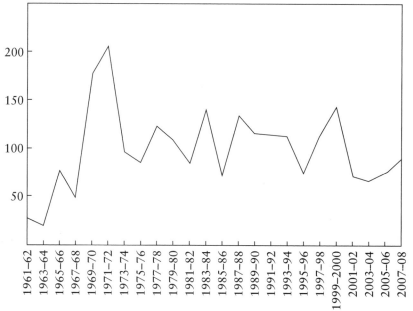

Source: Author's compilation using a series of LEXIS/congressional commands to identify hearings involving children, elementary and secondary education, Medicaid, and juvenile justice. Appropriations hearings are not included.

deal of children's legislation over the past four decades (see box 1-1). On the other hand, Congress has missed golden opportunities to transform the policy landscape in support of children. Occasionally, Congress has acted boldly, but the president has not. For example, during the Nixon administration, Congress passed the Comprehensive Child Development Act that would have established voluntary but universal child care throughout the country. President Richard Nixon vetoed the bill in December 1971, lamenting the bill's "fiscal irresponsibility, administrative unworkability and family-weakening implications."[23]

Fifth, while state legislatures have spent more money per capita on children than Congress has, they are severely constrained by constitutional requirements to balance their budgets annually. Some states, such

23. Cohen (2001, p. 51).

as California and Colorado, face additional constraints on tax increases to finance worthy programs. While state and local government officials can borrow money, by issuing bonds, to meet their physical capital needs, they may not do so to meet their human capital needs. Apart from these constitutional and legal limitations, state and local public officials face intense political opposition to tax increases that are needed to finance children's programs. As a result, children's advocates at the state and local levels must often settle for incremental progress at best.[24]

Sixth, the United States does not have strong government institutions explicitly designed to protect children. There is no cabinet-level department for children. Unlike ninety-three other countries, the United States does not have a national Youth Council. There is a Children's Bureau within the federal Department of Health and Human Services, but it has been transferred from one department to another over the years and is relatively small.[25] The House of Representatives used to have a Select Committee on Children, Youth, and Families (created in 1983), but it was abolished in 1993. By contrast, the Senate Special Committee on Aging, first created (as a temporary committee) in 1961, endures.[26] The states are not much better than the federal government in their institutional arrangements. Only twenty-nine states have a children's ombudsman office or an office of child advocate. Only sixteen states have children's cabinets—organizations that promote collaboration across state agencies with jurisdictions over children's issues. Only twelve states have a state youth council. In contrast, all fifty states have a nursing home ombudsman.[27]

In many ways, the deck is stacked against children in the United States. The country has a presidential system in which agreement between the legislative and the executive branches of government is necessary for significant policy change to occur. It has a federal system in which the level of government that focuses on children has to abide by constitutional constraints on spending, while the level of government

24. See Bartik (2011); Gainsborough (2010).

25. According to a staff member, the Children's Bureau employs 168 people, including both central and regional staff. Teferra (2012).

26. The creation of the Senate Caucus on Foster Youth in 2009 is a small step toward rectifying Congress's institutional weaknesses on children's issues, but its focus is quite narrow.

27. See Ferber (2010, pp. 42–43); Sardell (1990, pp. 277, 281); Cohen (2001); Davidson (2010, p. 75); National Governors Association (2004); National Long-Term Care (no date).

Box 1-1. *Selected Federal Laws Dealing with Children, 1965–2010*

Johnson administration
Head Start (Economic Opportunity Act), 1965
Medicaid (Social Security Act amendments), 1965
Elementary and Secondary Education Act, 1965
Child Nutrition Act, 1966
Child Protection Act, 1966
Child Health Act, 1967

Nixon administration
Women, Infants, and Children Program (Child Nutrition Act amendments), 1972
Child Abuse Prevention and Treatment Act, 1974

Ford administration
Juvenile Justice and Delinquency Prevention Act, 1974
Education for All Handicapped Children Act, 1975
Earned Income Tax Credit, 1975
Child Support Enforcement Program, 1975

Carter administration
Adolescent Health, Services, and Pregnancy Prevention and Care Act, 1978
Department of Education Organization Act, 1979
Adoption Assistance and Child Welfare Act, 1980

Reagan administration
Job Training Partnership Act, 1983
Comprehensive Child Development Act, 1987
Child Abuse, Prevention, Adoption, and Family Services Act, 1988
Family Support Act, 1988

---

that focuses on the elderly does not. The institutional arrangements to ensure that children's voices are heard are relatively weak. The general public has a soft spot for children, but it is easily placated by symbolic policies that do more to reassure than to solve the basic problems facing children. Under these adverse circumstances, the United States needs better arguments in support of children and children's programs than it has used in the past. Some features of the political system are relatively permanent and hard to change, but policy arguments in support

G. H. W. Bush administration
Children's Television Act, 1990
Child Care and Development block grants, 1990
Uniform Interstate Family Support Act, 1992

Clinton administration
Vaccines for Children Program (Medicaid amendments), 1993
Family and Medical Leave Act, 1993
Family Preservation and Family Support Services Act, 1993
Individuals with Disabilities in Education Act, 1995
Personal Responsibility and Work Opportunity Act, 1996
State Children's Health Insurance Program, 1997
Child Tax Credit (Taxpayer Relief Act), 1997
Adoption and Safe Families Act, 1997
Workforce Investment Act, 1998
Child Online Protection Act, 1998
Education Flexibility Partnership Act, 1999

G. W. Bush administration
No Child Left Behind Act (ESEA reauthorization), 2001
Promoting Safe and Stable Families Act, amended, 2001
Prosecutorial Remedies and Other Tools to End the Exploitation of Children Today, 2003
Adam Walsh Child Protection and Safety Act, 2006

Obama administration
Children's Health Insurance Program, amended, 2009
Patient Protection and Affordable Care Act, 2010
Healthy, Hunger Free Kids Act, 2010

of children can be changed for the better, if we know what works and if we resolve to do something about it.

Policy Arguments

The outcomes of debates over children and public policy depend in part on the policy arguments that are made in support of particular programs. Some arguments will be more persuasive than others, or more persuasive at a particular time, or more persuasive to a particular audience. This is not to diminish the importance of power, money, connections, and politics to the policymaking process.[28] Despite these forces, policy arguments play a significant role in what transpires. The argument that African Americans deserve an equal opportunity to share in the American dream helped to shape the outcome of federal civil rights legislation. The argument that air and water pollution threaten our health and our planet's health helped to stimulate passage of federal environmental legislation. The argument that the poor need a hand up and not a handout helped to shape the outcome of state and federal welfare policy debates.

What exactly is a policy argument? According to Giandomenico Majone, "argumentation is the key process through which citizens and policymakers arrive at moral judgments and policy choices."[29] This definition is instructive, because it highlights the importance of both value choices and public policy choices and the connection between the two. It does, however, neglect the importance of evidence, often a critical component of policy arguments. Thus I define a full-fledged policy argument as a statement that explicitly or implicitly connects values, evidence, and public policy choices.

A full-fledged policy argument may be many pages in length, with a clear exposition of value priorities, lots of tables and graphs, and specific public policy recommendations. In practice, however, most policy arguments are brief, and they often require the listener or the reader to connect the dots. A policy recommendation may be implied, rather than stated outright; relevant evidence may receive only passing attention; a reference to values may be oblique. In truth, most of the policy arguments that we digest as citizens are sound bites rather than treatises.

At the heart of most policy arguments is an issue frame, or what James Druckman refers to as an emphasis frame. An emphasis frame draws attention to a particular issue or value.[30] A frame in communication focuses on what a speaker says, while a frame in thought focuses on what

---

28. Lindblom (1977); Webb Yackee and Webb Yackee (2006); Baumgartner and others (2009).

29. Majone (1989, p. 2).

30. By way of contrast, an equivalency frame refers to a phrase that is logically equivalent to another phrase but that has a differential impact on listeners (such as a reference to an increase in jobs as opposed to a decrease in unemployment). See Kahneman and Tversky (1984).

a person thinks. As Druckman explains, "When a frame in communication affects an individual's frame in thought, it is called a *framing* effect."[31]

In table 1-1, I highlight differences in policy arguments for four widely used issue frames: the helping hand, equal opportunity, prevention, and investment. For any given frame, some policy arguments are more carefully delineated than others. An argument so brief that it can fit on a bumper sticker (in my lexicon, a truncated argument) may not be dense enough to change anyone's thinking. On the other hand, a memorable phrase, such as "the death tax" as a pejorative reference to the estate tax, can play a significant role in shaping some policy debates.[32]

Whatever their length, all policy arguments are not created equal. A helping-hand argument, with biblical roots, is easy to articulate and easy to understand. On the other hand, while it may help to mobilize supporters, it may not be powerful enough to convert skeptics into supporters. An equal opportunity argument, which appeals to shared values and evokes the American dream, enjoys some bipartisan appeal. On the other hand, its potency depends on the perception that equal opportunity has not been fully realized and that the policy in question promotes equal opportunity but not necessarily equal results. A prevention argument, which tries to avoid bad outcomes in the future, takes advantage of the fact that most of us are risk-averse.[33] It is also, in principle, empirically verifiable, but this is a double-edged sword—evidence must be convincing if the argument is to prevail. An investment argument, which seeks to promote good outcomes in the future, may be especially attractive in hard times, when difficult trade-offs must be made. However, like the prevention argument, it depends on good evidence, which may or may not be available.

For any of these arguments to make a difference in public debates, they must be covered by the mass media with some regularity and in some depth. Thus a key challenge to children's advocates is to make strong arguments that are also well publicized. If mass media coverage of good policy arguments on behalf of children is fleeting and fragmentary, children's policies are likely to remain weak.

In the pages ahead, I argue that children's policies differ from other public policies in two crucial respects. First, programs that benefit children

31. Druckman (2011, p. 282).
32. Graetz and Shapiro (2005).
33. Kahneman and Tversky (1979).

Table 1-1. *Policy Arguments, Children's Programs, Four Frames*

Frame	Truncated	Intermediate	Full
Helping hand	We should help the needy.	It is a moral obligation to help poor, disadvantaged, and handicapped children.	The test of a good and compassionate society is how it treats its most vulnerable citizens, including its children. We are all God's creatures, members of the same human race.
Equal opportunity	Every child deserves an equal opportunity.	Every child is entitled to develop his or her capacity to the fullest extent possible, in the pursuit of the American dream.	Every child deserves an equal opportunity to attend a good school, to eat three nutritious meals a day, to be healthy, and to go on to be gainfully employed. Everyone should have a fair chance at the American dream.
Prevention	Prevention makes sense.	Preventive health care spending on children today saves taxpayer money in the future.	If we spend money on preventive health care, children will grow up healthier, miss less school, and experience greater success in life. They will be more productive citizens and will require less hospitalization.
Investment	Preschool is a good investment.	Government spending on preschool today will yield self-supporting and productive members of society tomorrow.	Children who attend a high-quality preschool are better prepared for school, less likely to repeat a grade, less likely to drop out of high school, less likely to commit crimes, and more likely to become productive taxpayers.

are likely to have bigger long-run positive impacts on society than many other programs, because improvements in human capital early in life yield positive returns over a longer period of time. But second, programs that benefit children in the distant future are less likely than other programs to appeal to politicians, whose electoral time horizons direct their attention to the short run. Given these facts of life, hard-headed investment and prevention arguments have a special appeal, especially when combined with good evidence.

Plan for the Book

In this chapter, I focus on a puzzling paradox: we view children positively, but our public policies do not reflect that positive view. Across a wide range of indicators, children in the United States fare poorly when compared to children in other industrialized countries. Children in the United States also fare poorly when compared to senior citizens. I consider several possible explanations for such neglect of children. I also argue that one possible solution is for advocates to develop and publicize strong policy arguments in support of children's programs. As with a sports franchise facing formidable competition, children's advocates must work harder and think more creatively to even the odds.

In chapter 2, I contend that arguments used in support of children's programs and initiatives have changed significantly since the 1960s, from a heavy reliance on moralistic arguments (rights, obligations, compassion) to a growing reliance on economic arguments (societal benefits exceed societal costs). In support of that proposition, I document changes in congressional testimony by top administration spokespersons and congressional testimony by a leading child advocate, Marian Wright Edelman of the Children's Defense Fund. Rhetorical changes seem to have occurred in the 1980s as a response to the rhetoric of President Ronald Reagan. More broadly, the shift can be traced to growing awareness of budget deficits, a decline in religious sentiment and church attendance, changes in the racial and cultural composition of American society, and the rise of think tanks and empirical policy analysis. Unfortunately, although mass media coverage of economic arguments in support of children's programs has increased since the 1960s, mass media articles on children that reference an economic frame represent a relatively small fraction of all articles on children. A revolution in rhetoric has gone largely unnoticed by the general public.

In chapter 3, I show that despite a growing reliance on economic arguments, advocates deploy an economic frame more frequently in certain policy domains than in others. In early childhood education, advocates cite academic studies attesting to favorable benefit-cost ratios for early intervention programs, especially preschool programs. In child health, advocates stress the advantages of prevention, which avoids the high costs of hospitalization and emergency room care for those who become acutely or chronically ill. In contrast, child welfare arguments typically focus on the need to protect vulnerable children from harm and to provide them with safe and secure homes. Interviews with state-level child advocates confirm these differences. In short, advocates do not consistently use economic arguments.

In chapter 4, I shift the focus from policy domains to venues. Are rhetorical differences apparent when the judiciary and the political branches deal with the same kinds of children's issues? In contrast to the political branches of the government, the judiciary has long been associated with arguments that focus on legal rights and obligations. These arguments closely resemble moralistic arguments in their form and structure. Issue frames used by judges, advocates, and politicians are strikingly similar on certain issues, especially school finance, special education, school desegregation, and juvenile justice. In all of these issue areas, participants rely heavily on moralistic and legalistic, rather than economic, policy arguments.

Many studies attest to the ability of issue frames to affect both public perceptions and public support. But few framing studies focus on children, and fewer still juxtapose prochild arguments with protaxpayer arguments. In chapter 5, I report the results of two randomized experiments that do precisely that: a survey of 278 Georgetown University freshmen that focuses on a proposed Nurse-Family Partnership program; and an Internet survey of 1,039 Americans that focuses on a proposed expansion of Head Start. Newspaper articles were drafted that discuss these debates. All respondents were exposed to a protaxpayer argument; most respondents were also exposed to a prochild argument, which varied across respondents. Together, these two studies permit an assessment of the relative merits of moralistic and economic frames, in general and for specific subgroups.

In chapter 6, I use qualitative research techniques, including in-depth interviews with key public officials and advocates, to answer the question: Can issue framing make a difference in today's politically polarized and economically constrained state legislatures? Historically, state governments have done more to help children than the federal government. However, fiscal constraints and conservative values pose formidable obstacles to legislative proposals for new government programs or expansions of existing programs. How do policy arguments in support of children fare when they run up against budget deficits and political opposition in statehouses? Four case studies, in Connecticut (juvenile justice), Utah (early childhood education), North Carolina (taxes, education), and Pennsylvania (home visits to assist poor mothers with young children), help to place policy arguments in perspective. Powerful ideas can help, when combined with smart legislative tactics, strong gubernatorial endorsement, broad-based external support (especially coalitions), good empirical evidence, and favorable economic conditions. But in many situations a legislative victory secures only temporary benefits for children. As fiscal constraints worsen, even successful programs, like North Carolina's Smart Start and More at Four programs, find themselves struggling to survive.

Can issue framing affect children's policies at the national level? In chapter 7, I attempt to answer that question. In recent years Congress has become much more polarized along party lines, as moderates from both parties have lost at the polls. Interviews with twenty-seven Democratic and Republican congressional committee staff members who deal with children's issues reveal sharp party differences on arguments that promote children's programs and arguments that caution against them. In reflecting on congressional policymaking, staff members cite the power of compelling stories, personal experiences, evidence, and issue frames. Ultimately, though, judgments by the Congressional Budget Office matter more than evidence that programs work in the long run. As one staff member puts it, "Economic arguments matter, but what really matters is CBO scoring." Although CBO scoring in some ways epitomizes economic issue framing, it systematically undervalues early childhood intervention programs by excluding from consideration impacts beyond the first ten years.

Children's issue frames have helped to shape public policy in recent decades at both the federal and state levels. Thanks to winning issue frames, prekindergarten programs, children's health initiatives, juvenile justice reforms, home visitation programs, and other policies that benefit children have been adopted and sustained. In chapter 8, I attempt to place these findings in perspective. Although frames can make a difference, they sometimes collide with powerful political, social, and economic forces. Trends toward selective media exposure and hyperpartisanship in legislative bodies pose a threat to children's issue frames and children's programs, because they limit opportunities for persuasion. The growing national debt, and growing awareness of it, and the diminished role played by discretionary spending have also reduced opportunities for frames to make a difference. Despite these obstacles, issue frames will continue to matter, especially for certain subsets of the electorate. I conclude by discussing the relative potency of economic and moralistic frames and the relative importance of frames in general.

CHAPTER TWO

The Rise of
Economic Arguments

Protect the children!
Professor Harold Hill, River City, Iowa, 1962

In this chapter, I show that the arguments used in support of children's programs and initiatives have changed since the 1960s, from a heavy reliance on moralistic arguments to a growing reliance on economic arguments. Moralistic arguments remain prominent, however, especially in certain policy contexts, and the mass media have been slow to recognize the rise of economic arguments on social issues. Nevertheless, this shift is important because it signifies a possible change in societal values, interest group tactics, rhetorical choices by public officials, or all of the above.

Moralistic arguments are usually easy to spot, because they typically use such words as *ought, deserve,* and *entitled.* They sometimes include an explicit reference to rights (of individuals, groups) or the right thing to do. They are often accompanied by passionate rhetoric, though that alone does not distinguish moralistic from economic arguments. One straightforward way to think about moralistic arguments is that they are what ethicists would call deontological arguments.[1] A deontological argument is one that stresses moral obligations, irrespective of consequences. Thus a classic deontological argument would be Immanuel Kant's categorical imperative, which says, Act in such a way that your action could be considered a universal law for human behavior. From this point of view, stealing and lying are always immoral because they cannot be universalized as good behaviors, even if the consequences of stealing or lying in a particular instance might be good.

1. Frankena (1973).

Two contemporary examples of moralistic arguments are the helping-hand argument and the equal opportunity argument. The helping-hand argument says, in effect, that we should assist those who are weak, vulnerable, poor, disabled, or otherwise disadvantaged. Sometimes it is linked to religious themes or stories, such as the parable of the Good Samaritan, which praises a man for rendering assistance to a stranger in need of help. The underlying message is the core message of Christianity itself: Love thy neighbor as thyself! Arthur Flemming, President Eisenhower's secretary of the Department of Health, Education, and Welfare (HEW), embraced this view explicitly at the White House Conference on Children and Youth in 1960:

> As this Golden Anniversary Conference is about to pass into history, I find myself thinking of a spiritual law of life and of its relationship to your deliberations and to our hopes and aspirations for the future. The spiritual law to which I refer is this: Thou shalt love thy neighbor as thyself. It lies, as all of us recognize, at the heart of our Judeo-Christian tradition. It places upon us a common responsibility.[2]

Flemming went on to cite a sermon and to elaborate on his own personal religious faith.

The equal opportunity argument is just as familiar to most of us. It says that each of us is entitled to an equal opportunity to succeed in life and to enjoy the many benefits that life has to offer. As Arthur Okun notes, equal opportunity is generally understood to mean a "fair race," in which people are even at the starting line. Equal opportunity may apply to education, health, housing, employment, and other sectors as well. Equal opportunity is often distinguished from equal results: the government should not guarantee equal outcomes to everyone but should guarantee equal chances to excel, to succeed, and to be productive. This reflects the general view that most of us need some material incentives to be as productive as we can be; this leads to some inequalities in income. In Okun's words, "Any insistence on carving the pie into equal slices would shrink the size of the pie."[3] Even John Rawls, a strong proponent of equality, does not endorse equality at any price. His argument, in a nutshell, is that inequality is justifiable when it actually benefits the least advantaged

2. Flemming (1960, p. 308).
3. Okun (1975, pp. 48, 76).

members of society, as in the case of certain progrowth policies that help the rich more than the poor but that nonetheless do help the poor.[4]

Although I characterize equal opportunity arguments as moralistic, one could certainly view many such arguments as legalistic as well. Equal opportunity provisions have been included in many pieces of legislation, especially civil rights laws. When someone invokes equal opportunity, he or she may be saying, We need to provide equal opportunity because the law demands it. Of course, that is still a deontological argument, because it is rooted in an obligation (in this instance, a legal obligation), not in the perceived consequences of the action.

Economic arguments, as I characterize them, do not necessarily refer to the state of the economy. In a nutshell, economic arguments are what ethicists would call teleological arguments or what some policy analysts would call rational-instrumental arguments or socially efficient arguments. They justify action, in ethical terms, by focusing on the short-term or long-term consequences of that action. A classic example of teleological thinking is John Stuart Mill's utilitarianism. From Mill's perspective, we should promote "the greatest good for the greatest number." This is what economists today would call Pareto optimality. It is, in effect, the foundation of welfare economics, the cornerstone of microeconomics.[5]

Two contemporary examples of economic arguments are the prevention argument and the investment argument. The prevention argument says that we should adopt policies or programs that prevent bad things from happening in the future. These bad things include crime, disease, child abuse, and other pathologies. The virtues of prevention are embedded in our culture, as in Ben Franklin's famous epigram, An ounce of prevention is worth a pound of cure.[6] This adage is so popular that a children's advocacy group has adopted it as its name: the Ounce of Prevention Fund, based in Chicago, seeks to broaden access to a high-quality early childhood education for poor children from birth to age five.

Like the prevention argument, the investment argument focuses on future consequences (to all), not moral duties (to the individual) per se. The investment argument, in this context, refers not to savings but to expenditures on human capital that can be expected to benefit both the

---

4. Rawls (1971).
5. See Frankena (1973); Mucciaroni (2011, p. 191); Esterling (2004, p. 4).
6. Labaree (1960, p. 12).

individual and society in the long run. In effect, the investment argument says that a smart society develops the skills of its populace so that they can be productive taxpayers, competitive workers, and thoughtful citizens. The investment argument figures most prominently in debates over education policy (at various ages), but it also surfaces in employment policy (such as job training programs).

It is, of course, possible to apply the words *prevention* and *investment* to individual, not group, consequences. One can justify child immunization programs by noting the benefits that flow to those who get immunized as opposed to the benefits to those who otherwise would have to pay for the consequences of nonimmunization. One can justify government expenditures on education by noting the benefits that flow to those who get educated as opposed to the benefits that others experience from having neighbors who are productive workers and well-informed citizens. Depending on how they are phrased, these kinds of arguments sometimes blend moralistic and economic reasoning by arguing that the right thing to do (for individuals) is also the smart thing to do (for society).

In some respects, the investment argument, which offers the promise of positive consequences, is the flip side of the prevention argument, which threatens negative consequences. From this perspective, a summer school program for teenagers could be thought of as a way to prevent teenagers from dropping out of high school (prevention) or as a way to develop critical skills that will be useful later in life (investment). In many instances, advocates can convert a prevention argument into an investment argument or vice versa, through a modest change in phrasing. Some advocates even blur the distinction between the two arguments by recommending that we invest in prevention.

Moralistic Arguments and the Great Society

Equal opportunity was the cornerstone of President Lyndon Johnson's Great Society. It animated and justified his War on Poverty, civil rights legislation, the Head Start program, education reform, health reform, and other social policy initiatives. For Johnson, and for many public officials and activists in the 1960s, equal opportunity, in practice, meant equal opportunity for African Americans, who had long been deprived of equal rights. Johnson made this emphatic in his famous remarks at Howard University's commencement on June 4, 1965:

We seek not just freedom but opportunity. We seek not just legal equity but human ability, not just equality as a right and a theory but equality as a fact and equality as a result. For the task is to give 20 million Negroes the same chance as every other American to learn and grow, to work and share in society, to develop their abilities—physical, mental and spiritual, and to pursue their individual happiness. To this end equal opportunity is essential, but not enough, not enough.[7]

Note that in this remarkable speech Johnson actually embraced both equal opportunity and equal results. This is noteworthy—and unusual. In most of his public utterances, Johnson calls for equal opportunity, not equal results.[8] What he probably meant to convey in this particular passage was his conviction that equal opportunity must be more than just symbolic talk, that it must be taken seriously, that it should be a firm commitment, and that it should lead, eventually, to better outcomes for African Americans, who have long been victimized by discrimination.

In arguing for a War on Poverty, Johnson occasionally employed economic reasoning as well. In a private conversation with Representative George Mahon (D-Tex.), for example, he justified the War on Poverty this way: "I'm going to take tax-eaters and make taxpayers out of them." In public utterances, he sometimes referred to spending on poor youth as a "sound investment." When he signed the Economic Opportunity Act on August 20, 1964, he stressed both benefits to the poor and benefits to society as a whole: "Today for the first time in all the history of the human race, a great nation is able to make a commitment to eradicate poverty among its people. . . . In helping others, all of us will really be helping ourselves. . . . I firmly believe that as of this moment a new day of opportunity is dawning and a new era of progress is opening for us all."[9]

This same mix of moralistic and economic arguments is evident in Johnson's pleas for passage of the Elementary and Secondary Education Act of 1965, which pumped an unprecedented amount of federal funding into poor school districts. In justifying this bill to Congress, Johnson stressed both the moral imperative of equal educational opportunity and an economic rationale:

7. Johnson (1965a).
8. Davies (1996, pp. 30–53).
9. Johnson (1964, p. 989). See also McKee (2010, p. 11); Dallek (1998, p. 74).

I propose that we declare a national goal of full educational opportunity. Every child must be encouraged to get as much education as he has the ability to take. We want this not only for his sake—but for the nation's sake. Nothing matters more to the future of our country: not our military preparedness—our armed might is worthless if we lack the brain power to build a world of peace; not our productive economy—for we cannot sustain growth without trained manpower; not our democratic system of government—for freedom is fragile if citizens are ignorant.[10]

Nevertheless, in most of his public comments on poverty, education, and civil rights, Johnson stressed moral obligations. As he put it in defending the Civil Rights Bill, "This bill is going to be enacted because justice and morality demand it."[11]

Johnson was not the only public figure in the 1960s to speak passionately in support of equal opportunity. The Reverend Martin Luther King Jr. pleaded for equal opportunity for African Americans, in particular, in numerous speeches and in marches, protests, and boycotts, especially in the South. He was perhaps most eloquent in his remarks on the steps of the Lincoln Memorial on August 28, 1963:

I have a dream that one day this nation will rise up and live out the true meaning of its creed—we hold these truths to be self-evident, that all men are created equal. I have a dream that one day on the red hills of Georgia, the sons of former slaves and the sons of former slave-owners will be able to sit down together at the table of brotherhood. I have a dream that one day, even the state of Mississippi, a state sweltering with the heat of oppression, will be transformed into an oasis of freedom and justice. I have a dream that my four little children will one day live in a nation where they will not be judged by the color of their skin but by the content of their character. I have a dream today![12]

During the 1960s, scholars and public intellectuals proved valuable allies in the struggle for equal opportunity in the United States. In his book *The Other America*, Michael Harrington presents a scathing

---

10. Johnson (1965b, p. 26).
11. Dallek (1998, p. 112; also see pp. 54–121).
12. Garrow (1986, pp. 283–84).

portrait of a bifurcated society, in which some citizens live in wealth and comfort while others endure poverty and degradation. Harrington's take on widespread poverty in America is moralistic, not scientific. As he puts it, "In a nation with a technology that could provide every citizen with a decent life, it is an outrage and a scandal that there should be such social misery." In other passages, Harrington embraces what I call the helping-hand metaphor: "The other Americans are those who live at a level of life beneath moral choice, who are so submerged in their poverty that one cannot begin to talk about free choice. The point is not to make them wards of the state. Rather, society must help them before they can help themselves."[13]

Gunnar Myrdal, whose classic work, *The American Dilemma: The Negro Problem and Modern Democracy,* was republished in 1962 and published as a paperback in 1964, also contributed to the emphasis on moralistic rhetoric in the 1960s, by stressing the "moral" nature of race controversies in the United States. Although Myrdal examines the economic, social, and political aspects of race relations in painstaking detail, he regards the moral elements of race relations as fundamental. He also notes an embarrassing gap between moral practice, especially in the South, and what he calls the American Creed (a strong commitment to equality and liberty):

> From the point of view of the American Creed, the status accorded the Negro in America represents nothing more and nothing less than a century-long lag of public morals. . . . The Negro in America has not yet been given the elemental civil and political rights of formal democracy, including a fair opportunity to earn his living, upon which a general accord was already won when the American Creed was first taking form.[14]

Elite Discourse

Has the discourse of political elites changed over time? To answer this question, I systematically examined congressional testimony by key administration witnesses over time. To control for possible differences between Democrats and Republicans, I focused on testimony by witnesses

13. Harrington (1962, pp. 17, 162).
14. Myrdal (1944, p. 24).

representing four Democratic presidents: Kennedy, Johnson, Clinton, and Obama. I identify congressional hearings during each of these presidencies that focus on poverty and social services, elementary and secondary education, and child health. I coded testimony by key administration witnesses (mainly cabinet secretaries, but also some other top political executives), counting the number of policy arguments that could be considered either moralistic or economic. An example of a moralistic argument would be the assertion that all young people deserve an opportunity to share in America's abundance or that compassion requires us to eliminate or alleviate poverty or that we should help the needy. An example of an economic argument would be the assertion that returns on human capital are as great as returns on physical capital or that eliminating poverty will benefit taxpayers by decreasing welfare payments or that eliminating poverty will generate more consumer demand. In practice, congressional witnesses often use truncated arguments, invoking a key concept rather than spelling out a full-fledged argument. Given this reality, I was relatively generous in characterizing a statement as a policy argument.[15]

The War on Poverty

To begin our inquiry into elite issue frames, consider the genesis of the War on Poverty, as exemplified by the Economic Opportunity Act of 1964. In March and April of 1964, the House Education and Labor Committee, chaired by Representative Adam Clayton Powell (D-N.Y.), held hearings on the Economic Opportunity Act, as proposed by the White House. A number of witnesses appeared before this committee, including nine prominent Johnson administration spokespeople, who testified during the earliest days of the hearings. They included seven cabinet secretaries (McNamara, Celebrezze, Wirtz, Hodges, Kennedy, Freeman, and Udall), the head of the Economic Opportunity Office (Sargent Shriver), and the head of the Council of Economic Advisers (Walter Heller).

R. Sargent Shriver, the first director of the Office of Economic Opportunity and the opening witness, stressed themes of help and opportunity: "We want to give the young people a chance to escape from the cycle of

15. To ensure that my judgments could be replicated, I asked a research assistant to code a subset of ten congressional appearances using the same protocol that I used. The intercoder reliability coefficients were .849 for moralistic arguments and .889 for economic arguments, after two dress rehearsals using other transcripts.

poverty and to break out of the ruthless pattern of poor housing, poor homes, and poor education. We want to give them a way out." Willard Wirtz, secretary of labor, made an explicitly religious appeal: "The text for the bill could well be: Inasmuch as ye have done it unto one of the least of these, my brethren you have done it unto Me." Wirtz also quoted the Talmud, noting that "the father who does not teach his son a trade teaches that boy to steal." Some witnesses did make economic arguments. Walter Heller, the chair of the Council of Economic Advisers, argued that "returns on capital invested in human beings are fully as real and as great as those we realize on the money we invest in machines and equipment." Luther Hodges, secretary of commerce, asserted, "If we can make the low-income families in America more productive, and if we can provide an environment in which they can put their talents to work, we can greatly strengthen our domestic markets." However, Heller and Hodges, like other witnesses, also stressed the moralistic themes of help, self-help, fairness, and opportunity.[16]

As table 2-1 reveals, moralistic arguments outweigh economic arguments by a margin of 59 to 41.

Elementary and Secondary Education Act

Congressional hearings on the Elementary and Secondary Education Act, held in 1965, provide a useful baseline for education policy. Senator Wayne Morse (D-Ore.), chair of the Subcommittee on Education of the Senate Committee on Labor and Public Welfare, held seven days of hearings in January and February 1965. At the outset of those hearings, Morse made it clear that his goal was to promote "equality of opportunity" by enhancing the quality of education received by "youngsters which come from our poorest families."[17]

In the hearings that followed, Morse heard from three key administration witnesses: Anthony Celebrezze, the secretary of health, education, and welfare; Francis Keppel, the commissioner of education; and Willard Wirtz, the secretary of labor. Celebrezze, like Morse, stressed equality of opportunity through aid to the poorest children and the poorest communities: "This is the first order of the educational challenge which

16. See Shriver (1964, p. 21); Wirtz (1964, p. 185); Heller (1964, p. 29); Hodges (1964, p. 232).
17. See Morse (1965, p. 3).

Table 2-1. *Frame of Testimony, Administration Witnesses, Selected Congressional Hearings on Children's Issues, 1960s, 1990s, 2009–10*

Percent

Administration	Poverty and social services	Elementary and secondary education	Child health
1960s, Johnson, Kennedy	Moralistic: 59 Economic: 41	Moralistic: 67 Economic: 33	Moralistic: 33 Economic: 67
1990s, Clinton	Moralistic: 35 Economic: 65	Moralistic: 71 Economic: 29	Moralistic: 24 Economic: 76
2009–10, Obama	Moralistic: 23 Economic: 77	Moralistic: 45 Economic: 55	Moralistic: 10 Economic: 90

Source: Hearings: House Appropriations Committee, February 11, 1997. House Education and Labor Committee, March 17–20, April 7–10, and April 13–14, 1964; April 22 and September 23, 1993; May 20, 2009; March 17, 2010. House Energy and Commerce Committee, June 24, 2009; February 4, 2010. House Interstate and Foreign Commerce Committee, May 15, 1962; March 26, 1963. House Ways and Means Committee, May 6, 2009. Senate Appropriations Committee, March 4, 1997; March 10, 2010. Senate Health, Education, Labor and Pensions Committee, March 17, 2010. Senate Labor and Human Resources Committee, May 4, 1993; April 18, 1997. Senate Labor and Human Resources Committee and the House Energy and Commerce Committee (joint), April 21, 1993. Senate Labor and Public Welfare Committee, May 24, 1962; January 26 and February 1, 1965.

faces us—to give children of greatest need a better opportunity and to provide financial assistance to those communities that need it most." Keppel echoed the equal opportunity theme: "I propose we begin a program in education to insure every American child the fullest development of his mind and skills." To be sure, the administration's witnesses also made economic arguments. "We have come to see the clear link between high educational and high economic attainment," Celebrezze asserted. "If we fail to spend enough for good education today . . . we will . . . spend many times more on social services tomorrow," Keppel warned. However, as table 2-1 indicates, moralistic arguments exceed economic arguments by 2 to 1.[18]

18. See Celebrezze (1965, p. 78); Keppel (1965, pp. 630, 631).

Child Health

It is more difficult to find a good baseline for children's health policy debates. Although Medicaid was established in 1965, as an amendment to the Social Security Act, it generated virtually no attention at congressional hearings in 1965 or at reauthorization hearings two years later. During the Kennedy administration, however, congressional hearings were held on immunization, mental health, and dental disease. I coded testimony by HEW Secretary Abraham Ribicoff (1962), HEW Assistant Secretary Wilbur Cohen (1962), and HEW Secretary Anthony Celebrezze (1963).

In contrast to the other two policy domains, in which moralistic arguments predominate, child health testimony in the early 1960s tilts more toward economic arguments. At the hearings on immunization, for example, prevention figures prominently as a theme, along with other economic arguments. For example, Secretary Ribicoff defends a coordinated attack on disease as advantageous "from the standpoint of overall program efficiency and economy."[19] As table 2-1 indicates, economic frames actually outnumber moralistic frames, by a margin of 2 to 1.

Shifting Frames

Cabinet secretaries and subcabinet officials use a somewhat different mix of issue frames in their congressional testimony today (see table 2-1). Economic arguments were more prominent in the 1990s than in the 1960s, and they were more prominent in 2000 to 2010 than in the 1990s. A steady upward trend is more evident for child poverty and child health than for elementary and secondary education. For example, Secretary of Health and Human Services Donna Shalala makes this argument in support of the Clinton administration's antismoking efforts: "When we work to cut teen smoking by one-half over seven years, we are focusing on a huge public health challenge that, if successful, could save thousands of lives and dollars." Shalala offers this thought in support of child immunizations: "Great nations . . . invest in their people—and no investment is more fundamental and more cost-effective than immunizations."[20]

Similarly, Secretary of Health and Human Services Kathleen Sebelius makes a strong economic argument in support of comprehensive health

19. Ribicoff (1962, p. 46).
20. See Shalala (1993a, 1993b).

care reform: "Rising health costs represent the greatest threat to our long-term economic stability. . . . Solving this problem is essential to job growth, productivity, and economic mobility. We simply cannot become the nimble economy we need to be without health care reform." Sebelius also makes a case for "investments in prevention and wellness," citing the old adage that "an ounce of prevention is worth a pound of cure."[21]

I do not mean to exaggerate this trend. Many cabinet secretaries and other top administration officials stress moralistic claims in their speeches and testimony. In some instances, the moralistic claims predominate. In education policy in particular, administration spokespeople pay as much attention to moralistic arguments as to economic arguments. Secretary of Education Richard Riley, in his education testimony, urges Congress to "help all children" and cautions against "opportunities denied." Secretary of Education Arne Duncan makes economic arguments ("we have to educate our way to a better economy") but articulates moralistic arguments as well ("education is the civil-rights issue of our time").[22]

The timing of a shift in issue frames—unlike, for example, a change in corporate ownership or a change in party control of government—is difficult to pinpoint with precision. It is like a trend that catches on and then gains momentum, such as the growing use of cell phones or personal computers. But it is even more subtle than that, because it involves a change in rhetoric, including the rhetoric of public officials, advocates, and journalists. Fortunately, much of this is available in the public record, though some of it (private meetings between lobbyists and legislators, or private meetings between legislators and legislative staff members) is not.

The Children's Defense Fund's Changing Rhetoric

A good source of evidence for the change in the rhetoric of child advocacy is the congressional testimony of the leading child advocate of her generation, Marian Wright Edelman. Edelman, president of the Children's Defense Fund (CDF), was raised in Bennettsville, South Carolina, the daughter of a Baptist minister. A civil rights activist in the 1960s, she founded the CDF in 1973. In most of her public speeches, from the early 1970s to the present time, one detects a strong moralistic tone. She often conveys moral outrage and sprinkles her speeches with words like

21. See Sebelius (2009).
22. See Riley (1993); Duncan (2009a).

shameful, unconscionable, fairness, and *opportunity.* In testimony on the Emergency School Aid Act, she states, "The need for Federal legislative action which produces educational justice for the millions of children who are victims of racially isolated education is indisputable." In testimony on the Juvenile Justice and Delinquency Prevention Act, she says, "Children as a group are not treated equally to other groups in the population." In testimony on gun violence, she characterizes "the senseless killing of children" as a "moral tumor growing on the American soul." As one long-time admirer puts it, "Marian is a missionary, for children."[23]

But even Marian Wright Edelman makes economic arguments on behalf of children and has been doing so for many years. In discussing federal food assistance programs for women and children, she argues: "The cost of neglect exceeds, in my view, the cost of investing in healthy infants." In hearings on welfare reform, she pleads: "Please do not go cheap on child care, because we are just again assuring that the next generation will come up with lots of the same deficits of those we are trying to get off the welfare rolls now." Often, she cites specific benefit-cost ratios for particular children's programs. For example, in hearings on the plight of the working poor, she asserts: "One dollar of federal monies invested in preschool education returns about six dollars in savings because of lower special education and welfare costs and higher worker productivity."[24]

To chart Edelman's rhetorical odyssey more precisely, I coded all of her congressional testimony from 1970 to 2010, identifying those policy arguments that were moralistic or economic.[25] I should note that there are gaps: when Republicans controlled both the House and the Senate (1995–2000, 2003–06), Edelman did not testify at all, presumably because she was not asked.

An analysis of Edelman's congressional testimony, on a wide range of children's issues, suggests that attention to economic arguments—practically nonexistent in the early 1970s—first emerged during the last two years of the Carter administration (1979–80), escalated during the Reagan administration (1981–88), and oscillated a bit since that time (see figure 2-1). For Edelman, at least, economic arguments became more attractive in the late 1970s and the early 1980s. After that, economic arguments

23. See Edelman (1971, p. 35; 1973, p. 525; 1993, p. 61).
24. See Edelman (1987b, p. 5; 1987c, p. 64; 1989, p. 145).
25. As before, I asked a research assistant to code a subset of ten congressional appearances. The Pearson's correlation coefficient was .823 for moralistic arguments and .967 for economic arguments, after one dress rehearsal using other transcripts.

Figure 2-1. *Moralistic and Economic Themes in Marian Wright Edelman's Congressional Testimony, 1971–2010*

Percent

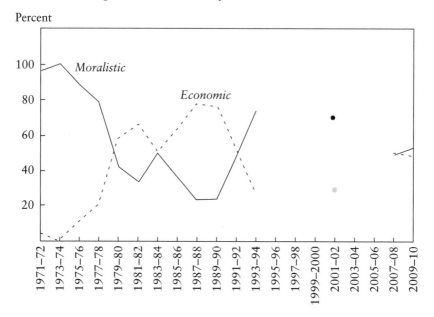

Source: Author's compilation based on content analysis of congressional testimony by Marian Wright Edelman, Children's Defense Fund. Gaps indicate years in which Edelman did not testify.

became a predictable feature of her congressional testimony, along with the moralistic arguments that enabled her to express her passion and her missionary zeal. One also sees this blend of moralistic and economic arguments, incidentally, in Edelman's public speeches and books. For example, in *Families in Peril,* published in 1987, Edelman argues: "As adults we are responsible for meeting the needs of children. It is our moral obligation. . . . We do not extend help to children solely because of moral obligations. . . . We invest in children because the cost to the public of sickness, ignorance, neglect, dependence, and unemployment over the long term exceeds the cost of preventive investment in health, education, employed youth, and stable families."[26] In Edelman's congressional testimony in 2009 and 2010, the first two years of the Obama administration, moralistic and economic arguments are equally prominent.

26. Edelman (1987a, pp. 30–31).

Why economic arguments during the waning days of the Carter administration? In fact, Carter initiated cutbacks in federal programs due to growing concerns about inflation. For example, it was during the final two years of the Carter administration that federal grants to state and local governments began to decline.[27]

As for Reagan, his cutbacks of social services programs were dramatic and unprecedented. In numerous congressional appearances, Edelman does not disguise her disdain for Reagan and his policies. "We are deeply concerned with the dismantling, under the guise of controlling the budget, of very fundamental rights and protections for the neediest children," she argues. The following year, she lambasts Reagan's additional budget cuts for children's programs as "unjust and unworkable . . . unrelenting and unfair." In these same appearances, however, Edelman argues that investing in prevention "can save money" and that many entitlement programs are "cost-effective." In response to proposed cuts in children's programs, she cites specific savings from child welfare programs in New York, Washington, Iowa, Pennsylvania, Minnesota, and California. In response to Reagan's arguments that we could not afford expensive social programs, Edelman responds that we cannot afford *not* to invest in children's programs, because the long-term benefits of such programs exceed the costs.[28]

It should be noted that the mix of moralistic and economic arguments in Edelman's congressional testimony varies not only across presidential administrations but also across policy domains. When discussing gun control, school violence, and juvenile delinquency, her arguments tend to be moralistic. When discussing welfare reform, child support enforcement, and teen pregnancy, her arguments tend to be economic. If we look beyond Edelman's testimony to other evidence, we see rhetorical shifts toward economic arguments at different points in time but especially during the 1980s.

When Did the Shift Occur?

For children's health debates, at the federal level, a key shift in elite discourse occurred in the early 1980s. Following the election of President Reagan and a Republican majority in the Senate in 1980, Congress enacted a series of budget bills that significantly reduced the scope of

27. Gormley (1989, pp. 173–93).
28. See Edelman (1981, pp. 218, 220; 1982, pp. 114, 143, 129–30; 1983).

federal social programs, including food stamps, employment and training programs, Aid to Families with Dependent Children (AFDC), and Medicaid. Key Democratic legislators in the House held hearings highlighting the extent of the budget cuts and their negative impacts on vulnerable constituencies, including poor women and children. Although traditional Democratic constituencies mobilized to oppose these cuts, they faced strong Republican opposition to government spending and some bipartisan concern over growing budget deficits.

Against this backdrop, Representative Henry Waxman (D-Calif.) conceived of a brilliant strategy aimed at expanding the Medicaid program. Some called it a children's strategy, which it was, because Waxman and his allies targeted infants and pregnant mothers as the first beneficiaries. But it was also an economic strategy, because Waxman used investment arguments to build support for this new initiative. As he recalled in 1989, "These expansions reflect a strongly held conviction on the part of many in the Congress that the nation must invest in the health of its children, and that the Medicaid program is an effective investment vehicle." Waxman also used budget reconciliation bills as vehicles for an unprecedented expansion in Medicaid coverage, from 25 million to 35 million persons. This enabled him to avoid debilitating floor amendments, given that budget reconciliation bills are handled through a single up or down vote.[29]

In education also, a key rhetorical shift appears to have occurred in the early 1980s. This is especially evident in presidential speeches on education. Like Lyndon Johnson, Jimmy Carter devoted more attention to "opportunity or civil rights" than to other education policy topics. Not surprisingly, Ronald Reagan devoted more attention to other education themes, when he discussed education at all. Interestingly, Bill Clinton devoted far less attention to opportunity or civil rights in his education policy speeches than either Carter or Johnson. Like congressional rhetoric on health policy, presidential rhetoric on education policy changed in the early 1980s. Also, one sees less attention to opportunity or civil rights in the 1980s and the 1990s than in the 1970s in both the Democratic and Republican party platforms.[30]

Rhetoric on poverty and welfare also shifted during the 1980s, though not in a direction preferred by many child advocates. The new idea that motivated Congress to pass the Family Support Act of 1988 and would

29. See Waxman (1989, p. 1217); Tanenbaum (1995).
30. See Manna (2006, pp. 58–59, 62–65).

eventually culminate in the dismantling of the AFDC program in 1996 was the proposition that welfare recipients should be required to work as a precondition for receiving government benefits.[31] Or as conservatives liked to put it, "What works is work."[32] One can interpret this shift in one of two ways: as a shift from moralistic arguments (help the needy) to economic arguments (welfare dependency is detrimental to both taxpayers and the poor themselves) or as a shift from one conception of fairness (help the needy) to another conception of fairness (help those who are willing to help themselves). In either case, the shift seems to have occurred during the mid-1980s and gathered momentum thereafter.

Other Accounts

My historical account, identifying key rhetorical changes in the 1980s, is roughly consistent with Mark Smith's, which situates key changes in the 1970s.[33] Smith believes that Republicans first embraced economic frames, which appeared in *National Review* columns, Republican Party platforms, and speeches by presidential candidates, in 1973, when the economy began to deteriorate. Democrats then responded, later, mimicking the Republicans' use of economic frames but using such frames creatively to promote their own policy goals and their own party fortunes. In his book, Smith focuses on reframing by Republican politicians in the 1970s; in this book, I focus on subsequent reframing by child advocates in the 1980s.

On the other hand, my argument differs from Smith's in three key respects. First, I define economic frames differently. For Smith, an economic frame is one that focuses on economic indicators, such as wages, unemployment, or deficits. For me, an economic frame is one that employs utilitarian logic, including both economic and social benefits. The distinction, in short, is between an economic focus (Smith) and economic reasoning (me). Second, in contrast to Smith, who looks at a wide variety of issues, I examine children's issues, which involve a segment of the population often regarded as "positively constructed."[34] With a positively constructed population, moralistic arguments—such as we should help those who need and deserve help—might be expected to work. Thus

31. Mead (1986).
32. Haskins (2006, p. 11).
33. Smith (2007).
34. Schneider and Ingram (1993).

it is especially striking to find a shift in rhetoric away from moralistic (or deontological) frames and toward economic (or teleological) frames in this policy domain, where it might be deemed less necessary. Third, Smith sees the Democrats' embrace of economic frames (such as Bill Clinton's support for deficit reduction) as a strategic choice that advances the party politically but perhaps at the expense of the party's core values. In Smith's words, "Republicans responded to economic insecurity largely by changing their arguments, whereas Democrats changed their positions."[35] In contrast, I believe that child advocates, including Democrats, can make an economic case for children's programs without abandoning their traditional concern for disadvantaged members of society.

The shift from moralistic to economic arguments is not unique to children's policy or to the United States. A study of arguments by capital punishment critics finds a shift away from moral arguments (such as forgiveness and redemption) and toward arguments that stress the wrongful imprisonment of innocent suspects. As Frank Baumgartner and colleagues put it, "The new innocence frame diverts attention away from theoretical and philosophical issues of morality to focus simply on the possibility of errors in the criminal justice system." A study of arguments by gay rights opponents also finds a shift away from moralistic arguments. As Gary Mucciaroni puts it, "Morality talk appears to have declined over time." A study of policy advocacy by Christine Mahoney—on a wide range of issues in the United States and Europe—finds that U.S. advocates, in 2002, were far more likely to make cost/economic arguments than fairness/discrimination arguments. European advocates also used cost/economic arguments more often than fairness/discrimination arguments, though the margin is not as great.[36]

Still, a key question remains unanswered: Why have advocates generally, and child advocates in particular, switched from moralistic to economic arguments over time?

Possible Explanations

Four possible explanations come to mind. First, a growing awareness of budget deficits encourages a search for cost-effective public policies.

---

35. Smith (2007, p. 176).
36. Baumgartner, DeBoef, and Boydstun (2008, p. 9); Mucciaroni (2011, p. 209); Mahoney (2008, p. 85).

State governments, constitutionally required to balance their budgets, have been sensitive to expenditure constraints for some time, but especially since the late 1970s, when taxpayer fervor swept California and a number of other states. The passage of forty-one antitax initiatives between 1978 and 1999 made it more difficult for advocates to argue for new social programs at the state level.[37] As for the federal government, budget deficit awareness grew noticeably in the 1980s, as the Reagan administration's budget deficits grew sharply and led to passage of the Gramm-Rudman-Hollings Balanced Budget and Emergency Deficit Control Act in 1985. Concern over budget deficits emerged again during the early Clinton years and led to the passage of significant, though controversial, legislation in 1993. Today, budget deficit reduction is once again on Congress's agenda, after alarming increases in the federal budget deficit and the national debt. The appeal of cost-effectiveness arguments is likely to increase.

Second, a decline in religious sentiment and church attendance has reduced the appeal of moralistic arguments. Church attendance declined during the 1960s and the 1970s, though it has stabilized since 1980.[38] The number of Americans with no religious identity increased sharply after 1968, stabilized, and then increased again in the first decade of the 2000s. In 2010, 16 percent of Americans professed no religious identity, as opposed to 2 percent in the 1960s. Despite the role that evangelical Christians have played and continue to play in American politics, American culture is increasingly secular.[39]

Third, as the United States has become increasingly a multiracial and multicultural society, moralistic appeals have become more problematic. The percentage of nonwhite children has risen sharply, with corresponding challenges to the country's social services safety net. According to the Census Bureau, 48.6 percent of children born between July 2008 and July 2009 were members of a racial or ethnic minority, as opposed to 35 percent of the overall population.[40] This change in the demographic landscape has profound political consequences. To be blunt, it is harder

37. Smith (2004).
38. The question was, Would you say you go to church regularly, often, seldom, or never?
39. See American National Election Studies (no date); Newport (2010); Wilcox (1992).
40. Dougherty (2010).

to make the case to white voters for policies that benefit other people's children when those children look and talk less like their own.[41]

Fourth, a growing number of policy-oriented think tanks and a growing number of rigorous empirical studies have generated an impressive supply of evidence on which advocates can draw when making economic arguments. The Great Society gave program evaluation a boost by creating new social programs that policy analysts wished to analyze and by mandating that evaluations be conducted. Think tanks proliferated, at both the national and state levels, and became independent sources of information and policy advice. Although the influence of public policy research on public policy itself can certainly be exaggerated, examples of influential public policy research abound.[42]

Mass Media Coverage

Of course, a change in the rhetoric of child advocates, inside and outside of the federal government, does not guarantee that the public's understanding of children's issues shifts as well. Of critical importance is whether the mass media, in covering children's issues, also change their emphasis from moralistic frames to economic frames. If not, then public opinion may remain unaltered.

To understand how the mass media's coverage of issue frames (or policy arguments) has changed over time, consider newspaper coverage of children and public policy over the past fifty years. To measure this, I focused on the *New York Times,* as measured by ProQuest, which has used a consistent algorithm for storing information on that newspaper's stories for the past fifty years. After identifying stories that discuss children and public policy or law or government, I distinguished such stories based on whether references to children were accompanied by references to help, opportunity, prevention, or investment.

As figure 2-2 indicates, stories that include an opportunity frame outnumber stories that include a prevention frame. Stories that include an investment frame increased over time, though not as sharply as stories that include a prevention frame. In short, the prevention frame and the

---

41. Cross-national comparisons suggest that racial heterogeneity discourages income redistribution (Alesina, Glaeser, and Sacerdote, 2001).

42. See Smith (1991); Rich (2004); Aaron (1978); Gormley (2007).

Figure 2-2. *Mass Media Coverage of Children's Issues, by Frame, 1960–2005*[a]

Number of stories

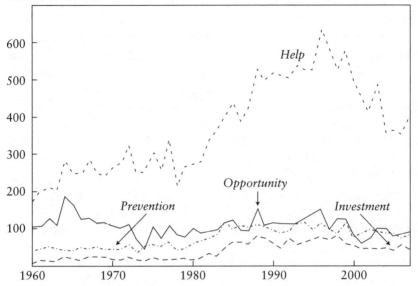

Source: ProQuest Historical Newspapers, *New York Times*.
a. Search was for child or children or youth w/15 [search term] and law or policy or program or Congress or legislation or legislative or legislator or government or governor or mayor and not classified ad, display ad, obituary, rebroadcast.

investment frame both increased in importance between 1960 and 2005, consistent with the change in elite rhetoric.

On the other hand, the help frame still predominates, and by a wide margin. Despite a change in elite rhetoric, a relatively small percentage of newspaper articles on children and public policy include an economic argument. In fairness, it should be noted that figure 2-2 exaggerates the gap between moralistic and economic arguments somewhat, because many articles that include the words *help* and *child* in close proximity do not feature a genuine helping-hand argument in support of children or children's programs. For example, an article on child support enforcement that explains why federal child support enforcement directives failed to help states collect more revenue gets counted, even though it contains no genuine argument on why child support enforcement should be strengthened. Similarly, an article on a proposed child health bill asserting that "curbs on Medicaid would help finance child health care" for the near poor gets counted, even though the strongest argument in support of the bill ("The President's proposal is a step in the right direction") is quite vague.[43]

Whatever the imperfections of newspaper content analysis, the bottom line is clear: the economic message is still struggling to be heard. That is because when children's issues are covered, normative arguments in support of children's issues get sporadic coverage at best. Also, only a subset of featured normative arguments use economic issue frames. Furthermore, as noted in chapter 1, most newspapers print far fewer stories on children's issues than the *New York Times,* featured here because of the consistency of its record keeping.

In short, children's issues struggle to receive attention in the mass media. As noted earlier, stories on children and public policy generally became less common after 1997. The failure of children's issues to rebound, despite increases in child poverty, child obesity, and other children's problems, is partly attributable to the rise of other major news stories over the past decade, including the September 11 terrorist attacks (2001), Hurricane Katrina (2005), the financial crisis (2008), and the rising national debt. It has been hard for children's issues to compete with these and other blockbuster issues for scarce news space. Also, for some news outlets—most notably, daily newspapers—agenda space has become even scarcer as revenues have declined. Do ordinary citizens pay enough attention to the mass media generally and to children's issue coverage in particular to detect and absorb a growing emphasis on economic issue frames by children's advocates? This is doubtful, given the mass media's stronger emphasis on other issues, the mass media's continuing reliance on a helping-hand frame when covering children's issues, the public's limited attention to news about public policy, and the public's growing reliance on social media and self-selected media.

Consider, for example, public awareness of two of the more significant and more highly publicized federal children's programs of the past two decades: the Children's Health Insurance Program of 1997 and the No Child Left Behind Act of 2001. Although these two programs received more publicity than most children's programs, only 17 percent of the general public claimed to be following news about the children's

---

43. Clymer (1997); Pear (1997).

health insurance bill "very closely" when Congress considered reauthorizing CHIP in 2007, and only 14 percent claimed to be "very familiar"
with NCLB when Congress considered reauthorizing that law in 2009.[44]
Regrettably, the public's familiarity with even the most visible of children's programs is limited at best.

Conclusion

In a major study of multiple interest groups and their policy arguments,
Frank Baumgartner and colleagues argue that issue reframing is relatively
rare. Of the ninety-eight issues examined, only four of them (or 4 percent)
underwent significant reframing from one session of Congress to the next.
The authors explain this finding by citing a plethora of constraints dis-
couraging reframing, such as sunk costs (you invest in a frame and stick
with it), ideology (a frame linked to a particular ideology is unlikely to
change because the ideology is unlikely to change), and credibility (legislators and legislative staff members may look askance at a lobbyist who
switches arguments as often as changing shoes).[45]

In contrast, I find evidence of significant reframing here and on a range
of children's issues, including poverty and social services, education, and
child health. A key methodological distinction is that I examine four
decades of policy arguments, while Baumgartner and colleagues examine
two to four years of policy arguments. Another distinction may be how
we define significant reframing. To me, a significant shift from moralistic
to economic frames does not necessarily mean that advocates abandon
moralistic frames but that such frames shift in importance from primary
to secondary arguments. Clearly, moralistic frames continue to be prominent weapons in the arsenal of children's advocates. Just as clearly, economic frames have become increasingly important.

On the other hand, the reframing of children's issues is much more
evident in testimony before congressional committees, by children's advocates and public officials, than it is in newspaper coverage of children's
issues. As with the proverbial tree falling in the forest that no one is
around to hear, one wonders what the impact of congressional testimony
on public opinion is if the mass media do not thoroughly cover the policy
arguments that witnesses make. Members of Congress and their staffs

44. Wolf (2007); Newport (2009a).
45. Baumgartner and others (2009, pp. 166–18, 178–86).

hear the arguments, and are conversant with them, but the general public has only limited exposure to them.

In this chapter, I focus on congressional testimony and national policy debates. But which issue frames do children's advocates use when trying to influence state legislatures? And which issue frames do children's advocates use when trying to influence the courts? I seek to answer these questions in chapters 3 and 4, respectively. As we shall see, rhetorical patterns are more mixed when we move beyond Capitol Hill.

CHAPTER THREE

Arguments in Different Policy Domains

Many younger children . . . are constantly arrested for petty thieving because they are too eager to take home food or fuel which will relieve the distress and need they so constantly hear discussed.

Jane Addams, 1912

The rise of economic arguments is more evident in some policy domains than others. These disparities, by policy domain, reflect differences in issue characteristics, historical paths, cultural expectations, repositories of scientific evidence, and levels of mass media interest (see table 3-1). In this chapter, I take a closer look at issue frames employed by children's advocates in three policy domains: child health, education, and child welfare. A key theme is that frames vary across issues and that some of this is due to the availability of good empirical evidence on the consequences of neglect, as opposed to the consequences of intervention. A related theme is that empirical evidence matters more if it points more or less in the same direction.

Child Health

For years, children's health advocates, inside and outside of government, have stressed the value of prevention. This is evident in legislative testimony from administration officials and in the arguments used by child advocates.

Academic experts have fueled this emphasis on prevention with numerous empirical studies that confirm the value to society of various preventive programs, including child immunization, early periodic screening, diagnosis, and treatment, nurse home visits to the homes of mothers and

43

Table 3-1. *Variables, Three Domains of Children's Policy*

Variable	Child health	Child education	Child welfare
Key values	Accessibility, affordability	Accessibility, accountability	Safety, security
Mass media interest	High	High	Intermittent
Scientific evidence	Extensive—consistent	Extensive—more consistent on pre-K than on K–12 interventions	Limited
Intergovernmental history	Strong federal role	Growing federal role	Limited federal role

Source: Author.

mothers-to-be, the federal Women, Infants, and Children (WIC) program, the National School Lunch program, food stamps, and the Obama administration's antiobesity campaign. Studies indicate that participation in the WIC program is associated with better pregnancy outcomes and higher test scores. A study of the school lunch program shows that it boosts educational attainment. A study of the food stamps program shows that it reduces the incidence of low-birth-weight births, which can have adverse outcomes later in life. Studies of the Nurse-Family Partnership Program demonstrate that it helps to prevent crime, among other positive outcomes.[1]

The concept of prevention, especially in health policy, has become so deeply ingrained that many advocates use a severely truncated policy argument, simply using the word *prevention* and hoping that listeners will make the connections—from public policy to service provision to service utilization to short-term impacts for direct beneficiaries to long-term impacts for society as a whole. That assumption may be mistaken. The concept of prevention is a powerful one, but it needs to be spelled out. Would a concerned parent simply tell a teenager to abstain from sex or instead talk in some detail about the consequences of an unwanted pregnancy? Would a priest committed to social justice give a short, abstract sermon on love or instead

1. See Devaney, Bilheimer, and Shore (1992); Bitler and Currie (2005); Currie (2009, p. 108); Hinrichs (2010); Almond, Hoynes, and Schanzenbach (2011); Olds and others (1997, 2007).

a ten-minute homily rich in examples, stories, and advice? A memorable word or phrase is a great motivator and an excellent mnemonic device, but it should complement an argument, not substitute for it.

Many advocates also assume a strong public consensus in support of extending health insurance coverage to more and more children. In this area, too, full-fledged arguments have sometimes morphed into truncated arguments. For example, in recent congressional debates over CHIP, members of Congress focused more on whether expanding CHIP would yield a commensurate increase in health coverage for children ("crowd-out" could prevent this from occurring) than on whether increased health coverage for children was socially desirable (this is commonly assumed to be true).[2] As one intimately involved congressional aide recalls, "People accepted the fact that it was better to insure kids than not."

One sees a truncated argument of this sort on the Children's Defense Fund's website: "For the past several years, CDF's top priority has been to guarantee affordable, comprehensive, accessible health coverage for *all* children. . . . Every child must be guaranteed access to all medically necessary health and mental health services from head to toe to maximize a child's health and development."[3] Note the absence of references to the long-term consequences for society as a whole. One sees such references in Marian Wright Edelman's congressional testimony but not in the most accessible parts of the CDF's website. Perhaps this is because websites attract a disproportionate share of interest from people already committed to the cause. Or perhaps the CDF is missing out on an opportunity for mass persuasion.

Clearly, health advocates have experienced messaging failures over the years. The Clinton administration's arguments for national health insurance were not strong enough to overcome some clever television ads (the famous "Harry and Louise" ads, aired in 1994) that portrayed the Clinton plan as a bureaucratic nightmare that robbed ordinary Americans of freedom of choice. The Obama administration's arguments for the Patient Protection and Affordable Care Act were strong enough to persuade Democratic members of Congress to enact the bill but not strong enough to persuade the American people to support it. Many Americans

2. The crowd-out hypothesis suggests that an expansion of public health insurance will result in a reduction of private health insurance. To the extent that this occurs, public insurance programs that cover x million persons may not result in a net increase of x million insured persons.

3. Children's Defense Fund (www.childrensdefense.org).

remain skeptical that the new law will lower health care costs. Also, most Americans oppose the individual mandate provision of the law, on which many of the bill's other provisions depend.[4]

On the positive side, some advocates have figured out how to frame health care debates more effectively. On its website, Families USA features a "Messaging Cheat Sheet," which succinctly rebuts many arguments against the Affordable Care Act. For example, it poses this question: "One major concern raised by Republicans and other opponents of the law is that it busts the budget. Did Congress burden our children with the cost of health reform?" Here is the answer:

> No. Prevention saves money. Controlling waste, fraud, and abuse in health care saves money. Controlling industry greed saves money. Patient-focused health care saves money. Efficient delivery of services saves money. Not depending on emergency rooms saves money. And all these improvements are part of the new law.
>
> In truth, the Affordable Care Act reduces the deficit. Congress's official scorekeeper—the nonpartisan Congressional Budget Office—estimated that the Affordable Care Act would reduce the federal deficit over the next 10 years. And earlier this year, when Republicans in the House wanted to repeal the Affordable Care Act, the official scorekeeper estimated that repealing the law would actually increase the deficit.
>
> Fixing health care will strengthen the economy by keeping more Americans healthy and by making coverage more affordable for families and for businesses. Healthier workers are more productive. American businesses will be more competitive in global markets.[5]

Notice the emphasis on repetition—prevention saves money, controlling abuse saves money, patient-focused care saves money. Even a casual reader is likely to remember that health reform saves money. But are these assertions credible? An endorsement from Congress's official scorekeeper—the nonpartisan CBO—suggests that the answer is yes. Finally, Families USA closes with a strong finish, emphasizing economic benefits for families and for American businesses. Its message is succinct and compelling.

Another advocacy group that can deliver pithy, persuasive messages is the Food Research and Action Center (FRAC). Here is its summary of

4. Johnson and Broder (1997); Serafini (2011); Kaiser Health Tracking Poll (2011).
5. Families USA (2011).

the strengths of the Supplemental Nutrition Assistance Program (SNAP), otherwise known as food stamps:

> SNAP has extraordinary strengths:
>
> —It reduces hunger and food insecurity by providing very low-income people desperately needed, targeted assistance to purchase food through an effective and efficient electronic benefit transfer system.
>
> —When the national economy or a regional, state, or area economy is in trouble, the program is among the most effective government responses. It reacts quickly and robustly to economic problems. . . .
>
> —There is the same responsiveness when disasters strike, as occurred in the aftermath of Hurricane Katrina in 2005. Disaster SNAP responded quickly and effectively to meet the increased need in Gulf Coast states.
>
> —Because SNAP benefits are so urgently needed by families, they are spent quickly—97 percent of benefits are redeemed by the end of the month of issuance—thereby bolstering local economies. Estimates issued by Moody's Analytics and others of the economic growth impact of SNAP during a recession range from $1.73 to $1.79 per $1 of SNAP benefits.
>
> —SNAP is targeted to go to the neediest people in our country: 93 percent of benefits go to households with incomes below the poverty line. This includes millions of working poor families.
>
> —It reaches key vulnerable populations—one-third of SNAP participants are in households that include senior citizens or people with disabilities; three-quarters of participants are in families with children.
>
> —SNAP lifted 3.6 million Americans above the poverty line in 2009, including 2.1 million children and 200,000 seniors. SNAP is as effective as the Earned Income Tax Credit in lifting families above the poverty line, and far more effective than any other program in lifting families out of deep poverty.
>
> —It relieves pressure on overwhelmed food banks, pantries, religious congregations and other emergency food providers across the country. They recognize SNAP as the cornerstone of national, state, and local anti-hunger efforts, and are the first to note their inability to meet added demand that would come from weakening SNAP.[6]

6. Weill (2011).

Although FRAC's plea for the SNAP program is less compact than Families USA's plea for the Affordable Care Act, it has the virtue of being strikingly specific. We learn that 97 percent of SNAP benefits are spent very quickly, "thereby bolstering local economies." We learn that 93 percent of benefits go to poor households, thus benefiting "the neediest people in our country." FRAC also establishes SNAP as a program that provides both routine (year-round) and emergency (hurricane relief) services. In addition to benefiting recipients, SNAP "relieves pressure" on worthy organizations, such as food banks, pantries, and religious congregations. Here, it seems, is a program that is effective, efficient, and far-reaching.

Education

Debates over education policy have long been informed by investment arguments. Even during the 1960s, when moralistic arguments reigned supreme, prominent economists urged public officials to think of education as an investment in human capital. As the University of Chicago economist Theodore Schultz puts it, "The rate of return to investment in schooling is as high or higher than it is to nonhuman capital. . . . Clearly, schooling can benefit some persons other than the student. Other families benefit as neighbors and as taxpayers."[7] These ideas surfaced in congressional hearings on the Elementary and Secondary Education Act, though they did not predominate.

Today the emphasis on education as an investment is even stronger. Consider the website of the National Education Association. On its home page, the NEA pleads for more education funding: "Funding public schools will strengthen the entire economy." Elsewhere, the NEA refines this argument: "NEA believes that, particularly in these troubling economic times, investing in education makes both good fiscal sense and good public policy. Funding targeted to quality public schools will see the greatest taxpayer return and will strengthen the entire economy."[8]

Of course, equal opportunity remains a powerful frame in education policy debates as well. In many of his speeches, Secretary of Education Arne Duncan stresses both moralistic (equal opportunity) and economic (investment) arguments. In his remarks upon being designated secretary of education, Duncan said: "Whether it's fighting poverty, strengthening

7. Schultz (1963, p. 11).
8. National Education Association (www.nea.org).

the economy or promoting opportunity, education is the common thread. It is the civil rights issue of our generation and it is the one sure path to a more equal, fair and just society." In a 2009 speech to the American Council on Education, he framed the issue once again as an economic issue *and* a moral issue: "Providing every child in America with a good education is both a moral imperative and an economic imperative." In a more recent speech, at the National Press Club, Duncan once again integrated economic and moralistic themes, emphasizing that "quality education—more than ever before—is the cornerstone of a strong economy in the 21st century," condemning high dropout rates from high school as "morally unacceptable and economically unsustainable" and arguing that "we have a moral obligation to take dramatic action."[9]

But which educational investments are likely to be most beneficial for children and for society? If we shift our focus from issues of affordability to issues of quality, the debate instantly becomes much murkier. Will school vouchers help disadvantaged children to experience the same educational opportunities that middle-class children enjoy? Some experts say yes, while others say no. Will charter schools, less shackled by rules and regulations than other public schools, improve educational quality for disadvantaged students? Some experts say yes, others say no, and still others say maybe. Will federally mandated testing requirements improve educational outcomes for students generally? Some experts say yes, while others say no. Will performance pay for teachers enable public schools to identify more effective teachers and to reward them for their performance, thus improving public education? Some experts say yes, while others say no, and still others say maybe. With these and other controversies, the absence of a scientific consensus makes it difficult for empirical research to inform public debates.[10]

Under such circumstances, debates are likely to shift away from investment and human capital frames to equal opportunity and freedom of choice frames. Or we may see two parallel sets of debates: a macroeconomic debate, in which investment arguments play a crucial role; and a microeconomic debate, in which other frames are paired—choice versus quality control, professional discretion versus political accountability,

9. See Duncan (2008, 2009b, 2010b).
10. See Peterson (1995); Howell and others (2002); Witte (2001); Krueger and Zhu (2003); Hoxby, Murarka, and Kang (2009); Center for Research on Educational Outcomes (2009); Buckley and Schneider (2007); Dee and Jacob (2009); Ravitch (2010); Lavy (2007); Rothstein (2008); Springer and others (2010); Esterling (2004).

compensation for credentials versus compensation for performance, and so forth.

Fortunately, empirical research is sometimes more consistent and more illuminating. In debates over early childhood education policy, "investment" arguments have become commonplace in recent years, thanks to two randomized social experiments (Perry Preschool, the Abecedarian Project), some well-designed quasi-experimental studies (Head Start, Chicago Parent Centers), and speeches by prominent economists (James Heckman, W. Steven Barnett, and Arthur Rolnick), who routinely invoke such arguments.[11] Although disagreements exist, multiple scientists, from multiple disciplines, have converged on a single bottom line—that investing in high-quality early childhood programs is the smart thing to do.[12]

James Heckman, the Nobel laureate from the University of Chicago, has been perhaps the most visible spokesperson for the human capital argument in favor of early childhood education. "Skill begets skill and learning begets learning," Heckman hypothesized in 2000.[13] In 2010 Heckman amplified this argument:

> If society intervenes early enough, it can raise the cognitive and socioemotional abilities and the health of disadvantaged children. Early interventions reduce inequality by promoting schooling, reducing crime, and reducing teenage pregnancy. They also foster workforce productivity. These interventions have high benefit-cost ratios and rates of return. Early interventions have much higher economic returns than later interventions such as reduced pupil-teacher ratios, public job training, convict rehabilitation programs, adult literacy programs, tuition subsidies or expenditure on police, or a variety of programs recently funded under ARRA.[14]

Much of Heckman's analysis builds upon empirical work by W. Steven Barnett, Lawrence Schweinhart, and others. In an analysis of the benefits and costs of the Perry Preschool Project, using data from participants and nonparticipants through age twenty-seven, Barnett estimates the benefits of the program at different discount rates and compares these to the

11. Kirp (2007).
12. Alberts (2011); Barnett (2011); Gormley (2011).
13. Heckman (2000, p. 50).
14. Heckman (2010).

established costs. Using a discount rate of 3 percent, he concludes that the benefit-cost ratio of the program is $8.74 per dollar invested, including $7.16 in benefits to the general public and $1.58 in benefits to program participants. Excluding benefits to program participants, the return to taxpayers is 7 to 1. In a subsequent report, focusing on participants and nonparticipants through age forty, Schweinhart and his colleagues estimate a benefit-cost ratio of $17.07 per dollar invested, using a 3 percent discount rate. Excluding benefits to program participants, the return to taxpayers is approximately 13 to 1. The authors conclude: "High-quality preschool programs for young children living in poverty contribute to their intellectual and social development in childhood and their school success, economic performance, and reduced commission of crime in adulthood."[15]

Arthur Rolnick, formerly vice president of the Federal Reserve Board's Minneapolis branch, has made similar arguments, on his own and in collaboration with Rob Grunewald. His research, based on the Perry Preschool Project, has found a 16 percent return on investment from a high-quality early childhood intervention focused on disadvantaged children. Benefits include more educated workers and less crime, among others. Like Heckman, Rolnick argues that earlier is better, and for economic reasons. As he and Grunewald put it, "Early childhood development programs are rarely portrayed as economic development initiatives, and we think that is a mistake. Such programs, if they appear at all, are at the bottom of the economic development lists for state and local governments. They should be at the top."[16]

Academic research on early childhood education has informed the arguments of children's advocates today. Fight Crime: Invest in Kids, an organization of more than 5,000 sheriffs, police chiefs, prosecutors, and violence survivors, founded in 1996, makes the following argument in support of more funding for high-quality preschool, Head Start, and child care: "Research shows that at-risk children left out of quality prekindergarten are five times more likely to grow up to become criminals by age 27 than comparable children in quality pre-kindergarten." Similarly, Pre-K Now, an organization launched by the Pew Charitable Trusts, puts it this way: "With local, state and federal budgets constrained, policy makers at every level are demanding that publicly funded programs

15. Barnett (1996, p. 85); Schweinhart and others (2005, pp. xvi, 214).
16. Rolnick and Grunewald (2003).

deliver results and yield returns on taxpayer dollars. Research shows that pre-k is unquestionably an efficient, effective investment."[17]

One of the most interesting organizations to embrace the findings of early childhood education researchers is the Committee for Economic Development, an independent research and policy organization of 250 business leaders and educators. Since 1985 the CED has issued reports supportive of preschool, full-day kindergarten, and high-quality child care. In a 2006 report, CED explicitly notes a shifting rationale for preschool: "The social equity arguments for preschool programs have recently been reinforced by compelling economic evidence which suggests that society at large benefits from investing in these programs. Broadening access to preschool programs for *all* children is a cost-effective investment that pays dividends for years to come and will help ensure our states' and our nation's future economic productivity."[18]

These conclusions, from a prominent business group, are significant because of the business community's reputation for hard-headed, dispassionate analysis focused on the bottom line.

Child Welfare

Historically, many of the arguments made in support of child welfare programs have been based on desert, not consequences. Through no fault of their own, some children find themselves without a functioning or supportive family or, for that matter, without any family at all. Under these circumstances, it is argued, society has an obligation to intervene.

In the United States these arguments can be traced back to Chicago's Hull-House, where Jane Addams and others cared for distressed mothers and neighborhood children and where they articulated a philosophy to support public initiatives on their behalf. The overriding sentiment that motivated Addams was a kind of "Christian humanitarianism" or "sympathetic knowledge" that viewed charity as a subjective necessity and a civic obligation. These moralistic sentiments encouraged the creation of the Children's Bureau in 1912, child labor laws, benefits for widowed mothers, public playgrounds for children, and many other initiatives at all levels of government.[19] As Jean Elshtain notes, "Nearly every major piece

17. Fight Crime: Invest in Kids (2012); Pre-K Now (2011).
18. Committee for Economic Development (2006, p. ix).
19. Lasch (1965, p. 29); Hamington (2009, p. 71); Skocpol (1992).

of social legislation or civic initiative having to do with the well-being of children from 1890 until the New Deal bears the Hull-House stamp in one way or another."[20]

Today one sees moralistic arguments on the websites of various organizations committed to child welfare. For example, the Baltimore-based Annie E. Casey Foundation proclaims: "All children need and deserve a family for life, as well as effective services and public systems that ensure, above all, their safety and well-being. Not all children in our country have these supports."[21]

In general, evidence on the consequences of various child welfare strategies has been conspicuous by its absence. There is, however, some evidence on this subject. Jane Waldfogel writes on the failures of our current child protective services delivery system and on the potential benefits of a "differentiated response" system such as that tried in Missouri. And David Finkelhor shows that school-based programs aimed at heightening awareness of sexual abuse can enhance knowledge, encourage disclosure, and reduce self-blame. Unfortunately, there is no firm evidence that it can also reduce victimization.[22]

A rare source of good information on child welfare is the University of Chicago's Chapin Hall Center for Children, a research and policy center that seeks to improve the well-being of children and youth. Although most of its work focuses on the incidence of certain problems and trends over time, it has produced some interesting empirical work on child welfare policy consequences. For example, in 2007 Chapin Hall reported results from an extensive comparison of foster youth in Illinois (where eighteen- to twenty-one-year-olds remained eligible for child welfare benefits) and foster youth in Iowa and Wisconsin (where eligibility stopped at age eighteen). The comparison finds that, after controlling for demographic characteristics, the Illinois foster youth were 3.5 times more likely to have completed one or more years of college than their counterparts in the other two states. The study also finds increased earnings and reduced pregnancy rates in Illinois, as opposed to the other two states.[23]

In public debates over child welfare, the typical pattern is that a horrible scandal (such as the death of an innocent child) triggers sharply

20. Elshtain (2002, p. 122).
21. Annie E. Casey Foundation (2011).
22. See Waldfogel (1998); Finkelhor (2009).
23. See Courtney, Dworsky, and Pollack (2007).

critical mass media coverage, temporary public outrage, a resignation or two, and some modest institutional reforms.[24] The focus, almost always, is a perceived moral obligation to come to the aid of vulnerable children who, through no fault of their own, find themselves in a dangerous home environment or shuttled from one foster home to another. Although short-term costs do receive some attention, long-term benefits seldom do. This could be because of the paucity of good empirical research on this subject, a consensus that society has a moral obligation to care for children whose parents are unable or unwilling to do so, or both. In short, child welfare frames tend to be moralistic (protect innocent children from harm) rather than economic (adopt policies that benefit society in the long run).

Table 3-1 summarizes some key differences across three children's policy domains. Some of these variables have important political implications. For example, when mass media interest is high, advocates can more easily expand the scope of conflict. When the federal government's role is strong, advocates understandably focus more attention on Washington. Nevertheless, the variable that shapes messaging most clearly is scientific evidence. With ample scientific evidence on the consequences of public policies, economic framing is possible; without it, economic framing is, frankly, speculative. In recognition of this fundamental fact, advocates have used economic frames more assiduously when discussing child health and education.

State Child Advocates

Differences across policy domains surfaced in interviews I conducted with fifty state-level child advocates (from forty states and the District of Columbia) in the summer of 2003. The groups contacted were affiliated with a national organization, Voices for America's Children, based in Washington, D.C.[25] I asked each advocate to identify the organization's top three issues that year and then to summarize the main argument used to justify their organization's position on each issue. The top issues that year were child health policy, early childhood care and education policy, and child welfare policy, in that order.

---

24. Gainsborough (2010, pp. 112–13).
25. Of fifty-nine organizations contacted, fifty agreed to an in-depth interview, for a response rate of 85 percent. For more on this research, see Gormley and Cymrot (2006).

Table 3-2. *Use of Issue Frames by State Child Advocates,*
by Policy Area, 2003[a]

Percent

Frame	Child health (N = 36)	Early childhood care, education (N = 29)	Child welfare (N = 12)
Prevention or investment	67	52	25
Parents' well-being	14	48	0
Fairness or morality	14	7	17
Safety	6	14	33

Source: Author.

a. Columns do not add up to 100 percent, because a relatively small number of arguments included more than one frame, while others could not be classified with the above four categories.

Economic arguments (investment, prevention) predominated in discussions of child health policy (two-thirds of all arguments) and early childhood care and education policy (one-half of all arguments) but were less common in discussions of child welfare policy (one-fourth of all arguments; table 3-2).

Child Health

Angela Jones, of D.C. Action for Children, made the following argument for more Medicaid and S-CHIP expenditures: "Kids need health insurance. Access to health insurance is a predictor of health outcomes. Kids with insurance are more likely to visit the doctor, less likely to visit the emergency room." Sharon Peters, of Michigan's Children, used a prevention argument, in support of health care programs for low-income children: "An ounce of prevention is worth a pound of cure. Public spending for children is far less than spending for the elderly. If we spend currently for children we save a lot for more costly interventions later. That's true of mental and physical health." Kathy Bigsby Moore, of Voices for Children of Nebraska, offered a similar argument in opposition to proposed cutbacks in Medicaid and S-CHIP spending: "Our argument was that dollars spent on preventive services save many more dollars later on. If prevention is not offered, children's health problems increase, and they are more likely to cost the state more money in the future." Jann Jackson,

of Advocates for Children and Youth (Maryland), argued against proposed cutbacks in the S-CHIP program: "Kids that get preventive care can
stay in school. It costs the states less money. Cutting it was the stupidest
thing you could do. You were losing federal dollars, lost jobs for doctors,
and you'd pay for it anyway through emergency room care."

Some advocacy groups blended their arguments. For example, Amy
Rossi, of Arkansas Advocates, which focuses on access to quality health
care for uninsured children, noted: "Our fundamental argument for this
is both moral and financial. Health insurance leads to preventive care,
which in turn leads to a lessening cost in chronic health problems. It
makes children more productive." Similarly, Jack Levine, of Voices for
Florida's Children, made a blended argument for greater health care
access: "The consistent argument around access to health care is always
the combination of moral and financial benefits. Early access prevents
pain and higher costs later. When we look at expanding Healthy Start
programs all the way through health insurance access, trying to broaden
dentistry services for children, the argument is always a twin between it's
the moral thing to do *and* the budgetarily sound thing to do."

Early Childhood Care and Education

Michael Reisch, of Children Now, in Oakland, California, recalled
making this argument for universal voluntary preschool for three-year-
olds and four-year-olds in California: "Preschool is an important component in school readiness and socialization and in providing a venue
for health, oral health, and mental health screening for children. Therefore, it not only produces children who are better able to learn, but also
healthier, and whose problems if any can be addressed at an early stage.
Better outcomes academically, better outcomes for the state financially."
Jerry Johnson, of Priority Children (Michigan), offered the following
argument for early childhood development expenditures: "We want to
invest in early childhood, quality care, better prepared provider workforce, and putting money into 0-5 programs. This is important because
investments in early childhood have greater payoffs and impact on child
development than any fix-it programs attempted later." Richard Rathge,
of North Dakota Kids Count, stressed economics: "From our work last
year, we found that what resonates best with legislators is the bottom-line
economics. The child care industry contributes to the economy, allows
parents to continue to work. Also, from the child's perspective, it helps

the education process." Ellie Goldberg, of the Maine Children's Alliance, explicitly referred to the celebrated Perry Preschool Project in arguing for more resources for infant and toddler care: "Child development information tells us that the way that babies start off is going to influence them for their whole life and the best care we can give them will have a monetary effect. For every dollar you invest in quality early care, you reduce costs by $7.16. That's the Perry Preschool Study. It just finished its 27th year and it found that they save $7.16 for every dollar invested."

Deb Miller, of Kentucky Youth Advocates, used a blended argument in support of better child care access and higher child care quality: "We make the child development kind of argument—the brain research argument. We also make the argument that for economic development and for parents to work, we need child care. We don't exclusively stick to one argument—I like to think we are being smart on our argument." Kappy Hubbard, of the Alliance for South Carolina's Children, also used a blended argument, in favor of early childhood education programs: "The argument has been all along that it is a great investment in terms of your dollars. The studies show that for every dollar invested, you are seeing dollars saved because of prevention. The notion of school readiness was also important. Early brain research shows that this is when children are ripe to learn."

Child Welfare

In contrast to child health and early care and education, discussions of child welfare are more varied. Gail Nayowith, of the Citizens Committee for Children of New York, stressed a child protection theme: "Children are supposed to be protected; otherwise, they die. Children are not always safe at home and with the people who love them. The city is responsible for providing quality foster care." In contrast, Dana Bunnett, of Kids in Common, a California-based advocacy group, stressed the value of family preservation: "The fundamental argument is that families are best if they remain together. We should provide a system that supports families rather than tearing them apart." Although some advocates used an economic frame (investment or prevention) when discussing child welfare, most did not.

The absence of strong empirical evidence on the long-term consequences of child abuse and neglect or prolonged foster care could help to account for the lower reliance on economic arguments in child welfare policy debates. Without credible evidence on social benefits and costs, it is difficult for advocates, outside or inside of government, to pin their hopes on economic arguments alone.

On the other hand, child welfare debates may lend themselves to moralistic arguments. Children whose parents have died, disappeared, or proven themselves unfit are both vulnerable and blameless. Traditional arguments in favor of parental responsibility simply don't apply here; like it or not, the state is already responsible for these children. Under these circumstances, an equal opportunity argument or a helping-hand argument may be compelling enough to carry the day.

Conclusion

Some children's issues lend themselves to economic arguments, while others seem to invite moralistic arguments. In general, child health and education issues seem better suited than child welfare issues to economic arguments. There are, however, variations within each of these broad issue areas. For example, economic arguments have been widely used in debates over early childhood education and childhood immunizations but are seldom used in debates over special education or kidney transplants for children.

Variations in the use of economic frames depend considerably on public perceptions of the legitimacy of government intervention. Americans remain ambivalent about the government's responsibility to care for or educate children under the age of five. For example, 75 percent of all Americans reject the idea that women should return to their traditional role in society, and 57 percent agree that both the husband and the wife should contribute to household income. On the other hand, 72 percent believe that too many children are being raised in day care centers these days. A strong economic argument might convince fence straddlers to get off the fence, which presumably is why advocates have shifted to such arguments.[26]

It is probably easier for children's advocates who prefer a stronger government role in helping children to become productive adults to persuade moderates (or fence straddlers) than conservatives, who believe that families should find their own way. In a fascinating study, Jonathan Haidt finds that both liberals and conservatives value fairness and protection

26. See Parker (2009).

from harm, while only conservatives value loyalty, authority, and purity. On crucial values, liberals and conservatives are poles apart.[27]

One might infer from this that liberals should highlight such values as fairness and protection from harm, which both liberals and conservatives embrace. Or one might infer that liberals should try to integrate such values as loyalty and authority into their arguments. A third option would be for liberals to abandon moralistic arguments altogether in favor of economic arguments, which conservatives might be tempted to embrace. These possibilities are investigated more fully in chapter 5.

In contrast to early childhood education and child health, where ideological fault lines remain visible, a rough consensus seems to have been reached that the government should assist children who are orphaned, abandoned, or exposed to physical or sexual abuse. A reminder of our moral obligations may suffice. The presence or absence of good empirical evidence on the consequences of government intervention also affects the viability of different issue frames. With considerable evidence in hand, an economic frame may be a better bet. With limited evidence available, a moralistic frame may make more sense.

Another possibility worth considering is that children's issue frames vary across venues and that this reflects institutional differences in the appeal of certain frames. For example, the utility of a given frame may depend on whether the venue is one of the political branches of government or whether the venue is the judiciary. The latter, in principle, should be receptive to rights-based (deontological) arguments, while the former should be receptive to more diverse types of arguments, including teleological arguments about consequences. In chapter 4, I explore this possibility.

27. Haidt (2007).

CHAPTER FOUR

Arguments in
Different Venues

*Reimbursement of private school tuition is essential to
enforcing IDEA's requirement that all children with disabilities be provided an education that is both free and
appropriate.*

Respondent's Brief,
Forest Grove School District v. *T.A.*,
March 25, 2009

In contrast to the political branches of the government,
the judiciary has long been associated with arguments focused on legal
rights and obligations. From the vantage point of federal judges, the key
question to be decided is not whether a particular policy is the best possible policy (or whether it is the most popular policy) but rather whether
it is consistent with the U.S. Constitution, relevant federal statutes, and
relevant judicial precedents. State judges, for their part, focus more on
their respective state constitutions and state statutes, though they must
also be mindful of the U.S. Constitution, federal law, and federal court
precedents. In child welfare cases, federal judges seek to determine
whether the persistence of abuse, neglect, and long stays in foster care
homes deprives children of their rights under the Fourteenth Amendment
to the U.S. Constitution. In school financing disputes, state supreme
courts wrestle with the meaning of key state constitution provisions guar-
anteeing an education to every child.[1]

Although framing has not received much attention in the judicial politics literature, Lee Epstein and Joseph Kobylka argue that how parties
frame legal arguments has important consequences for court decisions.

---

1. See Urbina (2009); Gainsborough (2010); Reed (2001); Hanushek and Lindseth
(2009, pp. 83–117).

For example, the NAACP Legal Defense Fund's decision to frame capital punishment as an issue of cruel and unusual punishment rather than due process may have contributed to an adverse Supreme Court ruling in *McClesky* v. *Kemp*. More recently, Justin Wedeking has documented strategic thinking in the use of issue frames, with petitioners choosing frames for Supreme Court briefs based in part on how lower courts reacted to similar frames.[2]

But do the courts welcome policy arguments that employ legalistic frames? Do they discourage or reject policy arguments that employ economic frames or science frames or moral frames that are not legalistic in nature? And do advocates take venue into account as they shift their focus from the political branches of government to the judiciary? If so, we should see different language being employed when the same issues are being addressed by different branches of government. To investigate this possibility, I consider four policy domains that often involve recourse to the courts: school finance, special education, school desegregation, and juvenile justice. My goal is to look for differences in issue frames between the judiciary and the political branches of government.

School Finance

Advocates of school finance reform at the state level use different frames in support of reform. In New Jersey, advocates articulated a compensatory frame, which stresses the need for relatively equal school district expenditure levels as a matter of fundamental fairness. In Kentucky, advocates presented a common school frame, which stresses the social benefits of a well-educated and well-informed citizenry. These different rhetorical appeals reflect the views and strategic calculations of reformers in the two states, not differences in the states' constitutions. In fact, the language of the two state constitutions is quite similar: New Jersey's constitution (1885) requires a "thorough and efficient education" for all children, while Kentucky's constitution (1891) requires "an efficient system of common schools" throughout the state.[3]

In 1981 the Education Law Center, based in Newark, New Jersey, filed a lawsuit (*Abbott* v. *Burke*) that built on a previous state supreme court victory in *Robinson* v. *Cahill*. In 1985 the New Jersey Supreme

2. See Epstein and Kobylka (1992, pp. 132–36); Wedeking (2010).
3. Paris (2010).

Court handed down a decision that technically favored the state defendant (the plaintiff must make his case before an administrative law judge, as opposed to a judge) but that in fact embraced the reasoning of the plaintiff that disadvantaged students may require greater than average resources in order to secure their constitutional rights. In early 1990 New Jersey's newly elected governor, Jim Florio, drafted an education reform law known as the Quality Education Act, or QEA. Although Florio viewed his legislation as providing benefits to everyone, including the "beleaguered middle class," this alternative frame never had a chance to develop. Florio announced that he would be proposing an education bill in March, unveiled the details in May, reconciled his proposal with the latest state supreme court decision in June, and signed the bill into law in July. Democratic legislators introduced Florio's bill on May 25, and the state supreme court handed down its *Abbott II* decision on June 5.[4]

In the public mind, the governor's education reform bill and the state supreme court's decision became virtually indistinguishable. As Michael Paris notes, "The Court's decision would only solidify the public's association of the QEA with Abbott, and its sense that together they represented a 'Robin Hood solution' that would steal from the rich (white) people to give to the (poor) black people."[5] Whatever message the governor and his aides hoped to convey, they found themselves closely linked to the Education Law Center, which brought the lawsuit, and to the supreme court decision that declared the ELC the victor in 1990.

In 1985 Kentucky's Council for Better Education filed a lawsuit contending that the state's school finance system was unconstitutional. Instead of a compensatory education frame, they embraced a common school frame, which stresses commonalities, not differences. Indeed, the council publicly rejected the idea of a Robin Hood approach to education. As one reformer, Arnold Guess, puts it, a redistribution of existing resources would only "redistribute mediocrity." The council articulated a common school frame in court and in politics, thus helping to ensure that the same relatively nonthreatening frame would be invoked in different institutional arenas. The Kentucky Supreme Court's opinion in *Rose v. Council for Better Education* (1989) closely mirrors language used by the plaintiffs. The following year, the Kentucky state legislature enacted the Kentucky Education Reform Act, which increased education aid to

4. See Paris (2010, pp. 90, 113).
5. Paris (2010, p. 114).

all school districts but which also channeled more funds to the neediest districts. A $1.3 billion tax increase, over two years, eventually supported by Governor Wallace Wilkinson, made all of this possible.[6]

While the principal frames in support of education finance reform differ between New Jersey and Kentucky, the frames within each state do not seem to differ much across venues. In New Jersey, the political and judicial debates look very similar: the emphasis is on compensation and redistribution. In Kentucky, the political and judicial debates also look quite similar: the emphasis is on shared values in support of a common school approach.

In one critical respect, however, the debate over school finance is framed differently in judicial and political settings. In legislative and executive branch deliberations, public officials are forced to confront competing claims on the public purse: elementary and secondary education versus other possibilities. In contrast, the issue before the courts is whether additional appropriations for education are required by the state constitution, not whether such appropriations are more or less deserving than appropriations for other purposes. As Eric Hanushek and Alfred Lindseth note, "Many educational advocates quite naturally prefer the courts because the discussion there is confined to a single issue: education. There are no competing demands, and advocates for other programs or taxpayers are excluded."[7]

Special Education

The federal judiciary's emphasis on rights and obligations is quite noticeable in recent Supreme Court rulings on special education. In *Forest Grove School District* v. *T.A.*, the U.S. Supreme Court had to decide whether a parent of an arguably disabled child could send that child to a private school and submit the bill to the local school district, even if the child never received special education services from the school district itself. A more routine situation would be one in which the child received special education services from the school district but either the school district or the parents subsequently decided that the child would be better served by a private school.[8]

6. See Paris (2010, pp. 173, 184, 207).
7. Hanushek and Lindseth (2009, p. 144).
8. *Forest Grove School District* v. *T.A.* (2009).

In *Forest Grove*, the Supreme Court decided, by a vote of 6 to 3, that parents are within their rights to send their disabled child to a private school (at the school district's expense) if this is necessary for the child to receive "a free appropriate public education." This language is the cornerstone of the Education of the Handicapped Act of 1975. The Court sidesteps language in more recent legislation, the Individuals with Disabilities Education Act of 1990, as amended in 1997, that seems to preclude parents from enrolling their child in a private school without first availing themselves of the school district's special education services. In this instance, the Court notes, the school district did not provide the child with an individualized education plan that would enable him to receive a free appropriate public education (FAPE). Ultimately, a majority of the Supreme Court concluded that the 1997 amendments do not constitute an absolute bar to reimbursement, especially since the all-important FAPE clause remained intact and since the overall intent of the 1997 amendments is to expand access to special education services.

In the Supreme Court's ruling, in the oral arguments before the Court and in the briefs submitted by the opposing sides, one sees no economic argument on behalf of handicapped children. Rather, one sees moralistic arguments—that these children need special help and that they are entitled to an equal opportunity.

Interestingly, one does see an economic argument by the school district, namely, that the cost of sending a special education child to a private school is unduly prohibitive. At oral argument, Justice Antonin Scalia drew attention to the cost of private schooling (in the school district's brief) by asking counsel for the school district to specify it. The counsel, Gary Feinerman, was happy to oblige, noting that private school tuition for a special education student cost taxpayers $5,200 per month, plus fees. Similarly, in his dissent, Justice David Souter (joined by Scalia and Thomas) notes that "special education can be immensely expensive, amounting to tens of billions of dollars annually and as much as 20 percent of public schools' general budgets." However, the overwhelming emphasis of the briefs, the oral argument, the majority opinion, and the dissent is on statutory interpretation, not costs or benefits.[9]

The preponderance of arguments heard by the Court and cited by the majority in its opinion are legalistic: for example, that states that accept federal funding agree to provide FAPE to handicapped students and that

9. *Forest Grove School District* v. *T.A.* (2009, pp. 7, 10).

a minor clause in a more recent law does not automatically eradicate a major clause in a less recent law.

Judicial Chambers versus Legislative Committees

A key question that arises when considering special education is whether the Supreme Court's inattention to economic analysis (as defined here) is characteristic of judicial behavior generally, special education debates generally, or both. Do members of Congress utilize economic frames when making the case for stronger special education policies? Do witnesses before congressional committees utilize economic frames when presenting testimony on special education policy proposals?

In fact, economic arguments have been largely absent from special education debates, not simply in Supreme Court decisionmaking but also in congressional debates. When Congress considered the Education of All Handicapped Children Act in 1975, members of Congress and witnesses eschewed economic frames in favor of moralistic frames. Representative John Brademas (D-Ind.), who chaired the Subcommittee on Select Education of the House Education and Labor Committee, regarded special education as an equal opportunity and a constitutional issue. Representative Albert Quie (R-Minn.), the ranking minority member of the subcommittee, also subscribed to the opportunity frame. Education Commissioner Terrel Bell made economic arguments of a sort, but in opposition to a strong piece of legislation. Citing fiscal deficits, Bell cautioned against spending a significant amount of money on new guarantees for handicapped children. He also cautioned against a federal takeover of activities traditionally reserved to the states. When expressing perfunctory support for some federal role, he cited equal opportunity arguments, though Brademas publicly questioned the depth of Bell's commitment to equal opportunity. In short, almost all of the arguments in favor of a strong new piece of special education legislation were moralistic in nature.[10]

In 1990 the Education of All Handicapped Children Act was renamed the Individuals with Disabilities Education Act (IDEA). In 1995 Congress held hearings on the reauthorization of IDEA. Representative Randall (Duke) Cunningham (R-Calif.), chair of the Subcommittee on Early Childhood, Youth and Families of the House Economic and Educational

10. See Brademas (1975, pp. 19, 135, 138); Quie (1975, p. 148); Bell (1975, pp. 135–38).

Opportunities Committee, expressed the view that programs for special education children should stress "preparation for a work force in later life so that they could earn a good living and not be on Federal programs." This could certainly be viewed as an economic argument. Other members of the committee, however, focused instead on the due process rights of special education children (Miller), the case for greater parental awareness of their legal rights (Kildee), and the need for even disruptive students to get a good education (Scott). IDEA was reauthorized in 1997.[11]

Secretaries of education have sometimes used economic arguments in support of special education initiatives. In a public address to an international Special Olympics group, Secretary of Education Margaret Spellings discussed the practical consequences of mainstreaming special education children. She cited research showing that when you put everyone together in the same classroom, both teachers and parents are more likely to see special education students as capable people. She also noted evidence of improvement in the math scores of fourth-grade students with disabilities following passage of the No Child Left Behind Act.[12]

In public speeches on the Individuals with Disabilities in Education Act, Secretary of Education Arne Duncan uses legalistic language, hailing IDEA as "a major civil rights victory." On the other hand, he also makes explicit allusions to economic consequences. Low expectations for special education students, he argues, are "terrible for our country's economic vitality." He further calls for investing more resources in special education so that these students, when older, will be "strong contributors to our national economy."[13]

Local politicians also sometimes use economic frames in discussing special education. Given the high costs of educating special education students, questions about cost-effectiveness are often raised. For example, Washington Mayor Adrian Fenty tried to reduce the size of the D.C. public schools special education budget by chipping away at the $280 million annual cost of sending special education students to private schools when the D.C. public schools could not accommodate them.[14]

In short, legalistic and moralistic arguments seem to predominate in debates over special education, in both the political branches and the

---

11. See U.S. House of Representatives (1995, p. 33).
12. See Spellings (2007).
13. See Duncan (2010c).
14. Turque (2010).

judiciary. Economic arguments occasionally surface, perhaps more so in the political branches, but thus far they have played a secondary role in these debates.

School Desegregation

In 2007, in a pair of decisions involving school systems in Seattle, Washington, and Louisville, Kentucky, the U.S. Supreme Court reconsidered its long-standing policy of encouraging racial and ethnic diversity in public school classrooms. In pursuit of that goal, the Supreme Court concluded, school districts may not take a student's race or ethnicity into account. To do so, the justices argued, is a violation of the equal protection clause of the Constitution. The Court's majority refused to distinguish between race-based approaches that promote integration and race-based approaches that promote segregation. In Chief Justice Roberts's words: "The way to stop discrimination on the basis of race is to stop discriminating on the basis of race." Four justices strongly disagreed. In an unusually long and biting dissent, Justice Breyer invoked the principle of stare decisis: "Since this Court's decision in *Brown,* the law has consistently and unequivocally approved of both voluntary and compulsory race-conscious measures to combat segregated schools." Condemning the majority for repudiating the Fourteenth Amendment's "moral vision," Breyer called the majority's decision a major setback to "the work of local school boards to bring about racially diverse schools." The justices' arguments, on both sides, are largely legalistic and moralistic.[15]

As some critics of the Court's decision predicted, the Supreme Court's decision has made it easier for local school boards to roll back long-standing policies and practices that facilitate school desegregation, such as the busing of students from one neighborhood to another. In March 2010 the Wake County school board, led by John Tedesco and three other newly elected school board members, voted to rescind Wake County's diversity policy in favor of a neighborhood schools approach. Because Wake County's diversity policy was, as of 2000, class based rather than race based, its decision was not mandated by the Supreme Court's 2007 decision. In fact, several school districts, including Pittsburgh's and Chicago's, switched from a race-based to a social class–based school

15. See *Brown* v. *Board of Education of Topeka* (1954); *Parents Involved in Community Schools v. Seattle* (2007, p. 864); Barnes (2007).

assignment system following the Supreme Court's decision. Nevertheless, the Wake County school board's decision is fully consistent with the Court's new skepticism toward proactive racial integration measures.[16]

At the school board's meetings, and in news media accounts, some of the arguments by opposing sides were more inflammatory than persuasive. For example, the Reverend Curtis Gatewood, second vice president of the state NAACP, called one member of the board a "white racist" and pleaded, "If you expect to go to hell, don't take our children with you."[17] A white member of the board, accused of racism, later defended himself by noting in a letter to the NAACP that, as a younger man, he had dated African American and Latino women. This comment did not improve the dialogue.

At the school board's meetings, diversity supporters relied primarily on moralistic arguments. William Barber, president of the state NAACP, put it this way: "Your plan is wrong. It's wayward. It will make things worse and you know it. Data doesn't support it. Morality doesn't support it." At least one member of the school board, Anne McLaurin, used an equal opportunity argument, stressing that North Carolina's constitution guarantees all North Carolina children "an equal opportunity for a sound basic education."[18]

In contrast, advocates of the new policy stressed freedom of choice, stability, and proximity. John Tedesco, the leader of the reform movement, argued that a neighborhood choice approach "will give parents more stability." One of the key complaints against the diversity approach was that it resulted in some students being uprooted again and again. A parent, Debbie Griffith Overby, invoked parental choice (freedom) as a value: "I'm against forced busing," she said. "This is the United States of America. People should not be forced in Wake County to do anything they don't want to do."[19]

As the Wake County school board prepared to implement its public school choice plan, it heard from Helen Ladd, a professor at Duke University, who cautioned that an unadulterated school choice plan could worsen racial segregation in the schools. Ladd noted that this seemed to have happened in the Charlotte-Mecklenburg school district following

16. See McCrummen (2011); Samuels (2011).
17. Hui (2010).
18. See Hui and Goldsmith (2010); Goldsmith and Hui (2010).
19. See Goldsmith and Hui (2010).

the introduction of a choice plan there in 2002–03.[20] On the positive side, Ladd cited a hybrid school choice plan in Boston, which combined a strong preference for socioeconomic and racial diversity, with a guarantee that 50 percent of available seats would be reserved for children who lived in the immediate neighborhood.

Nearly a year after the Wake County school board's tumultuous meetings, a member of the majority coalition switched her vote, which triggered further reconsideration. Under a compromise plan adopted in October 2011, current students would be allowed to stay where they are but parents would be free to choose from at least five elementary schools, two middle schools, and two high schools.[21] In November 2011 a school board election shifted the balance of power yet again, this time from a prochoice majority to a prodiversity majority. As of December 2011 the Wake County school board was actively reconsidering its prochoice decision.

In short, Wake County's elected officials and the U.S. Supreme Court both focused on moralistic and legalistic arguments. Should some students be coerced into being bused to a school in a different neighborhood? Should some students be deprived of equal opportunity because busing does not take place? These arguments were of central importance, as opposed to the question of whether majority or minority students would benefit from—or be harmed by—school integration.

On the other hand, it is true that the rhetoric employed in public hearings before the Wake County school board was more moralistic and less legalistic than the rhetoric employed in oral arguments before the U.S. Supreme Court. The rhetoric employed by ordinary citizens and community activists in Raleigh, North Carolina, was also more impassioned and histrionic than that employed by lawyers pleading before the Supreme Court. In this important respect, language did differ across venues, even if economic arguments received short shrift in both settings.

Juvenile Justice

The Supreme Court's emphasis on legalistic and moralistic criteria, as opposed to economic criteria, is evident not just in school desegregation cases but also in its most recent decision on the death penalty for

20. For good evidence on this point, see Clotfelter, Ladd, and Vigdor (2008). Also see Ladd (2010).

21. Hui (2011).

juveniles. In *Roper* v. *Simmons* (2005), the Supreme Court decided, by a vote of 5 to 4, that the Eighth Amendment (cruel and unusual punishment) and the Fourteenth Amendment (due process of law) effectively bar capital punishment for individuals who were under the age of 18 when their crime was committed.[22] This decision departed from a precedent set in 1989, in the *Stanford* v. *Kentucky* case.

A key point made by Justice Anthony Kennedy, who wrote the majority opinion, is that most states have abolished the death penalty for juveniles, with five more states joining that majority in recent years; most nations have abolished the juvenile death penalty as well. Kennedy frames the majority's conclusion in moralistic terms: "From a moral standpoint it would be misguided to equate the failings of a minor with those of an adult, for a greater possibility exists that a minor's character deficiencies will be reformed." He also rebuts an argument for retribution made by the other side: "Whether viewed as an attempt to express the community's moral outrage or as an attempt to right the balance for the wrong to the victim, the case for retribution is not as strong with a minor as with an adult." Kennedy dismisses deterrence arguments on the grounds that "juveniles will be less susceptible to deterrence" than adults. He cites the Court's opinion in another case (*Thompson*) that teenagers are extremely unlikely to engage in a "cost-benefit analysis that attaches any weight to the possibility of execution." In support of the majority's position, Kennedy cites scientific evidence that adolescents are less mature than adults, that they are more vulnerable to peer pressure, and that their character is not fully formed.[23]

In state legislatures in which the death penalty for juveniles was debated prior to the Supreme Court's decision in *Roper* v. *Simmons*, similar arguments were made. In Wyoming in 2004 Representative Jane Warren (D-Laramie) cites brain research as justification for abolishing the death penalty for juveniles. "There's a lot of data that can back up the idea that the death penalty is not an appropriate option for juveniles," she said. "The developmental level of a young person is not at the same point as an adult for making a decision." Representative Lorna Johnson (D-Laramie) offered a similar argument, but from personal experience: "There's been some push over the last few years that we need to get tough on kids. If part of that is going so far as to include the death penalty, I

22. *Roper* v. *Simmons* (2005).
23. *Roper* v. *Simmons* (2005, pp. 15–18).

really think we are looking at it from the wrong point of view. From my experience as a parent, I don't know kids that sit back and say, 'What is the law here? How severely am I going to be punished?' They don't think ahead. They may feel completely different after the fact." Wyoming abolished the death penalty for juveniles in 2004.[24]

In Virginia, where the death penalty for juveniles was debated in 2005, moralistic arguments also predominated. Representative Albert Eisenberg (D-Arlington) argued: "I think it's an international outrage. Anybody who has teenage children knows on a daily basis how bad their judgment can be."[25] Opponents, in contrast, argued that some crimes are so heinous that they deserve the death penalty. Virginia declined to abolish the death penalty for juveniles in 2005, though that decision was rendered moot by *Roper* v. *Simmons*.

Arguments Missing in Action

Moralistic and legalistic arguments have a special resonance in judicial tribunals, where justice, not efficiency, is the overriding concern. They also have a special legitimacy whenever and wherever questions of civil rights, broadly defined, are being discussed, whether that is in a courtroom, a legislative hearing room, or elsewhere.

The problem with debates over school financing, special education, school desegregation, and juvenile justice is not that moralistic and legalistic frames play a critical role in these debates but rather that economic frames are so thoroughly ignored.

In fact, economic frames and evidence on the consequences of alternative public policies could make a useful contribution to debates involving the welfare of children who suffer from mental or physical disabilities and children who belong to racial and ethnic groups that have been discriminated against in the past. The absence of such arguments in contemporary debates on children's issues is regrettable.

A key question in school finance debates ought to be whether differences in financial resources across school districts limit the ability of poorer school districts to achieve good results for their students. The Coleman Report raises some questions about this assumption, and at least one prominent researcher, Eric Hanushek, argues that the relationship between

24. See Olson (2004).
25. Green (2005).

school expenditures and school outcomes is generally weak. On the other hand, a careful meta-analysis of multiple studies concludes that per pupil expenditures (PPE) do make a considerable difference. Specifically, Larry Hedges, Richard Laine, and Rob Greenwald find that "an increase of PPE by $500 (approximately 10% of the national average) would be associated with a 0.7 standard deviation increase in student outcome." As the authors note, this would generally be considered "a large effect." The authors reach similar conclusions in a later meta-analysis of a more comprehensive set of studies. Even Hanushek and Alfred Lindseth concede that, in education, "there is mounting evidence that money, if spent appropriately, can have a significant effect." They cite the importance of recruiting and retaining effective teachers as a good example. Thus money does matter, though how we spend the money obviously matters as well. Advocates could do a better job of using empirical evidence and economic frames to support the view that in education, as in other policy domains, poorly funded programs are likely to produce poor results.[26]

The primary case for school desegregation can be found in the Fourteenth Amendment to the Constitution and in the Supreme Court's 1954 decision in *Brown* v. *Board of Education*. Separate schools are inherently unequal, they are unconstitutional, and they violate many of the moral premises of Judeo-Christian beliefs. But many questions about the pace of school desegregation and the mechanisms whereby school desegregation will be achieved are more practical in nature. For these questions, which arise in many school districts on a regular basis, empirical evidence and economic frames could be useful. A careful meta-analysis of ninety-three research studies finds that school desegregation enhances black achievement by approximately 0.3 standard deviation, if it occurs as early as first grade.[27] This has important implications, because it suggests that school desegregation delayed is school achievement denied. Advocates could do a better job of using empirical evidence and economic frames to support the view that school desegregation, from the very beginning of elementary school, promotes equal opportunity by reducing the black-white achievement gap. This in turn has important implications for black-white income disparities later on.

26. See Coleman and others (1966); Hanushek (1981, 1986); Hedges, Laine, and Greenwald (1994, p. 11); Greenwald, Hedges, and Laine (1996); Hanushek and Lindseth (2009, p. 57).
27. Crain and Mahard (1979).

Most debates over special education focus on legal requirements for students with disabilities to receive a "free appropriate public education" under federal law. Debates also focus on society's moral obligations to help highly vulnerable children who cannot succeed in school without generous financial and emotional support. As noted earlier, there is not much empirical evidence on the effects of special education programs.[28] However, there are some studies, including an excellent one by Eric Hanushek, John Kain, and Steven Rivkin, that analyze data from over 200,000 students in over 3,000 public schools in Texas.[29] This study finds that one year of special education results in a .1 standard deviation increase in students' math scores. Most important, exposure to special education students in the same classroom does not adversely affect the test outcomes of other students. More work needs to be done, including long-term studies on school achievement and studies that combine benefits and costs. In the meantime, however, advocates should use the results of this study to argue that special education programs improve school achievement for program participants, which should reduce costs to the rest of society down the road.

Conclusion

In contrast to framing differences across issue areas, which are relatively clear, framing differences across venues are relatively subtle, at least for those issues that routinely wind up in court. Debates over school finance, special education, school desegregation, and juvenile justice attract legalistic and moralistic frames in all three branches of government. Economic arguments surface occasionally, perhaps more so in the political branches than in the courts, but they play a less conspicuous role in these debates.

Why have economic frames generated less interest in the courts and in issue areas that lend themselves to judicial review? First, rights-based claims have a long history of being channeled into the courts. The same factors that push certain issues into the judicial arena—disputes over due process, equal protection, and legal rights—also shape the discourse surrounding these issues, whether they are debated in court or in the political

---

28. Aron and Loprest (2012, p. 111) reach similar conclusions: "Relatively little research has been conducted on the effectiveness of specific special education practices or programs."

29. Hanushek, Kain, and Rivkin (2002).

branches.[30] While the political branches seem to place more emphasis on costs and benefits and opportunity costs than the judiciary does, rights-based language remains important for the political branches.

Second, empirical evidence on the consequences of public policies in these areas is sometimes scarce. Certainly this is true of special education. While the short-term costs of special education are relatively easy to measure, the long-term benefits of special education have seldom been documented with precision. As a result, the data for a well-informed economic discussion are simply not available.

One can imagine a situation in which children's advocates switch their discourse from deontological to teleological reasoning when they shift venues from the judiciary to the political branches. Perhaps they should. But it is not easy to keep two sets of rhetorical books. Especially in the age of the Internet, rhetoric intended for one venue may easily be brought to the attention of another venue. For this reason, advocates must often choose a rhetorical strategy and stick with it.

But which rhetorical strategy should advocates choose? Are some issue frames more potent than others? Are economic frames more appealing to some subgroups, while moralistic frames are more appealing to others? And, in the case of economic frames in particular, how detailed must the supportive evidence be? Chapter 5, based on two randomized experiments, focuses on these critical questions.

30. Dworkin (1986); Glendon (1991).

CHAPTER FIVE

How Frames Shape
Public Opinion

I doubt this sign will change your opinion.
Placard observed at Rally to Restore Sanity
and/or Fear, Washington, October 30, 2010

A frame may be thought of as a speaker's emphasis on a subset of potentially relevant considerations when describing an issue or event.[1] When advocates and public officials self-consciously use particular frames in public debates over children and public policy, they are assuming that frames actually matter, that they shape how citizens think about a problem, and that they affect public support for a specific public policy remedy. Are these assumptions correct? Or are frames largely irrelevant to public opinion?

A Brief Review of the Framing Literature

A considerable body of literature attests to the ability of issue frames to shape both public perceptions and public support. Much of that literature utilizes randomized experiments, in which some citizens (often students) are exposed to one message while other citizens are exposed to a different message. A key advantage of randomized experiments is that they rule out many potential threats to internal validity. Another big advantage is that they enable the researcher to fashion a frame that closely corresponds to the theoretical construct being investigated.

Well-crafted experiments demonstrate that issue frames can shape public attitudes. Citizens who see a TV news clip that frames a KKK rally as a free speech issue are more tolerant of rallies and speeches than citizens who see a clip that frames that same rally as a public order issue.

1. Druckman (2001).

Citizens who read a newspaper article that stresses the risks to American soldiers from foreign intervention are less supportive of intervention than citizens who read an article that portrays the situation as a humanitarian crisis. In a series of experiments, Shanto Iyengar finds that episodic frames (highlighting specific events or individuals) and thematic frames (highlighting systemic or structural factors) differ in their impact. For example, episodic framing of poverty encourages respondents to attribute responsibility to individuals, while thematic framing of poverty encourages them to attribute responsibility to society. Episodic framing of crime also encourages attributions of responsibility to individuals—but only for certain types of crimes and certain types of criminals. Nonexperimental studies also attest to the importance of issue frames.[2]

Some framing studies have been criticized because they use one-sided issue frames that probably do not mimic political discourse in the real world. For example, the KKK study presents one set of students with a free speech perspective and another set of students with a public order perspective. In much mass media coverage of policy disputes, these two perspectives would be juxtaposed, thus diluting the impact of either frame. Scholars who measure responses to competing issue frames find evidence of framing effects.[3] Sometimes, however, they find that citizens exposed to competing frames offer opinions more consistent with their underlying values than citizens exposed to a single frame that challenges those values.[4] To the extent that this happens, frames reinforce opinions rather than changing them.

Another weakness of the framing literature is that many studies ignore the credibility or potency of evidence accompanying the frame. Although some framing studies suggest that people respond more to well-chosen human interest stories than to aggregate data that support a particular frame, there is some contrary evidence. In some situations (for example, a study of energy costs), adding factual information does not enhance the potency of the underlying frame. In other situations, however, factual information may enhance frames, if only for certain audiences (for example, better educated or more knowledgeable citizens). Clearly, we

---

2. See Nelson, Clawson, and Oxley (1997); Berinsky and Kinder (2006); Iyengar (1991, pp. 67, 44–45); Jacoby (2000); Stimson (2004, p. 48).

3. Brewer and Gross (2005).

4. Sniderman and Theriault (2004).

need to know more about the contextual factors that make frames more or less potent.[5]

Some citizens are more susceptible to frames generally or to particular frames than other citizens. Donald Haider-Markel and Mark Joslyn find that Democrats are more influenced by a frame that blames the Columbine shootings on weak gun control laws, while Republicans and independents are more influenced by a frame that blames the shootings on media violence. Shanto Iyengar finds that Democrats (and liberals) are more susceptible to frames stressing societal responsibility (thematic frames) than Republicans (and conservatives) are for stories on poverty, crime, and terrorism. Iyengar and Nicholas Valentino find that Republican voters rate Republican campaign ads more favorably when the ads focus on so-called Republican issues (drug abuse, crime, illegal immigration), while Democratic voters rate Democratic ads more highly when they focus on so-called Democratic issues (social security, welfare reform, health care). Jonathan Schuldt, Sara Konrath, and Norbert Schwarz find that Republicans are more likely to believe warnings about carbon dioxide emissions when presented as evidence of climate change as opposed to global warning. Scholars also study political knowledge—or policy knowledge—as an intervening variable, though they reach somewhat different conclusions.[6]

Although issue framing studies cover a wide range of issues, children's issues have not received much attention. A notable exception is some excellent work by Susan Bales and her colleagues at the FrameWorks Institute in Washington, which has conducted focus groups and Internet surveys focusing on children. In one such survey, of 4,200 registered voters who were randomly assigned to a treatment group or a control group, the FrameWorks Institute assessed the effects of seventeen frames on public support for various early childhood programs and initiatives.[7] Some of the frames sought to capture core values (such as prosperity, ingenuity, responsible management), while others introduced simplifying models or specific principles (such as toxic stress, pay now or pay later, brain

5. See Gilens (1999, p. 135); Kahneman and Tversky (1973); Nisbett and Borgida (1975); Dickson (1982); Baesler and Burgoon (1994); Druckman (2011).

6. See Haider-Markel and Joslyn (2001); Iyengar (1991); Iyengar and Valentino (1999); Schuldt, Konrath, and Schwarz (2011); Miller and Krosnick (2000); Druckman and Nelson (2003); Sniderman and Theriault (2004); Chong and Druckman (2007a).

7. Manuel (2009). A nationally representative sample was achieved by weighting for gender, age, race, education, and party identification.

architecture). Each survey participant was exposed to a one-paragraph narrative (one frame per participant) followed by thirty Likert-scale questions about policy support in five policy domains (mental health, child maltreatment, poverty and work supports, early care and education, health and health services). Some participants (the control group) were exposed to no particular frame, only the policy support questions.

Among the value frames, a prosperity frame and an ingenuity frame proved potent across several policy domains, including mental health interventions, abuse and neglect prevention, health and nutrition, early child care, and poverty and work supports.[8] In contrast, a frame featuring vulnerable child fairness fared poorly. Among the simplifying frames, a toxic stress frame produced the single biggest effect of all: an effect size of .38 for its impact on public support for prevention of abuse and neglect. A pay-now-or-pay-later frame in health care generated higher levels of policy support for abuse and neglect prevention policies, health and nutrition policies, and early child care policies. A return-on-investment frame generated higher support for abuse and neglect prevention policies and early child care policies. A brain architecture frame affected public support for the prevention of abuse and neglect but no others.[9] It should be noted that effect sizes were relatively small (usually .1 or lower) and that some of the statistical relationships were marginal ($p < .1$). It should also be noted that none of the frames was juxtaposed with a taxpayer frame or a limited government frame in this particular experiment. The absence of a counterframe could exaggerate framing effects.

Despite some weaknesses, the issue-framing literature has revolutionized our understanding of public debate. It has shifted our attention from the mass media's agenda-setting role to its opinion formation role. It reminds us that lobbyists are not merely arm twisters and campaign contributors but debaters and advisers as well. It recognizes that politicians, though they often pursue votes, sometimes pursue good public policies as well. Above all, it helps us to understand that the language we use in public policy debates may help to shape the outcome of those debates.

In this chapter, I posit that the presence of a child benefit frame (either moralistic or economic) will help to counteract a tax reduction frame, by

8. Prosperity: a short paragraph suggests that early investments in child well-being lead to societal prosperity (community and economic development) later on. Ingenuity: another short paragraph stresses positive results for children from innovative policies and programs adopted by selected states.
9. Manuel (2009, p. 19).

strengthening public support for public policies that are expected to help children. I also posit that the presence of an economic frame will have a greater positive impact on citizens than the presence of a moralistic frame, especially a helping-hand frame, which should be weaker than an equal opportunity frame. I predict that the addition of hard data to the economic frame will enhance support and that the addition of a luke-warm professorial endorsement will diminish support. Finally, I expect that positive framing effects will be stronger for moderates (or independents) than for liberals or conservatives (or Democrats or Republicans). As Dennis Chong and James Druckman argue, "Strong prior attitudes will attenuate framing effects." This suggests that swing voters or fence straddlers should be more susceptible to framing effects than ideologues or partisans.[10]

Nurse-Family Partnership Study

To test the effects of different issue frames on support for a particular public policy, I designed four mythical newspaper articles, supposedly published by the *Harrisburg Patriot News*, the newspaper of record in Pennsylvania's state capital.

Methods

Each newspaper article describes a debate in the Pennsylvania state legislature on the merits of establishing a nurse-family partnership (NFP) program modeled after a real program designed and implemented by David Olds of the University of Colorado–Denver.

The first newspaper article (frame A) includes only a negative argument, voiced by a state legislator and echoed by a lobbyist, opposing such a program on the grounds that it is too costly. That negative argument appears intact in all the other newspaper articles. The article based on frame B adds a moralistic argument, voiced by a state legislator, support-ing the program by invoking a helping-hand argument. The article based on frame C introduces an economic argument, voiced by a state legislator, supporting the program because "studies show that the program yields more benefits than costs." Finally, the article based on frame D makes a subtle change in the economic argument, substituting hard statistics for

10. Chong and Druckman (2007b, p. 110).

general claims: "studies show that this program yields $3 of benefits for every $1 of costs." These numbers, incidentally, accurately reflect Olds's research findings.[11] In the present study, frame A serves as the control condition, while frames B through D serve as the treatments.

To test the relative efficacy of these issue frames, I visited three introductory political science classes at Georgetown University in the fall of 2009 and distributed one article at random to every student. The article appeared on one side of the sheet. The reverse side asked students to indicate whether they supported or opposed the NFP program, using a 7-point Likert scale (strongly oppose = 1; strongly support = 7). It then asked students to rate arguments pro and con, by using a standard letter grade (including pluses and minuses). Finally, it asked students to identify their gender, their political party preference (Democratic, independent, Republican), and their ideology (liberal, moderate, conservative). A total of 278 students completed this exercise successfully.[12] A comparison of the four groups reveals relatively similar gender distributions.[13] There are no statistically significant differences in ideology or political party identification across groups.

To capture differences across frames, I used a simple difference-of-means test, with t statistics (two-tailed tests).

Findings

As table 5-1 indicates, students rate economic arguments (frames C and D) higher than moralistic arguments. There is, however, no statistically significant difference between an economic argument with hard numbers (frame D) and an economic argument without hard numbers (frame C).

For certain subgroups, the proprogram frame has an effect on the respondent's assessment of the antiprogram argument. For males, for example, the taxpayer argument receives a lower letter grade in the presence of a cost-benefit-with-evidence frame than in the presence of a

---

11. Olds and others (1998).

12. Nine of these students failed to identify their political party affiliation and four failed to specify their ideological orientation. As a result, the sample sizes are somewhat smaller for some of the results reported below.

13. There was a higher percentage of males in the first group than in the second group ($p < .05$) and the fourth group ($p < .10$). To correct for this, I present findings for men and women separately and I control for gender in a multiple regression equation.

Table 5-1. *Respondents' Ratings, Cost-Benefit and Moral Obligation Arguments*

Frame	N	Mean rating of argument (1–4 scale)
Frame A: No positive argument	70	. . .
Frame B: Help the needy	69	2.73
Frame C: Benefits exceed costs	72	3.04
Frame D: Benefits exceed costs (with numbers)	67	3.14
Summary statistic (p value)		Frame B vs. C = .05 Frame B vs. D = .01

moralistic frame ($p = .03$). For moderates, the taxpayer argument receives a somewhat lower letter grade in the presence of a cost-benefit frame than in the presence of a moralistic frame ($p = .07$). For Republicans, the taxpayer argument receives a somewhat lower letter grade in the presence of a cost-benefit-with-evidence frame than in the presence of a cost-benefit frame ($p = .09$). These differences could be important either because they contribute to proprogram sentiment or because they widen the gap between two policy options (program, no program).

But do issue frames also affect public policy support? One way to answer this question is to look at effect sizes, such as Cohen's d, which divides the mean difference in some variable (in this instance, policy support) between two samples by the standard deviation of the two samples combined.[14] If we use frame A as the baseline, then the effect sizes for the other frames are as follows: frame B: Cohen's $d = .233$; frame C: Cohen's $d = .362$; and frame D: Cohen's $d = .412$. Two of these differences (between frame C and frame A and between frame D and frame A) are statistically significant at an acceptable level ($p < .05$).

Although students exposed to an economic frame (either C or D) are more supportive of the NFP program than students exposed to no positive argument at all (frame A), there are no statistically significant differences between either of the economic frames and the moralistic frame (see table 5-2). However, we do see some differences when we disaggregate the data (see table 5-3). For females, there are no statistically significant

14. McCartney and Rosenthal (2000).

Table 5-2. *Support for Cost-Benefit Arguments*

Frame	N	Likert mean (1–7 scale)
Frame A: No positive argument	70	3.78
Frame B: Help the needy	69	4.17
Frame C: Benefits exceed costs	72	4.35
Frame D: Benefits exceed costs (with numbers)	67	4.42
Summary statistic (p value)		Frame A vs. C = .05 Frame A vs. D = .05

Table 5-3. *Support for Nurse-Family Partnership Program, by Issue Frame and Gender*

Frame	Male (N = 156)	Female (N = 122)
Frame A: No positive argument	3.58	4.17
Frame B: Help the needy	3.81	4.51
Frame C: Benefits exceed costs	4.51	4.13
Frame D: Benefits exceed costs (with numbers)	4.37	4.47
Summary statistic (p value)	Frame A vs. C = .01 Frame A vs. D = .05 Frame B vs. C = .10	

differences by issue frame. For males, on the other hand, issue frames do matter. Males exposed to an economic frame are more supportive of the NFP program than males exposed to a moralistic frame or males exposed to no positive argument at all.

For Democrats, as with females, issue frames do not seem to matter. However, they matter a great deal for independents: for them, economic frames evoke stronger support for the NFP program than moralistic frames; economic frames also evoke stronger support than no positive argument at all. For Republicans, we also see one statistically significant difference: Republicans exposed to the economic frame *with* statistics are more supportive than Republicans exposed to no positive argument (see table 5-4). For independents, differences, measured by effect sizes, are substantial: Cohen's d = 1.009 for frame C minus frame A, .620 for

Table 5-4. *Support for Nurse-Family Partnership Program,*
by Issue Frame and Party

Frame	Republican (N = 75)	Independent (N = 74)	Democrat (N = 120)
Frame A: No positive argument	2.63	3.40	4.54
Frame B: Help the needy	3.10	3.39	4.91
Frame C: Benefits exceed costs	3.23	4.97	4.76
Frame D. Benefits exceed costs (with numbers)	3.68	4.35	5.00
Summary statistic (*p* value)	Frame A vs. D = .05	Frame A vs. C = .01 Frame A vs. D = .10 Frame B vs. C = .01 Frame B vs. D = .05	

frame D minus frame A. For Republicans, Cohen's d = .698 for frame D minus frame A.

Moderates, like independents, do seem to respond to issue frames. Moderates exposed to an economic frame (either C or D) are more supportive of the NFP program than moderates exposed to a moralistic frame (B); they are also more supportive than moderates exposed to no positive argument at all (frame A). There are no statistically significant differences for conservatives. As for liberals, there is a marginally significant difference in the expected direction between liberals exposed to a moralistic frame and liberals exposed to no positive argument (see table 5-5). For moderates, differences are substantial. Cohen's d, for moderates, is 1.001 for frame C minus frame A, .892 for frame D minus frame A. For liberals, Cohen's d is .448 for frame B minus frame A.

It is possible, of course, that some of these independent variables are correlated. For example, it is well known that independents are much more likely to be men than women.[15] The same is almost certainly true of moderates. With my data as well, gender is correlated with political party identification. If one includes gender and political party identification and

15. Baldassare (2002, p. 206).

Table 5-5. *Support for Nurse-Family Partnership Program, by Issue Frame and Ideology*

Frame	Conservative (N = 70)	Moderate (N = 99)	Liberal (N = 105)
Frame A: No positive argument	2.57	3.38	4.76
Frame B: Help the needy	2.92	3.88	5.36
Frame C: Benefits exceed costs	3.15	4.71	4.93
Frame D: Benefits exceed costs (with numbers)	3.50	4.42	5.04
Summary statistic (*p* value)	Frame A vs. C = .01 Frame A vs. B = .10 Frame A vs. D = .01 Frame B vs. C = .05 Frame B vs. D = .10		

issue frames in the same multiple regression equation, the relationship between gender and policy preferences disappears (see table 5-6). However, the effects of issue frames remain.

Head Start Expansion Study

One limitation of the NFP study at Georgetown is that college students are not necessarily representative of the population as a whole. Do the same basic findings appear if we survey a representative cross-section of eligible voters instead? To answer that question, I contracted with Knowledge Networks to conduct an Internet survey, using the same basic strategy as before (fictional newspaper articles, random assignment, questions about policy arguments and policy support) but with some new twists and a national sample.

Instead of focusing on a relatively unknown program, being considered for the first time, I focused on a relatively familiar program, Head Start, being considered for expansion. This emphasis on an existing program may be more appropriate for the new reality of budget deficit concerns and government spending cutbacks. As with the previous study, I prepared several versions of the same newspaper article, each of which included a taxpayers' argument that we simply cannot afford to spend more money on worthwhile social programs.

Table 5-6. *Regression Analysis, Support for Nurse-Family Partnership Program*

Male	0.0004
Frame B: Help the needy	0.524*
Frame C: Benefits exceed costs	0.761***
Frame D: Benefits exceed costs (with numbers)	0.709**
Moderate ideology	−0.878***
Conservative ideology	−1.953***

Summary statistics
Adjusted R^2 = 0.25
N = 278

***$p < .001$, **$p < .01$, *$p < .05$.

The first article (using frame A) included only the argument against expansion. All remaining articles retained the negative argument but added a positive argument. The second article (frame B) included a moralistic argument—that we should help needy children. The third article (frame C) used a different moralistic argument—equal opportunity. The fourth article (frame D) used an economic argument—that the long-term benefits of Head Start exceed the costs. The fifth article (frame E) mimicked the fourth, except that I added a quote from a Harvard professor expressing qualified support for program expansion. The presumption was that this would dilute public support. The sixth article (frame F) substituted a science argument: that brain research confirms the critical importance of the early years to later success.

As with the Georgetown survey, I asked respondents to assign a letter grade to the protaxpayer argument and to the pro–Head Start argument (if asked). I also asked respondents to indicate their level of support for expanding Head Start, using a 7-point Likert scale.

Knowledge Networks administered the survey, on my behalf, in March 2011. The timing was fortuitous because a possible government shutdown had been averted a couple of weeks earlier. Just in case the ordering of the policy and policy argument questions might make a difference, I varied the sequence of these questions at random. Question order did not seem to affect policy support.[16]

16. The overall correlation between question order and policy support was −.004.

Table 5-7. *Support for Head Start Expansion, by Issue Frame*

Frame	Unweighted (N = 1,055)	Weighted (N = 1,039)
Frame A: Control group	3.73	3.87
Frame B: Equal opportunity	4.07	4.06
Frame C: Economic	4.12	4.36
Frame D: Economic, with qualified endorsement	3.97	4.01
Frame E: Science	3.92	4.12
Frame F: Helping hand	3.99	4.27
Summary statistic (p value)	Frame A vs. C = .10	Frame A vs. C = .05 Frame A vs. F = .10 Frame C vs. D = .10

A total of 1,039 respondents completed the survey, with a cumulative response rate of 0.06 (panel recruitment response rate times household profile rate times survey completion rate = .167 × .629 × .576 = .06). The random-assignment process worked rather well: demographic characteristics across the six groups of respondents receiving the six different articles were strikingly similar for key variables, such as gender, race and ethnicity, party identification, education, income, and age. Across frames, however, there was a marginally significant discrepancy for ideology.[17] For this reason, I present findings separately for respondents with different ideological predispositions. I also conduct a multivariate regression analysis below.

Do issue frames affect levels of public support? As table 5-7 indicates, framing matters, but effects are modest, at least for the sample as a whole. For the weighted sample, respondents express stronger support for expanding Head Start when exposed to an economic frame ($p < .05$). The helping-hand frame demonstrates a marginal advantage with respect to the control group, and the economic frame with qualified endorsement demonstrates a marginal disadvantage with respect to the economic frame. Cohen's d for the economic frame, compared to the control group, is .189 for the unweighted sample, .244 for the weighted sample.

---

17. I used a chi square test for categorical variables to determine statistical significance.

Table 5-8. *Regression Analysis, Support for Head Start Expansion*

	Unweighted sample (N = 1,043)	Weighted sample (N = 1,027)
Frame B: Equal opportunity	0.259	0.037
Frame C: Economic	0.333†	0.431*
Frame D: Economic, with qualified endorsement	0.206	0.050
Frame E: Science	0.319	0.301
Frame F: Helping hand	0.195	0.350†
Male	−0.130	−0.115
Moderate	−0.516***	−0.365*
Conservative	−1.672***	−1.383***
Age	−0.081*	−0.072*
Black	1.241***	1.245***
Hispanic	0.501*	0.337†
Summary statistic	Adjusted R^2 = 0.18	Adjusted R^2 = 0.15

***p < .001, **p <. 01, *p < .05, †*p* < .10.

Of course, other factors also influence levels of public support. To control for these other factors, I conducted a multiple regression analysis with policy support as the dependent variable, with each of the five treatment groups as independent variables (the control group serves as the residual category) and with several other variables as covariates. I selected these variables (ideology, race and ethnicity, age), as opposed to others (income, the presence of young children in the household), based on their predictive power. I also weighted the cases to bring the sample into closer alignment with the general population. As table 5-8 indicates, there is, for the weighted sample, a significant positive relationship between the economic frame and policy support and a marginally significant positive relationship between the helping hand frame and policy support.

Next, I turn to subgroups, focusing exclusively on weighted samples. As with the Georgetown study, the national sample can be broken down by ideology. As before, moderates seem more responsive to frames than either liberals or conservatives. As table 5-9 indicates, the equal opportunity frame, the economic frame, the science frame, and the helping-hand frame generate higher levels of support for Head Start expansion than the control group frame, for moderates. Cohen's *d* statistics for these frames,

Table 5-9. *Support for Head Start Expansion, by Issue Frame and Ideology*

Frame	Liberal (N = 273)	Moderate (N = 371)	Conservative (N = 399)
Frame A: Control	4.96	3.77	2.77
Frame B: Equal opportunity	4.65	4.36	3.23
Frame C: Economic	4.72	4.42	3.33
Frame D: Economic, with qualified endorsement	5.14	4.19	2.94
Frame E: Science	5.14	4.39	3.04
Frame F: Helping hand	4.82	4.71	2.74
Summary statistic (*p* value)		Frame A vs. B = .05 Frame A vs. C = .05 Frame A vs. E = .05 Frame A vs. F = .05 Frame D vs. F = .10	Frame C vs. F = .10

compared to the control group, are .286 for the equal opportunity frame, .316 for the economic frame, .301 for the science frame, and .456 for the helping-hand frame. Also for moderates, the helping-hand frame generates higher levels of support than the economic frame with a qualified professorial endorsement.[18] For conservatives, there is a marginally significant difference between the economic frame (more appealing) and the helping-hand frame (less appealing).

For party identification, there is, unfortunately, only a very small group of independents (N = 22). That is because Knowledge Networks uses a 7-point party identification scale, as opposed to the 3-point (forced choice) scale I used in the Georgetown study. Nevertheless, even with an extremely small subsample, statistically significant differences are evident for independents: the economic frame with a qualified endorsement is more appealing than the equal opportunity frame or the helping-hand frame or the science frame; the economic frame is marginally more appealing than the science frame; and the economic frame and the economic frame with a qualified professorial endorsement are more appealing than

18. Cohen's *d* is .456.

Table 5-10. *Support for Head Start Expansion, by Issue Frame and Party Identification*

Frame	Republican (N = 473)	Independent (N = 22)	Democrat (N = 560)
Frame A: Control	2.55	2.40	4.65
Frame B: Equal opportunity	3.32	3.50	4.71
Frame C: Economic	3.25	5.75	4.77
Frame D: Economic, with qualified endorsement	3.09	7.00	4.67
Frame E: Science	3.13	3.50	4.83
Frame F: Helping hand	2.88	4.00	4.85
Summary statistic (*p* value)	Frame A vs. B = .01 Frame A vs. C = .05 Frame A vs. D = .05 Frame A vs. E = .05	Frame A vs. C = .01 Frame A vs. D = .01 Frame B vs. D = .01 Frame C vs. E = .10 Frame D vs. E = .05 Frame D vs. F = .01	

no frame at all (see table 5-10). For Republicans, the equal opportunity frame, the economic frame, the economic frame with a qualified professorial endorsement, and the science frame generate more policy support than no frame at all.[19]

For men and women, considered separately, there are no statistically significant differences across frames (see table 5-11)—a notable difference from the Georgetown study, where men, but not women, responded differently to different frames.[20]

Unlike the Georgetown study, where education levels are identical, education varies significantly for members of the national sample. Unfortunately, the subpopulation of respondents with less than a high school degree is rather small (*N* = 90), making it difficult to discern statistically

19. The Cohen's *d*, compared to the control group, are .410 for equal opportunity, .372 for economic, .287 for economic with qualified endorsement, and .309 for science.

20. For men, there is a marginally significant difference between the equal opportunity frame and the control group (*p* < .10).

Table 5-11. *Support for Head Start Expansion, by Issue Frame and Gender*

Frame	Female (N = 488)	Male (N = 567)
Frame A: Control	3.87	3.63
Frame B: Equal opportunity	4.00	4.14
Frame C: Economic	4.33	3.87
Frame D: Economic, with qualified endorsement	4.15	3.82
Frame E: Science	4.15	3.72
Frame F: Helping hand	4.17	3.85
Summary statistic (p value)		Frame A vs. B = .10

significant differences there. However, for well-educated respondents, with a BA degree or higher, there is a marginally significant difference between the helping-hand frame and two other frames—the economic frame and the equal opportunity frame (see table 5-12). For well-educated persons, the economic frame and the equal opportunity frame have more appeal than the helping-hand frame ($p < .10$, in both instances).

For wealthier persons, one also sees some differences (see table 5-13). Specifically, the equal opportunity frame is more appealing than the helping-hand frame ($p < .05$), and the economic frame with a qualified professorial endorsement is marginally more appealing than the helping-hand frame ($p < .10$).

For relatively young and relatively old respondents, frames matter. For the relatively young (eighteen- to twenty-nine-year-olds), the economic frame with a qualified professorial endorsement is more potent, marginally, than either the economic frame or the equal opportunity frame (see table 5-14). Also, the economic frame with professorial endorsement is more appealing than the control group, and the helping-hand frame is more appealing than the control group. Apparently, an endorsement from a college professor has a positive impact on college-age individuals, even if the endorsement is lukewarm. For the elderly (over sixty years), the equal opportunity frame is marginally more attractive than either the helping-hand frame or no frame at all (that is, the control group).

Unlike the Georgetown study, this study distinguishes between respondents with or without having a child under five years old living in the

Table 5-12. *Support for Head Start Expansion, by Issue Frame and Education*

Frame	< High school (N = 90)	High school (N = 349)	Some college (N = 292)	BA and higher (N = 324)
Frame A: Control	3.47	3.72	3.74	3.78
Frame B: Equal opportunity	4.14	4.00	3.91	4.33
Frame C: Economic	4.20	4.10	3.88	4.31
Frame D: Economic, with qualified endorsement	4.06	3.95	3.86	4.07
Frame E: Science	4.47	4.13	3.60	3.86
Frame F: Helping hand	4.50	4.25	4.00	3.52
Summary statistic (*p* value)				Frame B vs. F = .10 Frame C vs. F = .10

Table 5-13. *Support for Head Start Expansion, by Issue Frame and Income*

Frame	< $25K (N = 160)	$25K–50K (N = 250)	$50K–100K (N = 359)	> $100K (N = 286)
Frame A: Control	3.80	3.65	3.71	3.78
Frame B: Equal opportunity	3.80	4.36	3.86	4.28
Frame C: Economic	4.53	3.92	4.23	3.87
Frame D: Economic, with qualified endorsement	4.23	3.76	3.95	4.04
Frame E: Science	4.41	3.67	4.04	3.73
Frame F: Helping hand	4.67	4.29	3.97	3.21
Summary statistic (*p* value)				Frame B vs. F = .05 Frame D vs. F = .10

Table 5-14. *Support for Head Start Expansion, by Issue Frame and Age*

Frame	18–29 (N = 160)	30–44 (N = 250)	45–59 (N = 309)	60+ (N = 336)
Frame A: Control	3.69	4.06	4.00	3.24
Frame B: Equal opportunity	4.09	4.11	4.05	4.05
Frame C: Economic	4.12	4.66	4.04	3.89
Frame D: Economic, with qualified endorsement	4.96	4.08	3.88	3.58
Frame E: Science	4.33	4.51	3.62	3.65
Frame F: Helping hand	4.52	4.35	4.17	3.24

Summary statistic (*p* value)	Frame A vs. D = .01		Frame A vs. B = .10
	Frame A vs. F = .10		Frame B vs. F = .10
	Frame B vs. D = .10		
	Frame C vs. D = .10		

home. For respondents who do have a young child living at home, a science frame is more potent than an equal opportunity frame, an economic frame, or an economic frame with professorial endorsement, and the helping-hand frame is more appealing than an economic frame with professorial endorsement (see table 5-15). Also, the science frame and the helping-hand frame generate more policy support than the absence of any positive frame at all (that is, the control group). For households with no young child, there is a marginally significant difference between the economic frame and the science frame, in favor of the economic frame, and a marginally significant difference between the economic frame and the control group, also in favor of the economic frame.

Finally, we can break our sample down by race and ethnicity (see table 5-16). For whites, the largest group of respondents by far (N = 803), there is a marginally significant difference between the economic frame and no positive frame at all, in favor of the economic frame. For Hispanics, there is a marginally significant difference between the helping-hand frame and the equal opportunity frame, in favor of the helping-hand frame. Some statistically significant differences are also apparent in the mixed-race

Table 5-15. *Support for Head Start Expansion, by Issue Frame and Young Children*

Frame	Child under 5 in home (N = 131)	No child under 5 in home (N = 924)
Frame A: Control	3.45	3.77
Frame B: Equal opportunity	3.81	4.12
Frame C: Economic	3.70	4.19
Frame D: Economic, with qualified endorsement	3.62	4.03
Frame E: Science	5.00	3.78
Frame: Helping hand	4.81	3.91
Summary statistic (p value)	Frame A vs. E = .01 Frame A vs. F = .05 Frame B vs. E = .05 Frame C vs. E = .05 Frame D vs. E = .05 Frame D vs. F = .05	Frame A vs. C = .10 Frame C vs. E = .10

categories. In absolute numbers, some of the differences across frames are bigger for blacks than for whites, but a relatively small sample size (N = 94) makes it difficult to detect statistical significance.

Although the key dependent variable here, as in the Georgetown study, is the level of policy support, it is also interesting to look at the letter grades given to particular frames, including both the positive frames (which varied) and the negative frame (which did not vary). A regression analysis—with the economic frame with qualified endorsement omitted—finds no statistically significant differences in the letter grade assigned to the positive argument, by positive frame. However, a regression analysis for the negative (protaxpayer) frame does reveal a statistically significant relationship between the economic frame and a letter grade assigned to the protaxpayer argument. Specifically, respondents exposed to the economic frame give the taxpayer argument a lower letter grade ($p < .05$), for the unweighted sample (see table 5-17). This is not true for any of the other frames.

Discussion

As predicted, economic frames appear to be stronger than moralistic frames. In both the NFP study and the Head Start expansion study,

Table 5-16. *Support for Head Start Expansion, by Issue Frame and Race and Ethnicity*

Frame	White (N = 803)	Black (N = 94)	Other, non-Hispanic (N = 42)	Hispanic (N = 91)	2+ races, non-Hispanic (N = 25)
Frame A: Control	3.54	4.87	3.86	4.25	4.67
Frame B: Equal opportunity	3.86	5.27	4.92	3.80	5.00
Frame C: Economic	3.95	5.73	3.20	4.5	3.50
Frame D: Economic, with qualified endorsement	3.76	5.38	3.67	4.45	3.33
Frame E: Science	3.61	5.69	3.50	4.31	6.25
Frame F: Helping hand	3.76	5.65	3.50	5.05	1.67
Summary statistic (p value)	Frame A vs. C = .10		Frame B vs. C = .10 Frame B vs. F = .10	Frame B vs. F = .10	Frame A vs. F = .10 Frame B vs. F = .05 Frame C vs. E = .05 Frame D vs. E = .05 E v. F (.01)

Table 5-17. *Regression Analysis, Assessment of Argument for Protecting Taxpayers*

	Unweighted sample (N = 1,030)	Weighted sample (N = 1,027)
Equal opportunity	–0.065	0.065
Economic	–0.266*	–0.149
Economic, with qualified endorsement	–0.001	0.142
Science	–0.036	0.051
Helping hand	–0.044	0.008
Male	0.107	0.042
Moderate	0.277**	0.185*
Conservative	1.009***	0.826***
Age	–0.013	–0.016
Black	–1.057***	–1.028***
Hispanic	–0.254†	–0.232*
	Adjusted R^2 = 0.18	Adjusted R^2 = 0.16

***$p < .001$, **$p < .01$, *$p < .05$, †$p < .10$.

economic frames generated higher levels of public policy support, when paired with a protaxpayer argument, for respondents as a whole. In short, arguments that stress favorable benefit-cost ratios for children's programs can have an impact on public opinion, even when juxtaposed with anti-spending arguments.

Economic arguments also matter most for those voters who arguably matter most. For swing voters—moderates, independents—economic frames trigger stronger policy support. This is important, because in the last two federal election cycles (2008, 2010) it has been independents who have determined the outcome. In 2008 independents leaned Democratic, yielding Barack Obama's election as president and substantial Democratic increases in the House. In 2010 independents leaned Republican, yielding substantial Republican gains in the House and less substantial gains in the Senate.[21]

21. It should be noted, however, that independents do not always determine the outcome of federal elections. See Abramowitz (2011).

More broadly, it is independents (or moderates) who determine shifts in public opinion over time. In James Stimson's words, they are "scorekeepers" or "nonideological pragmatists," who distrust both liberals and conservatives, Democrats and Republicans.[22] Unlike party partisans, scorekeepers can be swayed by policy arguments and by public policies that tilt too far in a given direction. Unlike the apathetic or uninvolved, scorekeepers pay enough attention to politics that their views matter. Because economic frames can shape the thinking of citizens in the middle (independents, moderates, scorekeepers), they are undeniably important.

Other voters who matter a lot include the well educated, the wealthy, and senior citizens, all of whom participate in politics more than other citizens. For the well educated, the economic frame and the equal opportunity frame have special appeal. For the wealthy, the equal opportunity frame and the economic frame with qualified professorial endorsement are attractive. For the aged, the economic frame resonates best. Thus the economic frame is not alone in having strong appeal to attentive and active voters. The equal opportunity frame, which helped to justify the Great Society in the 1960s and which has been invoked on many occasions since then, continues to have considerable appeal today.[23]

The inclusion of hard evidence did not strengthen the potency of the economic frame in the Georgetown survey. A benefit-cost argument fared just as well without an actual benefit-cost ratio as with one. This is consistent with research on public opinion on emerging technologies by James Druckman and Toby Bolsen, who find that facts do not enhance frame strength.[24] Of course, the content of the facts might matter. If the benefit-cost ratio for the NFP program were 15 to 1, as opposed to 3 to 1, perhaps this would have left a deeper impression. Prior expectations might also matter. If respondents expect a program to be ineffective, the inclusion of hard evidence may help to dislodge negative expectations. Hard evidence also matters even if not included in an official mass media report, in the sense that the absence of such evidence would reduce the likelihood of a favorable comment in the first place.

At least three surprises surface in the national survey. First, the helping-hand frame, which fares poorly in the Georgetown survey, does well enough in the weighted sample to have a marginally significant

---

22. Stimson (2004, p. 163).
23. Haskins and Sawhill (2009).
24. Druckman and Bolsen (2010).

positive impact. This appears to reflect the helping-hand frame's relative attractiveness to the poor, the poorly educated, blacks, and Hispanics. Second, the science frame does not do particularly well in the national survey, compared to other arguments in support of children's programs. Although the science frame demonstrates some appeal to certain subgroups (moderates, Republicans, parents with a young child at home), when compared to no positive frame at all, it does not fare well when compared to other prochild frames. Third, the addition of a qualified professorial endorsement (wonkish, with reservations) deflates the appeal of the economic frame, but not as much as expected. For young people (ages eighteen to twenty-nine), this is actually the most attractive of all the frames, possibly because college-age individuals are more sensitive to messages from college professors. In the end, the lukewarm endorsement detracts only somewhat from the overriding message, which is that expanding Head Start is a good thing.

In general, the national survey finds no gender differences for the population as a whole. However, the two surveys are best regarded as complementary, not contradictory, in their gender findings. Georgetown students represent a slice of the wider society—younger, better educated, and more affluent. If one focuses on such subgroups within the national sample, one sees sharper differences between men and women. For example, for wealthy respondents and for well-educated respondents the equal opportunity frame is significantly more appealing for men than for women. For young respondents, the economic frame with a qualified endorsement is more appealing for both men and women. In both the Georgetown survey and the national survey, the helping-hand frame does not fare well with elite respondents.

One can imagine situations in which a moralistic frame might evoke greater sympathy or support—such as a visual image of a disadvantaged child coupled with a helping-hand or an equal opportunity argument. Had I used television news clips with evocative images rather than newspaper articles, a moralistic frame might have fared better. On the other hand, the use of individual stories and visual images highlighting an individual's suffering may divert attention away from government solutions to systemic problems.[25] Instead, people may blame the child's parents for his or her misfortune.

25. Susan Bales, interview with author, Washington, September 27, 2010.

Is it possible that economic frames matter less for certain children's issues? For special education or for school desegregation debates, rights-based arguments might be more compelling than for other issue areas. Any threat to children's civil or constitutional rights could be regarded as serious and legally actionable.

Similar considerations may apply to the realm of juvenile justice, where judgments of moral culpability hinge on evidence but not the sort of evidence that characterizes welfare economics. In two recent Supreme Court decisions, for example, a majority of the Court explicitly embraced new research highlighting limitations of the adolescent brain. The arguments that persuaded the Court in both cases focus on individual rights, moral desert, and the anatomical characteristics of teenagers' still-developing brains.[26]

For many children's issues, however, economic frames seem to matter. As people have become more cost conscious (less tolerant of tax increases, more concerned about budget deficits), the appeal of economic frames has probably increased. In at least two areas (early care and education, child health), economic issue frames are now widely used by child advocates.

Clever advocates and public officials who frame children's issues in economic terms are likely to enjoy greater political success than those who do not. This is true even as consumers exercise selectivity in their news choices, a phenomenon that is growing in importance. An economic frame, unlike a moralistic frame, is unlikely to be screened out by conservative media. Indeed, conservatives have shown a penchant for using economic frames, dating back to the 1970s.[27]

This is not to say that moralistic frames, like equality opportunity frames, have lost their power in public debate. Public opinion polls suggest that norms of racial equality have grown in strength since the 1960s and are strong today. But these norms coexist uneasily with negative racial predispositions. Because of this ambivalence, support for equality can diminish when implicit racial appeals give white citizens an excuse to reduce their support for strong public programs aimed at enhancing the prospects of inner-city blacks.[28]

---

26. *Roper* v. *Simmons* (2005); *Graham* v. *Florida* (2010). See Haider (2006); Steinberg and Scott (2003).

27. See Iyengar and Hahn (2009); Smith (2007).

28. See Schuman, Steeh, and Bobo (1985, pp. 71–138); Mendelberg (2001, pp. 113–15); Hurwitz and Peffley (2005).

Allusions to budget constraints, budget deficits, opportunity costs, or the taxpayers' burden need not be racist in intent to activate negative racial predispositions. These negative predispositions are much less likely to be triggered if citizens are persuaded that proposed public policies benefit everyone or, more technically, that their long-run benefits exceed their short-run costs. These same considerations apply to negative dispositions toward the poor, even if devoid of racial prejudice.

Conclusion

Framing matters. The introduction of a prochild frame dilutes the impact of a protaxpayer frame. But the extent of impact depends on which prochild frame is employed. The extent of impact also depends on who is being exposed to the frame. In general, an economic frame and an equal opportunity frame appeal the most to those voters who matter the most, while a helping-hand frame appeals the most to those voters who matter the least. Frames also matter more for swing voters, who are less likely to be locked into fixed positions.

Both the NFP survey and the Head Start expansion survey try to replicate real-world conditions: positive and negative arguments compete for voters' approval and support. Both surveys also guard against threats to validity by using random assignment. The national survey also scores high in external validity because it uses a nationally representative sample (and because it replicates the way that many Americans obtain their news these days: via the Internet, and in haste).

Despite relatively clear findings, three questions remain. First, do the impacts of issue frames persist over time, or do they fade after exposure to other issues and other issue frames? Second, does selective exposure to preferred media insulate many voters from issue frames that might run counter to their ideological predispositions? Third, do political elites respond as affirmatively to issue frames as the general public does?

In the next chapter, I ask what happens when a powerful prochild issue frame encounters powerful political obstacles, including resource constraints, conservative values, legislative opposition, and indifferent mass media. I do so through four case studies, in four states where a legislative proposal to better conditions for children sought crucial political support.

CHAPTER SIX

Battling for Kids in State Capitols

When our kids read things early, we're more competitive.
Jim Calhoun, head coach of men's basketball,
University of Connecticut, 2008

Children's policies occupy a prominent place on the agendas of governors and state legislators. The role of state governments in funding and regulating elementary and secondary education has long been of critical importance, and state expenditures on child health, through Medicaid and the Children's Health Insurance Program (CHIP), have increased significantly in recent years. More than the federal government, state governments devote a substantial percentage of their time and their financial resources to children. In fact, state governments account for two-thirds of all government spending on children.[1]

In principle, economic frames ought to matter quite a bit to state government officials. As is often noted, state governments, unlike the federal government, must balance their budgets due to state constitutional mandates. This sensitizes state officials to the need to economize and to seek efficient solutions to policy problems. At the same time, state taxpayers hold state officials on a relatively tight leash. When politicians do not hold taxes down, the voters often punish them at the polls. Sometimes, they pass initiatives—not allowed at the federal level—restricting state taxes.

In this chapter I take a closer look at the connection between children's politics and state politics. I focus on four diverse states: Connecticut, Utah, North Carolina, and Pennsylvania. These states differ in their political ideology, their political party preferences, and their child friendliness.

1. Golden (2011).

Two of them (North Carolina, Pennsylvania) also recently experienced abrupt political transformations, permitting comparisons over time.

In the previous chapter, experiments demonstrated the capacity of economic issue frames to shift public opinion in a prochild direction. In this chapter, I chronicle the interplay between economic issue frames and other powerful forces in the real world, including the party identification and ideological preferences of public officials, the budget constraints imposed by state constitutions or a weak economy, public opposition to higher taxes, and other challenges. In the real world, economic frames fare better in some states, in some years, and in some policy domains than in others.[2]

Connecticut

Connecticut is one of the wealthiest states in the United States. It benefits greatly from its proximity to New York City and its close ties to Wall Street. In recent years, both houses of its legislature have been controlled by Democrats, while the governor has been Republican.[3] Party polarization is relatively low in Connecticut. Although Democratic legislators are relatively liberal, Republican legislators are more moderate than their counterparts in many other states.[4]

In many ways, Connecticut is a child-friendly state. It was among the earliest states to adopt a high-quality preschool program (in 1997). Its spending per capita for elementary education is very high, and its funding fairness across school districts is relatively high. It was one of only six states to receive a grade of A from the Pew Charitable Trusts for its policies promoting access to dental care for children. According to Kids Count, many of its child well-being indicators compare favorably to the national average.[5]

On the other hand, Connecticut was, in 2006, one of only three states to treat sixteen-year-olds and seventeen-year-olds accused of crimes as adults, to be tried in adult courts and, if convicted, to be placed in adult

2. My analysis of the case studies leans crucially on many of their main actors, who were interviewed during 2010 and 2011. For a list of those interviewed, see appendix A.

3. That changed when Democrat Daniel Malloy became governor in January 2011.

4. Shor and McCarty (2010, p. 19).

5. See Cavanaugh (2010); Lucchese (2010); Kids Count (2010). Overall, Connecticut ranked eighth in child friendliness in 2010.

prisons. The other two states were New York and North Carolina.[6] The vast majority of crimes committed by sixteen- and seventeen-year-olds are relatively minor. Nevertheless, these young people were being transferred out of the juvenile justice system. Studies show that teenagers who receive treatment in the juvenile justice system are less likely to recidivate or to commit more serious crimes than those who go through the adult system. A comparison of New York, where adolescents are tried in adult courts at age sixteen, and New Jersey, where adolescents are kept out of adult courts until age eighteen, finds that New York adolescents are likely to be rearrested more often and more quickly for serious offenses.[7] Thus the debate over the age of adult jurisdiction is potentially quite significant.

The key players in addressing this issue were the Connecticut Juvenile Justice Alliance, led at the time by Hector Glynn, and State Representative Toni Walker. The Connecticut Juvenile Justice Alliance—founded in 2001 with start-up funds from the Tow Foundation—wanted to raise the age of adult jurisdiction from sixteen to eighteen years, but it needed a strong legislative champion. Walker, an African American Democrat from New Haven, first elected to the General Assembly in 2002, fit the bill perfectly. Intelligent, articulate, and personable, she was widely respected and well liked. An administrator at an alternative high school in New Haven, Walker was quite familiar with adolescent behavior: "I work with them one on one. I see the issues they struggle with." She also saw the potential benefits to all parties of raising the age of adult jurisdiction from age sixteen to age eighteen, except for those accused of serious crimes. Walker, like everyone else, believed that if adolescents are accused of serious crimes, they should be treated as adults. In fact, in all fifty states, young offenders who commit especially violent crimes may be prosecuted as adults.[8]

When Representative Walker looked into this in 2005, she learned that efforts had been made to raise the age of adult jurisdiction to eighteen years over a period of two decades but that these efforts had failed. In Connecticut, as elsewhere, the perception in the 1990s had been that juvenile crime was on the increase, that it posed a serious threat, and that this

6. In eleven other states, the threshold for treatment as an adult is seventeen years of age (Secret 2011). In the remaining states, the age is eighteen.

7. See Anderson (no date); Hammond (2008).

8. See Crutchfield, Kania, and Kramer (2011, p. 40); Walker interview, appendix A; Secret (2011).

required a tough governmental response. This thinking received a boost from John DiIulio's widely cited article warning of the rise of "morally impoverished juvenile super-predators" who "are perfectly capable of committing the most heinous acts of physical violence for the most trivial reasons."[9] During the 1980s and the 1990s a number of states passed laws allowing the criminal prosecution of young teenagers accused of serious crimes.[10] Connecticut passed tough anticrime legislation creating a new class of offenders—serious juvenile offenders—who were not given the same level of protection as other juvenile offenders. Thus anti-crime sentiment, stoked by some heated rhetoric during the 1990s, was a potential obstacle to reform.

Another key obstacle to any effort to raise the age of adult jurisdiction to eighteen was the perceived cost. A legislative report issued in early 2004 estimated the cost of raising the age to eighteen at $160 million or more. That figure proved a conversation stopper for many state legislators and a major obstacle to advocates who believed that the best way to deal with juvenile crime was through "balanced and restorative justice."[11]

Representative Walker probed a little and discovered that the $160 million cost estimate was very rough and that the report contained few details. How many juveniles are processed every year? How many are incarcerated? How many slots are available for sixteen-year-olds? What are the costs? Walker requested a systematic study but was rebuffed. Too costly, she was told.

Undeterred, Walker began the tedious process of seeking allies inside and outside the legislative branch. She approached Speaker Joe Amman. She also spoke with House Judiciary Committee Chairman Mike Lawlor, who agreed to convene a joint hearing with the Senate Judiciary Committee on the question of raising the age of adult jurisdiction. The hearing, on February 21, 2006, featured a variety of witnesses identified by the Connecticut Juvenile Justice Alliance.

A turning point in the hearings occurred when Abigail Baird, then an assistant professor of psychology at Dartmouth, testified on the adolescent

9. At least one study showed that exposure to a "superpredator news frame" on TV news increased the fear of crime among viewers. For whites and Asians, it also increased support for harsher public policies. DiIulio (1995, p. 23); Gilliam and Iyengar (1998).

10. Fagan (2008); Shaddox (2008).

11. See Francis interview, appendix A; Bazemore and Umbreit (1997).

brain.[12] Baird's PowerPoint presentation combined good science with good humor. She joked with legislators about differences between male and female adolescents. She also reported that adolescents and adults react differently to demonstrably bad ideas, like setting your hair on fire or eating a cockroach. To underscore the point, she showed legislators a video clip focused on a shark tank. Asked whether it was a good or bad idea to swim with a shark, the assembled adolescents seriously considered the possibility and wanted to know more: Have the sharks eaten recently? Could someone else jump in with me and distract the shark? Baird effectively made the point that the adolescent brain was not fully developed. The public policy implication: that adolescents accused of a crime should be treated differently from adults.

With support from legislative leaders, Walker secured approval to establish a task force on juvenile jurisdiction, with Walker and Senator Toni Hart as cochairs. The task force met fourteen times between August 2006 and February 2007. It invited parents, children, lawyers, judges, and various experts to testify. Abigail Baird, who had made such a deep impression on legislators earlier, was invited to testify again.

Meanwhile, Walker was working hard on getting a new cost estimate. With input from the Urban Institute, she determined that the $160 million cost estimate was way off base. In fact, it was likely that raising the age to age eighteen would save money, by diverting youths out of the adult correctional system and by giving them a meaningful chance to rehabilitate themselves. John Roman, at the Urban Institute, estimated that the benefits of raising the age would exceed the costs by 3 to 1 (see table 6-1).

"Connecticut doesn't like to be first out of the box, but we don't like to be last either," Walker commented in her interview. She remarked that she had reminded her colleagues that Connecticut was one of only three states to try sixteen- and seventeen-year-olds as adults: "That stopped everybody."

Walker continued her campaign, enlisting support from both juvenile court and adult court judges. In March 2007 the Connecticut Juvenile Justice Alliance organized a rally at the Capitol that drew an estimated 350 enthusiastic supporters.[13] Legislative comfort levels with the pro-

12. Baird (2006). For a good account of Baird's testimony, see Crutchfield, Kania, and Kramer (2011, p. 41).
13. Francis interview.

Table 6-1. *Benefit-Cost Ratios, Raising the Age of Adult Jurisdiction from Sixteen to Eighteen, Connecticut*

Assumption	No construction	With construction
One recidivism offense	2.94	0.39
Two recidivism offenses	5.88	0.77
Expected number of offenses	21.09	2.78

Source: Roman (2006).

posed legislation noticeably increased. Transitional costs emerged as a potential deal breaker. Sensing that victory was at hand, Walker and her supporters agreed to phase in the reform, starting with sixteen-year-olds in 2010, seventeen-year-olds in 2012. These changes gave state agencies and local governments time to prepare for the switch and to keep short-term budget costs down.

In 2007 the House and the Senate approved a budget bill that included a provision to raise the age of adult jurisdiction to eighteen. The bill passed, by wide margins, in both the House and the Senate. Republican governor Jodi Rell, though not viewed as supportive of raising the age, signed the bill on June 29, 2007. In fact, she didn't have many options, because the margins of victory in both chambers were veto proof.

Looking back on it, Bob Francis of the Regional Youth Adult Social Action Partnership gives a lot of the credit to Walker: "She has a charm about her. People liked working with her, an awful lot. She always came to meetings. She did her homework. And she's a natural politician." With characteristic grace, Walker gives credit to others. "The movement was bigger than me. It was something everybody did." But Walker acknowledges that this perspective was strategic too. "I didn't want it to be per ceived as *my* agenda but everybody's agenda. When we did press conferences, I tried *not* to be the one to talk." On the floor of the General Assembly, Walker sought out tough-minded colleagues like Mike Lawlor to defend the bill. "They're skilled lawyers. Everybody says I'm warm and fuzzy. They're not warm and fuzzy!" Walker was also conscious about the racial aspects of juvenile crime. "I didn't want the TV to see a black person defending the bill."[14]

14. Francis and Walker interviews.

Utah

Utah is teeming with children. Due to a very high birth rate, it has a higher percentage of children than any other state: 31 percent, as opposed to the national average of 24 percent. Utah has a reputation for being well managed and for having a high quality of life. According to one study, Utah residents are happier than residents of any other state.[15] Some of this is surely good for children.

On the other hand, Utah ranks dead last in its per capita state expenditures for elementary and secondary education. Utah is one of only twelve states with no state-funded preschool program (two of these states, Alaska and Rhode Island, have pilot programs). It is one of five states to receive a grade of D or F from the Pew Charitable Trusts for its failure to provide good access to dental care for children.[16]

Two factors conspire against well-funded children's programs in Utah. The first is strong fiscal conservatism, as manifested in relatively low public spending across the board. Low levels of public spending are, of course, closely related to low levels of taxation. When economic conditions worsened in 2009 and 2010, in Utah as elsewhere, the state's leading politicians resisted calls for income tax, sales tax, or severance tax increases. They did approve a $1 per pack increase in the state's cigarette tax, effective July 1, 2010, but this was expected to raise only $43 million a year in new revenue.[17] Without higher taxes, it would be difficult for Utah to fund new children's programs or to strengthen existing programs.

The second constraining factor is strong social conservatism, as manifested in considerable public commentary against abortion, same-sex marriage, and the dangers of "the nanny state." This social conservatism reflects the spiritual and political power of the state's strongest institution, the Mormon religion, as exemplified by the Church of Jesus Christ of the Latter-day Saints, based in Salt Lake City. Approximately 61 percent of all Utah residents are Mormons. Mormons are more supportive of traditional gender roles than members of other religious groups. Mormons are more active politically than Catholics or Southern Baptists, and they vote Republican more reliably than any other religious group. Since

15. Clark (2010). See also U.S. Census Bureau (2012).
16. U.S. Census Bureau (2010, table 253); Barnett and others (2010); Lucchese (2010, p. 4).
17. Roche (2010).

1966 Utah's state legislature has been controlled by the Republican Party; since 1984 Utah has elected only Republican governors.[18]

In the summer of 2005 a Republican state legislator and high school special education teacher, Kory Holdaway, decided to fight for all-day kindergarten. The following year, he proposed a bill that would authorize local school districts, at their discretion, to offer publicly funded full-day kindergarten. He also proposed that $7.5 million a year be set aside for that purpose. Several nonprofit groups, including Voices for Utah's Children and United Way, helped Holdaway with talking points and suggested witnesses for legislative hearings, which were held in February 2006. According to Holdaway, the key argument in favor of full-day kindergarten was economic: "A dollar paid today will save us money down the road, in terms of remediation, special ed, and crime."[19]

Somewhat surprisingly, Holdaway was successful, though not immediately. It helped that Holdaway had secured Republican governor Jon Huntsman's strong support during a conversation in the summer of 2005. Huntsman, who had become quite interested in early childhood education as a result of some National Governors Association meetings on the subject, was extremely enthusiastic and agreed to include all-day kindergarten in his budget request. According to Holdaway, "We were singing Kumbaya together." On the other hand, the Eagle Forum and other groups voiced strong objections. "They said we were taking children from the wombs of their mothers, that it was a family responsibility, and that full-day kindergarten was too taxing for young kids," Holdaway recalls. Although the House passed the bill in the spring of 2006, it languished in the Senate Rules Committee.

To succeed the following year, Holdaway and his allies decided that they needed a strong supporter in the Senate. They found such a person in Senator Lyle Hillyard, cochair of the Executive Appropriations Committee, a key House-Senate committee. Hillyard's support was conditional: he would "carry" the bill in the Senate if it included a "sunset" provision. If the legislature failed to act four years later, the program would expire in 2011. This clause made it easier for skeptical legislators to support the bill, and the bill became law in 2007.

Four years later, child advocates and supportive legislators had to work even harder to renew the full-day kindergarten program because

18. See Newport (2009b); Campbell and Monson (2007, pp. 107–09, 111).
19. Holdaway interview, appendix A.

Utah faced serious budget constraints (though less serious than most other states) and because some legislators preferred to spend education dollars on classroom computers. Although some legislators preferred technology to full-day kindergarten, the legislative leadership eventually crafted a compromise that appropriated $7.5 million annually, as before, but that allowed local school districts, at their discretion, to spend some (or all) of their money on computers. They called this "optional extended-day kindergarten," with an emphasis on the word optional. A key factor was strong support from Republican governor Gary Herbert. According to Senator Hillyard, "If the governor hadn't been as adamant, we wouldn't have gotten the kindergarten appropriation through the legislature." His advice to his colleagues: "We're all Republicans up here. We ought to be nice to a fellow Republican." Given the state's financial situation, the possibility of another multiyear appropriation for all-day kindergarten was not actively discussed.[20]

In contrast to the all-day kindergarten campaign, efforts to promote a state-funded preschool program in Utah have been unsuccessful. A Democratic state legislator, Patricia Jones, explains: "It's not just about money. A core of ultraright people believe that kindergarten and earlier is the responsibility of the parents."[21] Prevailing values are a big constraint. In Senator Hillyard's words, "Some of the more conservative members think that every mother ought to be home taking care of their children."

North Carolina

North Carolina has been one of the nation's leaders in early childhood education. In 1993 Democratic governor Jim Hunt established Smart Start, a locally based public-private partnership program aimed at providing comprehensive early childhood services to children ages birth through five years. In 1999, with Hunt's support, North Carolina inaugurated a quality rating system for its day care centers and family day care homes, assigning stars (one to five) as a measure of quality to help guide parents in their choices. In 2001 Democratic governor Mike Easley established More at Four, a state-funded preschool program that serves at-risk four-year-olds.

20. Hillyard interview, appendix A.
21. Jones interview, appendix A.

Some of these programs seem to have paid off. An evaluation of the More at Four program by University of North Carolina–Chapel Hill researchers finds that disadvantaged third graders who attended More at Four as preschoolers had significantly higher math and reading scores than disadvantaged third graders who did not attend More at Four. A subsequent evaluation by Duke University researchers finds that third graders who attended Smart Start or More at Four had significantly higher math and reading scores than other third graders and were less likely to have been assigned to a special education classroom.[22]

In early 2009 North Carolina's education policy gains and other social programs were imperiled when it was announced that the state faced a deficit approximately 20 percent the size of its general funds budget.[23] Without tax increases, sharp cutbacks in education, child health, and other social services programs would be necessary. Elaine Mejia, a policy analyst with the North Carolina Justice Center, based in Raleigh, took the lead in establishing a coalition of over a hundred organizations that sought to protect North Carolina's social programs by raising more revenue.

Unlike previous efforts to galvanize public support for tax increases in North Carolina, which sought to evoke sympathy and support for disadvantaged citizens, the coalition in 2009 stressed the benefits to *all* citizens that flow from a strong social infrastructure.[24] The North Carolina Justice Center summed up its viewpoint in a newspaper ad:

> North Carolina is a great place to live—because our state has made wise investments in education, children's healthcare, job training and a clean environment. Now is the time to protect these investments. That means raising the revenue we need—and in a fair and sustainable manner—to get us out of this recession and help working families across the state. We know it won't be easy in this time of budget crisis. But just as surely, we know that it's worth it. It's worth it to educate our kids. . . . It's worth it to keep our communities safe. . . . It's worth it to provide quality health care.[25]

The coalition's efforts succeeded, thanks to a strong message and support from key politicians, including Governor Bev Perdue, House Speaker

22. See North Carolina Department of Public Instruction (2010); Dodge, Ladd, and Muschkin (2011).
23. Mejia (2009).
24. Mejia interview, appendix A.
25. North Carolina Justice Center (2009).

Joe Hackney, Senate President Pro Tem Marc Basnight, and House Appropriations Committee member Jim Crawford. In August 2009 the state legislature agreed to a two-year sales tax increase of one penny, temporary income tax surcharges, and permanent sin tax hikes that, together with some spending cuts, brought the budget into balance. The additional revenue was estimated to yield approximately $1 billion a year. Without the new revenue, North Carolina would have been forced to lay off approximately 10,000 teachers and make other cuts as well. This was a remarkable achievement. North Carolina was one of only twelve states to raise taxes more than 5 percent, from 2008 to 2010.[26]

The political climate changed abruptly, however, in November 2010. For the first time since Reconstruction, Republicans took over the North Carolina General Assembly. Republicans won control of the state Senate as well, giving them comfortable working majorities in both houses (67–52 House; 31–19 Senate).[27] Many Republican legislative candidates promised that, if elected, they would not vote to raise taxes. At the same time, economic conditions worsened—the state faced an annual budget deficit of $3.5 billion and would need to make substantial cuts even if it retained the temporary tax increase.

The new Republican leaders of the state House and Senate announced early on that they would oppose making the temporary tax increases permanent. They also opposed a more modest tax extension recommended by Perdue. As Senator Richard Stevens explains, "My party had run on a platform of not raising taxes, no matter what . . . that was in stone."[28] A House bill proposed $1 billion in education cuts, requiring layoffs and larger classes. A Senate bill proposed somewhat smaller cuts but eliminated teaching aide positions in public schools to permit some new hires, smaller classes, and a longer school year. Senate Republicans were impressed by studies showing a link between smaller class sizes and educational achievement and by international comparisons suggesting that countries with longer school years experienced better test scores.

The House and Senate passed a budget bill by wide margins on June 4, 2011.[29] Although Governor Perdue vetoed the budget bill in June 2011 (the first veto of a budget bill in North Carolina history), both houses

26. See Associated Press (2009); Lav and Grundman (2011).
27. Campaign contributions from a conservative businessman and philanthropist, Art Pope, contributed to the Republicans' electoral success; see Mayer (2011).
28. Stevens interview, appendix A.
29. Dalesio (2011).

Figure 6-1. *Cuts to Education Spending, North Carolina,*
by Category, 2011

Percent

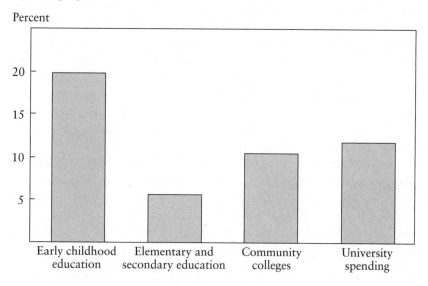

Source: North Carolina General Assembly (2011).

overrode the veto and enacted it into law. The final bill cut elementary
and secondary education spending by 5.8 percent, community college
spending by 10.7 percent, university spending by 12 percent, and early
childhood education spending by 20 percent (see figure 6-1).

Why were Smart Start and More at Four cut even more severely than
other education programs? Former governor Jim Hunt, arguably the most
popular politician in the state, held a press conference in support of preschool programs in March 2011 and vigorously lobbied key Republican legislators behind the scenes. The Duke University study touting the
benefits of Smart Start and More at Four was released in March 2011.
Nevertheless, both programs were cut by 20 percent.

Senator Stevens, chair of the Senate Appropriations Committee, concludes from the Duke research that the evidence on North Carolina's
early childhood education programs was "mixed" and that "this was
not the best thing since sliced bread." He notes especially that immediate
gains seemed to erode over time. Former House Speaker Joe Hackney
(D-Chapel Hill) believes that both programs suffered from a close association with Democratic politicians: "Smart Start is a signature program of

Democratic governor Jim Hunt and More at Four is a signature program of Democratic governor Mike Easley. They came in with a big target on their backs."[30] Hackney believes that the Duke University research "made no difference" in the debate, but he does think that Hunt's intervention helped to prevent both programs from being cut even more deeply: "What Governor Hunt did behind the scenes was more important than what he did publicly. He made it clear that Republicans would pay and pay substantially for deeper cuts in Smart Start. If cuts had been deeper, Hunt would have gone after them." According to other sources, the threat was that Hunt would actively campaign against recalcitrant legislators in the next election.

The structure of Smart Start also made it difficult to dismantle. Unlike many state programs, it has deep roots in local communities, where key programmatic decisions are made and where political support from businesses, schools, and churches is strong. According to Gary Pearce, a former Hunt staff member, when Hunt designed the program twenty years before, he advocated a "cementing" strategy, which Pearce defines as "getting so many people committed to the program at the local level that they'll scream if it's threatened."[31] In 2011 that cementing strategy was instrumental in preventing the program from being dismantled, but in the age of the Tea Party it was not enough to prevent it from being deeply cut.

Pennsylvania

Pennsylvania has produced many individuals who have helped to shape children and our images of children over the years, including Fred Rogers (from Pittsburgh), Bill Cosby (from Philadelphia), and Marc Brown (from Erie), who gave us *Mister Rogers' Neighborhood, The Cosby Show,* and *Arthur the Aardvark,* respectively. Jonas Salk, who invented the polio vaccine, taught for a while at the University of Pittsburgh, as did Benjamin Spock, the author of an enormously popular—and controversial—book on raising children.

Overall, Pennsylvania ranks somewhat above average in its child friendliness. For example, its child poverty rate is somewhat better than the national average. It ranks twelfth in the nation in the percentage of two-year-olds immunized and fourteenth in the nation in the percentage

30. Hackney interview, appendix A.
31. Pearce interview, appendix A.

of children who have health insurance. Its child maltreatment rate was the lowest in the United States. On the other hand, it received a grade of F from the Pew Charitable Trusts for its provision of dental care to children.[32]

Pennsylvania established its Nurse-Family Partnership program in 1999, one of the first states in the nation to do so. The program originated with tacit support from then governor Tom Ridge, a Republican, who would later become the first secretary of homeland security. Feather Houstoun, Ridge's secretary of public welfare, recalls that the idea of establishing an NFP program in Pennsylvania owes its beginning to a U.S. Department of Justice report and a chance remark by John Perzel (R-Philadelphia), then leader of the Republicans in the General Assembly: "Perzel was giving me a hard time about something when he said, 'You guys should find out ways for moms to be good mothers.' I got off the phone, reported it to somebody, and one of our staff members said, 'You ought to see this pamphlet.'"[33] The pamphlet, from the Office of Juvenile Justice and Delinquency Prevention, was titled "Blueprints for Violence Prevention." As Houstoun recalls, "Blueprints" identified ten programs that really work, as opposed to about ninety that don't. At the top of the list of successful programs was the Nurse-Family Partnership program. Houstoun resolved to start the program immediately, at three sites.

By the end of the Ridge administration, in 2002, the program had extended to twenty-three sites. At first, the program was financed with state funds from the Pennsylvania Commission on Crime and Delinquency. Later, federal TANF dollars were added to the mix. In 2006, thanks to the leadership of Representative Phyllis Mundy (D-Luzerne) and Senator Pat Browne (R-Allentown), the NFP was included as a line item in the state budget. As Mundy notes, "Making it a line item in the budget makes it a lot easier to watch." This would prove especially important in 2011, when big budget cuts were enacted.[34]

When Ed Rendell, a Democrat and former mayor of Philadelphia, became governor in January 2003, he brought with him a strong commitment to early childhood education and a team of people committed to carrying out that vision. Rendell launched a campaign to expand state-funded prekindergarten in Pennsylvania and to integrate children's programs run by the state's Department of Public Welfare and the state's Department of

32. See Kids Count (2010); U.S. Census Bureau (2010); Lucchese (2010, p. 4).
33. Houstoun interview, appendix A.
34. Mundy interview, appendix A.

Table 6-2. *Benefits of the Nurse-Family Partnership Program for Mothers and Children, Fifteen Years after Intervention, Elmira, New York*
Percent

Benefits to mothers	
Arrests	↓ 61
Convictions	↓ 72
Days in Jail	↓ 98
Benefits to children	
Abuse and neglect	↓ 48
Arrests	↓ 59
Adjudications for incorrigible behavior	↓ 90

Source: Olds (2007).

Education. Toward that end, he appointed Harriet Dichter, a prominent early childhood expert from Philadelphia, to bridge the gap between those two departments, heading up the new Office of Child Development and Early Learning, which spanned both departments. Dichter would later serve as secretary of public welfare. Dichter was familiar with evidence from Elmira, New York, which indicated strong positive effects from the NFP program, across a wide range of indicators (see table 6-2).

The Rendell administration proposed and achieved an expansion of the Nurse-Family Partnership program, in terms of both resources and the number of children being served (see figure 6-2). As Dichter recalls, "We knew this program, understood the value added, and grasped the relationship between the home visit model and the broader idea of a continuum of early childhood education and learning." The Rendell administration also diversified the funding base for the NFP program, supporting it with Medicaid dollars for the first time, and commissioned a study of the program by David Rubin of Philadelphia. That study finds that NFP clients in Pennsylvania have significantly fewer births within two years after the birth of their first child than a comparable group of nonclients.[35]

Despite a worsening economy, in 2010 the Rendell administration's final budget protected the Nurse-Family Partnership program and other early childhood programs from cuts. Throughout this period, the NFP

35. See Dichter interview, appendix A; Rubin and others (2010).

Figure 6-2. *State Funding for Nurse-Family Partnership Program, Pennsylvania, 1999–2012*[a]

$ Million

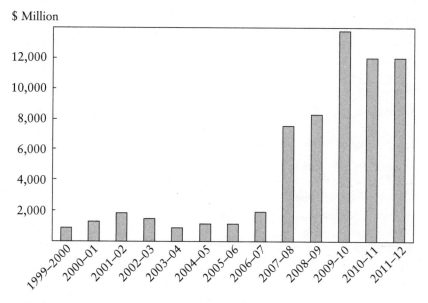

Source: Pennsylvania House Appropriations Committee, July 11, 2011.
a. Years are fiscal years.

received critical support from Representative Mundy, a strong champion of the NFP. Mundy became a convert to NFP when she accompanied a nurse on a visit to a home in Wilkes-Barre, part of her district. On that visit, and later, she learned of many success stories, one of them about a heroin addict who gave birth at age eighteen, kicked the heroin habit, ended an abusive relationship, found a job, and raised a healthy daughter who met all the benchmarks for a two-year-old after two years of home visits. More broadly, early learning programs, according to Jay Costa, fared "very, very well" during the latter years of the Rendell administration.[36] It probably helped that advocates could point to studies showing that program benefits substantially exceeded program costs (see table 6-3).

The election of Tom Corbett, a Republican, as governor in November 2010, and the takeover of the General Assembly by the Republican Party, posed a potential threat to early childhood programs, including the

36. Costa interview, appendix A.

Table 6-3. *Nurse-Family Partnership Program for Low-Income Families, Benefit-Cost Analysis*
Dollars

| Benefits by area | Benefits and costs from different perspectives | | | |
| | Program participants | Non-program participants | | Total |
		Taxpayers	Nontaxpayers	
Crime	0	4,877	8,533	13,410
High school graduation	672	299	169	1,141
Test scores	5,572	2,480	1,403	9,454
K–12 special education	0	0	0	0
K–12 grade repetition	0	11	0	11
Child abuse and neglect	3,212	661	0	3,873
Out-of-home placements	0	0	0	0
Alcohol (disordered use)	107	57	2	167
Illicit drugs (disordered use)	44	26	0	70
Total benefits	8,936	8,112	9,938	26,986
Program costs	0	–8,931	0	–8,931
Net benefit	8,936	–819	9,938	18,054
Total dollars of benefits per dollar of cost				3.02

Source: Lee, Aos, and Miller (2008).

NFP, because Corbett and other Republicans had taken a pledge not to raise taxes. But Corbett promised to protect early childhood programs in his first budget, and in key respects he did exactly that. Specifically, he "level funded" the state's child care quality program (Keystone Stars), the state's prekindergarten program (Pre-K Counts), and NFP. However, he proposed to eliminate the education accountability block grant, which enables school districts to fund a variety of education programs, including all-day kindergarten and prekindergarten. According to Costa, this block grant had lost popularity with Republicans, who thought that local school districts could have done a better job of managing the public's money.

When state legislators confront a tight fiscal environment, they must make some difficult decisions. According to Jake Corman, chair of the Senate Appropriations Committee, they must ask three big questions: "First, what is the need and is there another way to fill that need? For example, sometimes the private sector or the nonprofit sector can help.

Second, if a program has no value, why not eliminate it? Third, is a program a core responsibility of the government? We should do those things first and do them right." According to Corman, "the governor is a big player in all of this." Corman also believes in examining the evidence on program effectiveness, though he concedes that the legislature does not often do this.[37]

Ultimately, the budget bill approved by the legislature left the NFP program intact, at $12 million annually (exclusive of federal funding); the legislature made more modest cuts in early childhood education than in education generally. According to Kathy Vranicar, funding for Pre-K Counts and the Head Start supplemental assistance program declined by 2.9 percent, while funding for child care declined by 9 to 10 percent. In contrast, higher education funding declined by 13.9 percent, and the basic education budget declined by 7.3 percent (if federal funds from the American Recovery and Reinvestment Act are considered). Although the education accountability block grant was not eliminated, as proposed by Corbett, funding was reduced by 62 percent, according to Lisa Fleming. Some of these cuts are almost certain to affect early childhood education, because 75 percent of Pennsylvania's school districts were using block grant funds for prekindergarten, full-day kindergarten, or class-size reductions in the early elementary grades.[38]

Why did NFP survive untouched after a brutal budget battle? Although Governor Corbett had not promised to protect the NFP program in particular, he had supported early childhood intervention in his gubernatorial campaign. Also, this program stood out from other programs in its strong evidentiary base. As Representative Mundy puts it, "It's research based. It's been proven to be effective in terms of preventing later problems and costs. It remains a high priority." Although House Republicans originally proposed a reduction in the NFP's appropriation, the money was restored in negotiations with the Senate. Senator Browne, a longtime supporter of the NFP, recalls that no arm twisting was necessary: "It wasn't a program that required a lot of advocacy."

More broadly, specific early childhood programs escaped severe cuts, thanks in part to evidence on program effectiveness. As Senator Jay Costa, the Senate Democratic leader, puts it: "The evidence shows that targeted investments in early learning programs work very well. They make sense,

37. Corman interview, appendix A.
38. See Vranicar and Fleming interviews, appendix A.

and there's clear evidence that they work." Most observers agree that Pennsylvania's elected officials tried to spare early childhood programs (at least those targeted to early childhood), although sharp cuts in the education accountability block grant may have had the practical consequence of hurting those programs. As Senator Corman observes, "Early childhood programs did fairly well in a year when there were big cutbacks."

Discussion

These cases help to remind us that the policymaking process is a turbulent brew of political, economic, and social ingredients. Although issue frames play a role in the outcome of debates, that role ranges from important to irrelevant. To make sense of these variations, it may be useful to distinguish between new and old policies and between direct and indirect effects.

New versus Old

In Connecticut and Utah, the state legislatures had to decide whether to adopt new policies: an increase in the age of adult jurisdiction for most criminal offenses (Connecticut) and the establishment of all-day kindergarten on a voluntary basis (Utah). In North Carolina and Pennsylvania, in contrast, the state legislatures had to decide whether to continue to fund established programs (the Nurse-Family Partnership program, Smart Start, and More at Four) at their prior levels. Did this distinction between new and continuing policies matter for issue framing?

The Connecticut case illustrates exactly what one would expect of a brand-new social policy—lots of data gathering, hearings with in-state and out-of-state witnesses, rallies and protests, and a full-throated legislative debate. The stakes were high, the questions were numerous, and the state legislature behaved like a genuinely deliberative body. In this setting, an economic frame and a scientific frame both made a difference. A benefit-cost analysis by the Urban Institute effectively rebutted an earlier legislative analysis of the financial impacts of raising the age of adult jurisdiction. Instead of spending money, experts argued, Connecticut would actually be saving money. Graphic evidence of the immaturity of the adolescent brain also shaped legislators' perceptions. The scientific research, presented by a developmental psychologist with humor and folksy charm, won many converts by connecting new scientific insights into the changing human brain with familiar glimpses of adolescent immaturity that legislators had witnessed themselves. Although other factors also contributed to the success of the raise-the-age campaign, including especially the adroit legislative leadership of Representative Toni Walker, framing was undeniably important.

The Utah state legislature's approach to full-day kindergarten also featured a legislative hearing and economic framing, but Utah's approach to potential policy change was more casual, informal, and superficial. Instead of bringing in out-of-state experts, the House Education Committee invited Patti Harrington, the state superintendent for public instruction, a gubernatorial aide, and representatives of three school systems. Harrington helped make the case for full-day kindergarten by citing national research showing that full-day kindergarten contributes to school readiness and reduces the costs of grade retention and remediation later on. Yet some legislators remained skeptical. Representative Margaret Dayton (R-Orem) was one: "What about childhood? At what point are we going to say that childhood matters and time at home matters and we shouldn't get society in the mind-set that we should turn our kids over to school as early as we can?"[39]

Full-day kindergarten would not have been possible in Utah were it not for the enthusiastic support of Governor Jon Huntsman and the more reluctant, more conditional support of a well-respected conservative legislator, Senator Lyle Hillyard. Before Huntsman jumped on board, the bill was languishing in committee. With the governor's strong endorsement, the bill rocketed through the House of Representatives, but the Senate's consent remained uncertain. An agreement to "sunset" the bill won Hillyard's backing and the full Senate's support the following year.

With a new, untested public policy, one expects careful scrutiny, expert testimony, and thorough legislative debate. With an established policy, one expects rhetorical shorthand, truncated arguments, and allusions to past decisions. In Pennsylvania, supporters of early childhood education and the Nurse-Family Partnership program appealed to shared understandings that had developed during previous gubernatorial administrations—namely, the governorships of Tom Ridge (a Republican) and Ed Rendell (a Democrat). It was not necessary to revisit these issues with a full-scale legislative debate, because a rough consensus already existed that nurse home visits and high-quality preschool were beneficial to young children and economically beneficial to the state. It certainly

39. Erickson (2006).

helped that the new governor, Tom Corbett, not only agreed that the early years were of critical importance but had said so emphatically during the gubernatorial campaign. It also helped that Senate Republican staffers reminded House Republican staffers that the NFP was popular with the governor, with high-ranking state senators, and with folks back home. In short, there was no need to reframe the debate on home visits or early childhood education, nor was there much need for any debate at all on these issues. There was, however, a need to remind some legislators of the reasons for generous funding of early childhood programs in the past. When the House proposed to cut NFP, reminders from the Senate helped to restore the funds.

In North Carolina, the situation was quite different. Shared understandings were shattered and existing programs were threatened by stunning economic and political developments. An economic tsunami hit North Carolina in the fall of 2008, and a political tsunami hit the state in the fall of 2010. With both chambers of the state legislature controlled by the Republicans for the first time since Reconstruction, tax increases were off the table and budget cuts were inevitable.

The state's early childhood education programs—Smart Start and More at Four—were generally popular, and they seemed to be working. However, they were closely associated with two former Democratic governors (Hunt and Easley), which did not endear them to Republican legislators. Policy researchers at Duke University used an economic frame and new scientific evidence to make the case that Smart Start and More at Four were working. Former governor Hunt, still as captivating as a good preacher, made a strong appeal:

> If you're gonna have good business and good jobs and lots of jobs
> . . . you've gotta have good education. During the 1990s our NAEP
> scores went up more than any state in America. The people from the
> RAND Corporation told me that was because of early education.
> . . . Smart Start is looked at across America as the best early childhood program there is. When you've got something this good, you
> don't want to mess it up![40]

Hunt's intervention, especially his personal lobbying, may have saved the programs from extinction, but it could not save them from deep budget cuts (20 percent). An investment frame worked well in previous years,

40. Hunt (2011).

but in 2011 North Carolina Republicans were in no mood to invest any more of the taxpayers' money than absolutely necessary in programs launched by Democratic governors.

Direct versus Indirect

Direct appeals to public officials utilize lobbying, committee hearings, and other forms of direct personal contact with legislators and other decisionmakers. Indirect appeals rely on rallies and protests, newspaper and broadcast ads, and other strategies to generate public support for a proposed course of action. Indirect appeals seek to "expand the scope of conflict" through "outsider" strategies, while direct appeals seek to change public policy by persuading public officials themselves.[41] Of the four cases discussed, outside appeals were most prominent in Connecticut and North Carolina.

In Connecticut, the Connecticut Juvenile Justice Alliance played a key role in generating publicity and public support for raising the age of adult jurisdiction. In February 2006 the alliance produced 150 people for what was billed as "educate the legislature day." In March 2007 the group reprised educate the legislature day, this time with 350 orange-shirted supporters. Hector Glynn, then executive director of the alliance, recalls being both gratified and apprehensive: "If you looked out, you'd see a sea of orange in the elegant statehouse building. There were so many people, a lot of them were teenagers, and they were really noisy. We were afraid the sheriffs would kick people out. You had enough intensity, but it could have turned ugly. After that, most legislators were convinced that (we) had public support."[42]

In North Carolina, a coalition of a hundred groups played a significant role in generating public support for a temporary tax increase in 2009 The frame was the high quality of life in North Carolina, which depends significantly on government spending, which in turn depends on taxes. By emphasizing that something highly valued by most citizens (quality of life) could be lost if taxes weren't raised, the alliance relied on Amos Tversky and Daniel Kahneman's well-known argument that citizens fear losses more than they value equivalent gains.[43] That argument helped the

41. Schattschneider (1960).
42. Glynn interview, appendix A.
43. Tversky and Kahneman (1981).

state's political leaders to secure passage of a controversial tax increase, though some legislators believe this would have happened anyway.

The coalition suffered a serious loss when Elaine Mejia left the state in 2010. However, even a master strategist would have found the political challenges of 2011 daunting: a strong Republican majority in both chambers of the North Carolina legislature united in their opposition to anything resembling a tax increase. Former governor Hunt and his supporters did expand the scope of conflict in March 2011 in an effort to protect early childhood education programs. However, experts agree that it was Hunt's inside lobbying that ultimately persuaded key Republican legislators to limit cuts to 20 percent.

In Utah and Pennsylvania, the critical debates over children's issues took place inside the state capital. The general public was not courted or mobilized, the mass media were not actively engaged, the scope of conflict was not expanded in any significant way. Conversations among legislators, between legislators and the governor's office, among legislative staffers, and between legislators and lobbyists helped to determine the outcome of public policy debates involving children.

In Utah, strategically situated legislators took the initiative and sought out key politicians in an effort to win their endorsement. Supporters of full-day kindergarten were fortunate that Jon Huntsman was the sitting governor. In contrast to other Utah politicians, Huntsman was more progressive, more activist, and more child oriented. He was highly receptive to arguments that all-day kindergarten could be a good investment for the future because he had already warmed to such arguments at meetings of the National Governors Association. Other legislators also played a key role in launching full-day kindergarten and in sustaining it when it expired. On the other hand, the coalition in support of full-day kindergarten is fragile. Experts agree that it will be severely challenged when the latest version of full-day kindergarten runs its course.

In Pennsylvania, the key debates over the Nurse-Family Partnership program also involved state public officials. From the outset, both legislators and executive branch officials participated actively. The very idea for a Pennsylvania version of an NFP seems to have originated in a casual conversation between a prominent Republican legislator and a cabinet secretary for Governor Ridge. Legislators from both parties and members of Governor Rendell's administration successfully engineered a growth spurt for the program. Republican legislators and members of Governor Corbett's administration protected the NFP from cuts during a very difficult budget year. Lobbyists also played a role in these debates, including lobbyists for the NFP and children's lobbyists generally.

Conclusion

In chapter 5, which focused on two randomized experiments, I demonstrated the efficacy of children's issue frames, most notably, an investment frame and an equal opportunity frame. In this chapter, which examines four case studies, we also see evidence of framing effects. In Connecticut, a benefit-cost frame and a science frame proved useful in persuading the Connecticut General Assembly to raise the age of adult court jurisdiction for criminal offenses from age sixteen to age eighteen. In Pennsylvania, a benefit-cost frame helped to convince Governor Ridge and the Pennsylvania General Assembly to establish a pilot program for the Nurse-Family Partnership program years ago. Occasional reminders, using the same frame, have helped the program to grow over time and to avoid cutbacks in 2011. In North Carolina, a public relations campaign that warned of imminent threats to quality of life helped to persuade the North Carolina General Assembly to support temporary tax increases in 2009. These tax increases protected children's programs from significant cutbacks for two years.

Still, a key theme of this chapter is that good issue frames do not always carry the day. Strong economic arguments and good empirical evidence were not enough to persuade the North Carolina General Assembly to protect its early childhood education programs from severe budget cuts in 2011. Strong economic arguments and some good empirical evidence were not enough to persuade the Utah state legislature to adopt a state-funded prekindergarten program in the first place. Although the Nurse-Family Partnership and some early childhood education programs survived a declining economy and a Republican takeover of the statehouse in Pennsylvania, substantial K–12 budget cuts did occur.

Several factors pose obstacles to children's advocates who seek to launch or strengthen children's programs at the state level. First, budget constraints, especially in a bad economy, make it difficult to justify new programs or to grow existing programs. Constitutional requirements to balance state budgets reinforce these constraints. Second, ideological objections threaten certain children's programs and children's policy proposals. Although conservatives generally support public education for kindergarten through twelfth grade, they often oppose early childhood education on the grounds that parents should be taking care of young children at home. Also, conservatives have taken aim at teachers' pay, teachers' benefits, and teachers' tenure in recent years. Third, party polarization has worsened in state government. This phenomenon makes compromise difficult and makes it difficult to get children's programs approved or strengthened.

Are these constraints stronger or weaker at the federal level? Which issue frames for children's issues are most appealing on Capitol Hill? Beyond issue frames, what other rhetorical strategies help to move congressional debates? I turn to these questions in chapter 7.

CHAPTER SEVEN

Capitol Hill Debates
about Children

> *One of the searing memories in my life is being in a children's hospital in Boston, when my son who had lost his leg to cancer (was being treated). . . . And I listened to these (other) families, whose children had the same kind of affliction that my child had. . . . I knew that my child was going to have the best because I had the health insurance of the U.S. Senate. And I knew that no parent in that hospital had the kind of coverage that I had. That kind of choice for any parent in this country is absolutely unacceptable and wrong.*
>
> Ted Kennedy, May 20, 2008

Although notoriously porous and accessible, Congress represents a more daunting battleground for children's advocates than state legislatures do. Historically, Congress has allocated far more resources to senior citizens than to children. Congress has also authorized tax expenditures for numerous favored constituencies, including the health industry, the defense industry, and the financial industry. These patterns are hard to change, especially because powerful lobbyists are strongly committed to the status quo. Even critics of incrementalism as a metaphor for the policy process acknowledge the power of inertia: "Defenders of the status quo usually get what they want: No change."[1]

Another challenge facing children's advocates on Capitol Hill is the rise in party polarization that has occurred in recent years. The growth of the Republican Party in the South since 1964 has decimated the ranks of conservatives within the congressional Democratic Party while increasing the ranks of conservatives within the Republican Party. In other

---

1. Baumgartner and others (2009, p. 241). Also see Lindblom (1959).

regions, moderates in both parties have lost ground to extremists. As Nolan McCarty, Keith Poole, and Howard Rosenthal put it, "Compared to the 1960s, extreme conservative as well as extreme liberal positions are more likely to be represented in Congress."[2] By contrast, moderates have virtually disappeared. They took a particularly hard hit in 2010, with moderate Republicans losing to conservatives in Republican primaries and moderate Democrats losing to Republicans in the general election.

Although many state legislatures are polarized along party lines, party polarization in Congress is far worse. Both turnover and conversion contribute to rising polarization. Party leaders are more partisan, and the use of restrictive procedural rules offers little encouragement to members to craft middle-of-the-road compromises that might be accepted as amendments on the House or Senate floor.[3]

One advantage Congress does possess over many state legislatures is a large, well-educated, knowledgeable staff, which can supply expertise on a wide range of issues, including children's issues. In addition to personal staff and committee staff, Congress has access to some formidable support agencies, including the Government Accountability Office (3,100 employees), the Congressional Research Service (900 employees), and the Congressional Budget Office (235 employees).

On the other hand, many congressional staff members are strikingly partisan. Indeed, committee staffs are organized along party lines, with majority staff members serving the majority party, minority staff members serving the minority party. Staff partisanship is not simply an unintended side effect; it is actively promoted by members who have chosen to organize their world this way.

Partisanship is not the only challenge facing Congress. As congressional campaigns have become much more expensive, members now spend a considerable amount of time back in their home districts and states. This could actually be a good thing, from a democratic perspective, but it detracts from the amount of time available to engage in legislative activity, now effectively limited to two or three days a week. More subtly, it also means that members are less likely to socialize with other members than they did a generation or two ago. Such socialization, in and around Washington, facilitated coalition building in the "good old days." As David Obey, the Wisconsin Democrat who recently retired from the

2. McCarty, Poole, and Rosenthal (2006, p. 23).
3. See Shor (2008, p. 10); Theriault (2008).

House after forty-one years of service, put it: "It's a lot harder to kick the hell out of somebody on the House floor if you know you're going to see their wife and kids on Sunday."[4]

Does all of this affect the quality of congressional debate? In a fascinating study, Gary Mucciaroni and Paul Quirk analyze the quality of congressional debate on the floor of the House and the Senate, focusing on three areas: welfare reform, estate tax repeal, and telecommunications deregulation. They find that the quality of debate is high about a fourth of the time, low about a third of the time, mediocre the rest of the time. Although they occasionally encountered serious efforts to rebut bad arguments, they observe that rebuttals tend to focus on repeated arguments rather than bad arguments per se. Their overall conclusion: "Congressional debate is typically no better than moderately informed."[5]

Party Differences on Children's Issues

To get a better sense of how children's issues are framed on Capitol Hill, and to better understand how congressional staff members think, I interviewed twenty-seven congressional staff members during the summer of 2010. They had two things in common: they worked for a congressional committee, and they focused a good deal of their attention on children's issues. I deliberately included both Democrats and Republicans, House and Senate staffers. (For the list of congressional staff members interviewed, see appendix B.)

The interviews were primarily open-ended, which enabled me to explore the nuances of congressional debates with which particular staff members were intimately familiar. The issues included, among others, elementary and secondary education, early childhood education, child health, teenage pregnancy, foster care, home visitation programs, child nutrition, and child tax credits. All interviews were conducted on a not-for-attribution basis.

I began every interview with a closed-ended question that elicited staff members' reactions to twelve policy arguments (or frames). The twelve policy arguments, each two sentences in length, include six arguments often made in support of children's programs and six arguments often made in opposition to children's programs. Each congressional staff

4. Pershing (2010).
5. Mucciaroni and Quirk (2006, p. 197).

Table 7-1. *Congressional Staff Views of Policy Arguments for Children's Programs*[a]

Policy argument	Democratic mean (N = 16)	Republican mean (N = 11)
Every child should have an equal opportunity to succeed in our society; the government should do what it takes to ensure that.	6.8	4.8*
For every dollar the government devotes to children today, society gets back even more money in return; children's programs are a good investment.	6.4	3.8[a]
Every child has the right to a decent standard of living; the government should guarantee that to every child.	6.2	3.0*
Our children need help, the kind of help that only the government can provide; we have an obligation to assist the needy.	5.8	3.4*
Other nations do a better job of providing valuable social services to children than we do; we must do better.	5.4	3.7*
We devote too few resources to children, as opposed to senior citizens; children deserve a larger share of government spending.	5.4	4.3**

a. Respondents were asked to rate each policy argument on a 7-point Likert scale, with 7 signifying strongly agree and 1 signifying strongly disagree.
*$p < .001$, **$p < .10$.

member was asked to respond to each argument, using a 7-point Likert scale, with 7 signifying strong agreement and 1 signifying strong disagreement. Before each interview, I randomly sorted the twelve policy arguments so that their sequencing was strictly due to chance.

As table 7-1 indicates, Democratic and Republican staff members react very differently to policy arguments in support of children's programs. Despite a small sample size, Democrats and Republicans differ in their levels of agreement in five of six cases, and there are marginally significant differences in the sixth case. As table 7.2 indicates, Democratic and Republican staff members also differ, in six of six cases, in their levels of

Table 7-2. *Congressional Staff Views of Policy Arguments against Children's Programs*[a]

Policy argument	Democratic mean (N = 16)	Republican mean (N = 11)
A lot of children's programs are well intentioned but they simply don't work. We should not spend money on programs that don't work.	4.5	6.3*
The most innovative programs for children are those developed by the private sector and non-profit organizations. Let's give them a chance to work.	3.9	5.2*
Most government programs for children start out small but soon become much bigger. We need to be wary of potentially costly initiatives.	3.6	6.0*
Primary responsibility for helping children to reach their potential belongs to the parents. Government should not be involved.	2.5	5.5*
Taxpayers are already overburdened. We can't afford to spend more money on children's programs.	1.6	5.2*
Most government programs for children are wasteful and inefficient. We're better off relying on the private sector and faith-based organizations.	1.5	4.2*

a. Respondents were asked to rate each policy argument on a 7-point Likert scale, with 7 signifying strongly agree and 1 signifying strongly disagree.
*$p < .001$.

support for six policy arguments that question the wisdom of allocating more government resources to children's programs. Clearly, there is a chasm that divides Democratic and Republican staff members, even those whose jurisdiction includes children's issues.

Just as clearly, all policy arguments are not created equal. For the Democrats, the most potent argument of those presented is: Every child should have an equal opportunity to succeed in our society; the government should do what it takes to ensure that. The next most potent argument is: For every dollar the government devotes to children today, society gets back even more money in return; children's programs are a good investment.

The fourth most potent argument is: Our children need help, the kind of help that only the government can provide; we have an obligation to assist the needy. In terms of our frames, it would seem that an equal opportunity frame does better than an investment frame, which in turn does better than a helping-hand frame. For Republicans, also, an equal opportunity frame fares better than an investment frame, which in turn fares better than a helping-hand frame. A prevention frame was not directly tested, though conceptually it has a good deal in common with an investment frame.

Among the first six policy arguments, the one that divides Democrats and Republicans most sharply is: Every child has the right to a decent standard of living; the government should guarantee that to every child. Republicans hate that argument, while Democrats love it. The argument that comes closest to triggering similar reactions from the two parties is: We devote too few resources to children, as opposed to senior citizens; children deserve a larger share of government spending. Both Democrats and Republicans react lukewarmly to this argument, though Democrats are marginally more supportive.

The View from the Hill

Closed-ended questions are useful to get comparable, standardized reactions to issue frames of theoretical interest. But open-ended questions are better at illuminating congressional views of how public policy is made, how issue frames contribute to the resolution of policy conflicts, and what other important considerations are at work. In wide-ranging interviews with congressional staffers I found frequent references to compelling stories, personal experiences, evidence, and issue frames. Not unexpectedly, I also heard numerous references to interparty differences.

Compelling Stories

Many politicians love to tell stories about individual hardships that could be alleviated by government intervention (usually Democrats) or that have been aggravated by government intervention (usually Republicans). President Reagan—the great communicator—was famous for doing this. Having done this professionally, as the host of *Death Valley Days*, which chronicles true stories of heroes from the wild, wild West, he was extraordinarily good at telling a personal story laden with broader social and political significance. As CBS newsman Dan Rather notes, "If

Hollywood taught Mr. Reagan anything, it was the value of a good story . . . and a good punch line." Many other presidents and presidential candidates have done this as well. Abraham Lincoln, for example, was a renowned storyteller. It was said of Lincoln that his stories, though charming and amusing, always had a purpose.[6]

Politicians also appreciate a good story when they hear one. Congressional hearings often feature testimony by someone who has endured a health hardship or someone who lost a loved one who was unable to afford timely medical care or someone who benefited from a government program. These personal stories dramatize the impacts of public policies, for better or for worse, on people's daily lives. They often generate mass media interest and attention and pluck at the heartstrings of members of Congress. They also help to "expand the scope of conflict." As Gary Mucciarioni and Paul Quirk put it, "Legislators prefer claims that permit dramatic appeals and personal anecdotes." For example, proponents of estate tax repeal told stories of family farms and small businesses being threatened or destroyed by the tax. Kristin Goss, who has studied the reframing of the gun control issue in the late 1990s, puts it this way: "Not only must issue entrepreneurs collectivize the benefits of individual goods, they also must individualize the benefits of collective goods. When that happens, individuals can see a benefit to participating in social reform and recognize the cost of doing nothing."[7]

In my interviews, several congressional staffers mentioned the sad story of Deamonte Driver, whose personal tragedy played a role in the CHIP debate of 2007. Driver, a twelve-year-old boy from Prince George's County, Maryland, died in February 2007 from a fatal brain infection brought on by an untreated tooth abscess. According to the *Washington Post,* a simple tooth extraction (costing about $80) could have saved the boy's life.[8] But Driver's family was unable to afford dental care.

Senator Barbara Mikulski (D-Md.), Senator Ben Cardin (D-Md.), and others used the Deamonte Driver tragedy to make a case for extending CHIP to more children. In a spirited debate on August 1, 2007, Driver's fate received a good deal of attention. Senator Tom Harkin (D-Iowa), pointing to a picture of Deamonte Driver, summed up his story and its implications:

---

6. See Hirsch and Van Haften (2010, p. 75); also see Rather (2004).

7. See Schattschneider (1960); Mucciarioni and Quirk (2006, p. 157); Graetz and Shapiro (2005); Goss (2006, p. 108).

8. Otto (2007).

We all know too well what it means when a child does not have health insurance, when they don't even have access to basic medical care. Earlier this year, the *Washington Post* reported on 8-year-old (sic) Deamonte Driver of Prince George's County, MD. Deamonte was suffering from an abscessed tooth, but his mother could not afford to take him to a dentist. Eventually, the abscess spread to Deamonte's brain. He was taken to an emergency room, but tragically, after two operations and more than 6 weeks of hospital care costing upwards of $250,000, Deamonte—this young guy right here, Deamonte Driver—died. He died from an abscessed tooth. In the 21st century in the United States of America, this child died because he had an abscessed tooth because he is so low-income, he didn't have health care and mom didn't have any money. Not until he got so sick that they rushed him to the emergency room, and he died. Why in the world would President Bush want to cut more than a million children from the rolls of the Children's Health Insurance Program and put them in jeopardy—the kind of jeopardy that took Deamonte's life? What is the real cost of denying children access to basic health care? Well, in the case of Deamonte Driver, if you want to know just in money terms, a quarter of a million dollars in emergency hospital bills, and, most importantly, it deprived Deamonte of his life and a very happy future.[9]

A Democratic congressional staff member put it this way: "Deamonte Driver died because of a tooth abscess. If things had been different, and his family had gotten him to a dentist, it would not have been fatal. CHIP covers dental care. Not to be cynical, but that sounds better on the floor of the Senate than a report saying the average kid covered by CHIP gets more time with doctors. Personal stories resonate with all members of Congress."

Republican staff members acknowledged that the Deamonte Driver story played a role in the congressional debate over CHIP, but they drew a different moral from the story: "Deamonte Driver was used by both sides. Democratic members of Congress pointed to his death and said we need funding to help kids like him. We also cited his case. At various points, he was eligible for Medicaid but couldn't get access to Medicaid because no primary care dentists in Prince George's County were taking Medicaid patients."

9. Harkin (2007).

In short, the Democratic inference from the Deamonte Driver tragedy was that we should expand access to Medicaid and CHIP, to help ensure that poor children receive essential dental care. In contrast, the Republican inference was that we should ensure that those children who are currently eligible for Medicaid and CHIP actually receive medical and dental services, as opposed to expanding eligibility to additional children who may or may not receive the services for which they are eligible.

Deamonte Driver's story was not the only one to get mentioned in the Senate's CHIP debate. Senator Harkin also discussed Jenci Ruff, from Knoxville, Iowa, who might have gone blind without medical care under CHIP. Senator Deborah Stabenow (D-Mich.) and Senator Sherrod Brown (D-Ohio) mentioned Kitty Burgett, from Ohio, whose daughter received medical treatment for bipolar disorder under CHIP; the daughter, now employed and married, with a child of her own, is a productive member of society; her illness is under control. Senator Patty Murray (D-Wash.) mentioned Sydney DeBord, of Yakima, Washington, who, despite cystic fibrosis, is able to sing and dance, thanks to CHIP and life-saving antibiotics.[10]

Personal Experiences

As Arthur Lupia and Mathew McCubbins note, "People who want to make reasoned choices need knowledge."[11] To acquire knowledge, they may learn from others, or they may draw upon personal experience. If a compelling personal story gets the attention of members of Congress, direct personal experience with a problem (or program) can be even more compelling, provided that the policy implications of personal experience are clear.

Some members of Congress have served as foster parents or have friends who have served as foster parents. Tom Delay, former House majority leader and a former foster parent, actively championed foster care reform and child welfare legislation when he served in the House of Representatives. For example, he sponsored the District of Columbia Family Court Act, aimed at providing stronger protection for abused and neglected children. He also supported training vouchers for children exiting the foster care system, to help them adapt to real-world challenges.

10. See Harkin (2007); Stabenow (2007); Brown (2007); Murray (2007).
11. Lupia and McCubbins (1998, p. 7).

Sometimes, just being a parent is enough to change a member's outlook on a public policy choice. As one staff member observes, "Many members of Congress were parents—they knew that at age eighteen their kids weren't independent. Kids bouncing from one foster care home to another foster care home were unlikely to meet a higher standard than other kids. It was just unrealistic." For example, Representative Shelley Berkley (D-Nev.) remarked at House deliberations on foster care that she had two children, ages twenty-two and twenty-three, who were no closer to going to the moon than they were to getting out of her home! The moral of that story, as one congressional staffer explained, was succinct and compelling: "No one stops parenting at the age of eighteen. Why should we stop foster care at the age of eighteen?" With support from Berkley and many others, Congress passed a Fostering Connections bill in 2008 that provides continuing benefits to foster children beyond the age of eighteen.

Many members of Congress can also relate to child health issues from a parental perspective. As Senator John Kerry (D-Mass.) put it in a debate over CHIP: "I know most of the Senators here have families, have children, and are deeply concerned about kids and understand these issues."[12] A Democratic congressional staff member echoes this refrain: "It helps that almost every member of Congress is a parent. They know that a healthy kid does better, they're happier, they do better in school." Arguably, this made it easier to win support for expanding CHIP, though that process was long and painful.

In 2007 Congress twice approved legislation reauthorizing and expanding the S-CHIP program. In October and December 2007 President George W. Bush vetoed that legislation, citing cost concerns and fears that the bill was a stalking horse for national health insurance. One of President Obama's first acts as president was to sign new legislation enacted by Congress in February 2009 reauthorizing and expanding the CHIP program.

Evidence

Although personal stories and personal experiences help to generate legislative and public support, they do not always suffice. There are many worthy causes on Capitol Hill. In an era of scarce resources, it helps to be able to characterize a program as demonstrably effective. A congressional

12. Kerry (2007).

staff member puts it this way: "The most persuasive arguments for children's programs are those that show outcomes—economic costs and benefits, health costs and benefits, academic costs and benefits. If we show a positive outcome, we seem to do better." Another staff member agrees: "Scientific evidence on program effects is incredibly important!"

Of course, evidence alone is seldom enough. To make a difference on Capitol Hill, evidence should be credible, accessible, and timely. It helps if a consensus exists on the consequences of a particular policy. Also, researchers and intermediaries who supply evidence are more likely to find their evidence used if they have nurtured good relationships with potential users.[13]

Evidence on program effectiveness is of special interest to members of Congress who serve on the House or Senate Budget Committee. As one budget committee staff member comments, "Our committee members want to know which programs provide some bang for the buck." Evidence may matter most when a new idea is being hatched. A staff member explains: "I think that research can play a huge role when Congress is doing something really *new*. If you get to the stage where members of Congress don't know the answer and they are looking for an answer. But the path for research from the researcher to Congress is very torturous. . . . Once the battle lines get drawn around here, the research doesn't matter much."

A number of congressional staff members spontaneously cite evidence of program effectiveness, and some even cite the source. Occasionally, staff members mention benefit-cost ratios in support of a particular program's effectiveness (such as for the Women, Infants, and Children's program and home-visiting programs). Some staff members cite the Drug Abuse Resistance Education (DARE) program as an example of a well-intentioned program that simply doesn't work. Others cite sexual abstinence programs aimed at reducing teen pregnancy as ineffective.

More than any other president, Barack Obama has articulated a strong commitment to evidence-based research. His first Office of Management and Budget director, Peter Orszag, strongly advocated this as director of the Congressional Budget Office and then as OMB director. Obama's earliest budgets included proposals that give special priority to programs that are vindicated by the strongest possible research evidence. Orszag explains the rationale for a two-tiered approach:

13. See Bogenschneider and Corbett (2010, pp. 34, 194–98); Esterling (2004).

First, we're providing more money to programs that generate results backed up by strong evidence. That's the top tier. Then, for an additional group of programs, with some supportive evidence but not as much, we've said: Let's try those too, but rigorously evaluate them and see whether they work. Over time, we hope that some of those programs will move into the top tier—but, if not, we'll redirect their funds to other, more promising efforts.[14]

Perhaps the leading example of the new evidence-based approach is home-visitation programs, like the Nurse-Family Partnership (NFP) program, originated years ago by David Olds. The program provides regular home visits, by a registered nurse, to expectant mothers and mothers of infants and toddlers from disadvantaged backgrounds. Its goals are to empower poor, first-time mothers, enhance their parenting skills, and improve outcomes for both mothers and children.

In a series of randomized experiments, in Elmira, New York, Memphis, Tennessee, and Denver, Colorado, Olds demonstrates impressive short-term and long-term benefits for children and their families. In the short run, outcomes are better for both mothers (less smoking, fewer pregnancies) and children (fewer injuries, earlier language development). At age fifteen Elmira treatment group children were less likely to be arrested and consumed less alcohol than control group children. Their mothers were also less likely to have engaged in child abuse and neglect. At age nine Memphis treatment group children had higher math and reading achievement test scores and fewer behavioral problems than control group children. Over a twelve-year period, the government spent approximately $1,000 less a year on social services for nurse-visited than for control families in Memphis. Although the long-term effects of the Denver randomized trial are not yet known, its short-term effects are very impressive. Of special interest, the Denver study finds that home visits by registered nurses are more effective than home visits by paraprofessionals. A key reason seems to be that parents are more willing to open their doors to a registered nurse than to someone who lacks that credential.[15]

But do the benefits outweigh the costs? That is the key question, from an economic perspective. Studies by the RAND Corporation and by the Washington State Institute for Public Policy conclude that the benefits do

14. Orszag (2009).
15. See Olds (2010); Olds and others (1997, 1998, 2004, 2007, 2010).

outweigh the costs—and by a substantial margin. The Washington State study, for example, finds a benefit-cost ratio of $2.88/1, with an even higher benefit-cost ratio for higher-risk children.[16]

In President Obama's proposal to Congress, the NFP program enjoyed a privileged status because of its unusually strong evidentiary base: three randomized experiments in different settings, each of which demonstrated impressive long-term consequences for poor children and their families. Based on that evidence, Obama and the OMB recommended that all visits be conducted by registered nurses, as in the NFP. Both Democratic and Republican members of Congress were impressed by the NFP program and sympathetic to proposals to expand it to other states (though Democrats and Republicans disagreed on funding for such an expansion and on the most appropriate legislative vehicle for getting such legislation passed). Despite this basic agreement, however, members of Congress in both the House and the Senate fought, successfully, to lower the eligibility threshold so that programs that lacked the NFP's strong record of success and its insistence on a home visit by a registered nurse would still be eligible to participate.

Why? On the Senate side, two senators—Kit Bond (R-Mo.) and Patty Murray (D-Wash.)—were strong supporters of the Parents as Teachers (PAT) program. In fact, in 1984 Bond, then governor of Missouri, signed into law the first statewide PAT program in the country (the program originated as a pilot program in Missouri in 1981). Murray, a preschool teacher before embarking on a political career, has long supported early intervention programs. An intriguing idea, the PAT program was heralded by the Kennedy School of Government and the Ford Foundation as an outstanding "innovation." Unfortunately, empirical studies suggest that it has not been effective in altering the course of children's lives.[17] Nevertheless, the program continues to enjoy congressional support. Another factor in congressional deliberations is the general view that states should be free to fund indigenous programs that enjoy political support in their

16. Aos and others (2004).

17. For example, two randomized experiments (one in northern California, the other in southern California) find that children experience no gains in child development or health despite some positive impacts on parent knowledge, attitudes, and behavior (Wagner and Clayton 1999). Similarly, a study by Mathematica Policy Research Inc. for the U.S. Department of Health and Human Services (Paulsell and others 2010) finds that the Parents as Teachers program was less effective than other home-visiting programs, such as the NFP program and the Healthy Families America program.

part of the world. As one Democratic staff member explains: "Politically, we had states that were enamored of their existing programs. We didn't want to alienate them." Politics aside, members of Congress and their staffs liked the idea of giving states some discretion, provided that the legislation pushes funds in the direction of programs with the strongest evidentiary base.

Eventually, a home visitation program was included in the omnibus health reform bill, with provisions that give states discretion while emphasizing the need to fund programs that work. Health and Human Services (HHS) also enjoys some discretion. The total funding level is $1.5 billion, over five years. In July 2010 HHS announced its first grants—$88 million to forty-nine states and Washington, D.C.—under the Affordable Care Act.

Issue Frames

When David Obey, now retired, became chair of the House Appropriations Committee after many years of congressional service, he ordered that two quotes be prominently displayed in the House Appropriations Committee hearing room. The first, from President Dwight D. Eisenhower, states: "There should be an unremitting effort to improve those health, education and social-service programs which have proved their value." The second, from Senator Hubert H. Humphrey, states: "The moral test of a government is how it treats those who are at the dawn of life, the children; those who are in the twilight of life, the aged; and those who are in the shadow of life, the sick and the needy, and the handicapped." Intentionally or not, Obey juxtaposed an economic frame and a moralistic frame. Congressional appropriators cannot fund everything. They must economize, taking program effectiveness into account. But they also have moral obligations to the most vulnerable members of society. In effect, Obey was saying that both frames have merit.

One Democratic congressional staff member believes that economic arguments are increasing on Capitol Hill, partly because there are more empirical studies available: "As more studies get done, maybe there's a slight tendency towards that evidence. But what is the quality of that evidence? There is a greater effort to use economic reasoning. But that reasoning is usually misapplied. For example, 'jobs' bills actually create fewer jobs than WIC or Food Stamps." Going one step further, that staff member distinguishes between children's programs and programs that benefit kids. From his perspective, "Some adult programs, like unemployment benefits and food stamps, actually benefit kids more than programs that are aimed directly at kids."

Although economic arguments and cost-benefit analyses capture the attention of members of Congress and their staffs, the calculations that *really* shape legislative outcomes are the scores assigned to particular legislative proposals by CBO analysts. As one Democratic staff member puts it: "Economic arguments matter, but what really matters is CBO scoring." She notes, for example, that what really boosted the home visitation program promoted by President Obama and others was not the scientific evidence provided by David Olds's randomized experiments but rather the CBO's conclusion that home visitation programs merited a good score. That can never be taken for granted. The same staff member elaborates: "We need help proving to CBO that investments in these children's programs yield savings in other programs."

A key problem with CBO's scoring of proposed legislation is that it normally halts its projections after the first ten years of implementation. Because many of the benefits from education, health, and other programs do not accrue until later in life, this standard operating procedure systematically underestimates the benefits of many social programs. For example, a recent study of diabetes prevention and management interventions finds that the benefits are much more impressive in a twenty-five-year projection than in a ten-year projection.[18] One reason that President Obama's health care reform bill was passed is because the CBO broke with tradition and calculated benefits beyond the standard ten-year period. A reappraisal of the ten-year-projection norm could lead to much more accurate scoring in the future.

In some congressional debates, both parties use economic and moralistic arguments. This was the case in the CHIP debate. Democrats argue that expanding health coverage to include more children, including near-poor children and the children of illegal immigrants, is both the right thing to do and the smart thing to do. Republicans, for their part, raise the specter of crowd out, or government health insurance displacing employer-provided health insurance. It is not smart for taxpayers to pay for health insurance that is already being provided by employers, they argue. On coverage for illegal immigrants, they argue that it is not fair for people who emigrate to the United States illegally to have their children's

18. Marks (2010, p. 129).

health coverage paid for by taxpayers, while individuals who play by the rules struggle to pay these costs themselves.

Occasionally, however, one party uses economic arguments while the other party uses moralistic arguments. The teenage pregnancy debate illustrates this nicely. Conservative Republicans favor abstinence-only programs aimed at preventing teenage pregnancy, on the grounds that sexual intercourse outside of marriage is immoral. But studies show that abstinence-only programs have generally been ineffective in preventing teenage sexual activity, pregnancy, or HIV infection. A congressionally mandated and federally funded study by Mathematica Policy Research, released in April 2007, shows that abstinence-only programs fail to reduce the incidence of sexual intercourse. A literature review published in the *British Medical Journal* in July 2007 reaches similarly disappointing conclusions. At the time these studies were released, the federal government was spending $176 million a year on abstinence-only education programs. Aware of this evidence, at least fourteen states have decided not to accept federal funding for abstinence-only education programs.[19]

Democrats, citing the evidence, argue that Congress should fund programs that work, more specifically, programs that actually reduce the number of teenage pregnancies in the long run. For example, Representative Lois Capps (D-Calif.) notes that 40 percent of evaluated comprehensive education programs delay the initiation of sex and that more than 60 percent reduce unprotected sex.[20]

Given weak empirical support for abstinence-only education programs, one might expect Republican members of Congress to switch from evidence-based (economic) arguments to faith-based (moralistic) arguments. Yet interestingly enough, that is not what happened. At a House hearing where numerous witnesses cited the disappointing results of abstinence-only education, Senator Sam Brownback (R-Kan.) persisted in characterizing abstinence-only programs as effective: "There are a large and growing number of studies showing that youth participating in abstinence programs have lower rates of sexual activity when compared to youth who do not receive abstinence education." Brownback's position has remained steadfast over time. As late as December 2010, just before Brownback's retirement from the Senate (he's now governor of Kansas),

---

19. See Stepp (2007); Underhill, Montgomery, and Operario (2007); Stein (2007).
20. Capps (2008, p. 16).

his website proclaimed: "Repeated evaluations show that abstinence education programs substantially reduce teen sexual activity."[21]

This rhetoric illustrates an important point made by Gary Mucciarioni and Paul Quirk—namely, that members of Congress often make factually inaccurate assertions that are not effectively rebutted (or rebutted at all) by their colleagues. Inaccurate or unsupported claims are more likely when issue salience is high. Also, because legislators prefer making claims to rebutting opponents' claims, many questionable assertions go unchallenged in legislative debate.[22]

In 2009 President Obama and his OMB director, Peter Orszag, proposed an evidence-based teenage pregnancy program, rooted in the same principles as the home-visitation program: a strong preference for programs that work but some opportunities for other programs to demonstrate their effectiveness through program evaluations funded by the federal government. Led by Representative Lois Capps (D-Calif.), the House accepted this formula: abstinence-only programs would continue to be eligible for federal funding but only if they demonstrate their effectiveness. The Senate, however, rejected evidence-based language in favor of two separate programs: one for abstinence-only programs ($50 million), another for evidence-based programs ($75 million). Following Scott Brown's election to replace Senator Edward Kennedy in the Senate, the House was forced to accept the Senate's language on this and other health care provisions, because the Democrats no longer enjoyed a filibuster-proof majority in the Senate.

Intergenerational Equity

In their discussions of children's issues, congressional staff members seldom invoke an intergenerational equity frame. In fact, if the issue arises, staff members generally make it clear that they are not interested in a frame that pits children against senior citizens. As a Democratic staff member puts it: "We've moved beyond a 'children versus seniors' frame. Members steer clear of that. Nobody on our side wants to put two vulnerable populations against each other." Another Democratic staff member cautions: "Intergenerational equity arguments tend to lead towards cutting programs. . . . There's a pretty strong bias on this subcommittee for

21. See Brownback (2008, p. 27; 2010).
22. Mucciaroni and Quirk (2006, pp. 156–80).

children, rather than seniors. But a decent society needs to spend money on the elderly."

One Democratic staff member accepts the political premise that zero-sum thinking should be avoided if possible but also predicts that the national debt crisis will force members of Congress to confront trade-offs much more explicitly:

> The pace of growth for programs for the elderly is threatening other things. Lawmakers don't want to take on the AARP. But lawmakers are on the cusp of realizing that's what you have to do. Most children's programs are discretionary. Most elderly programs are formula driven. If we continue spending as much as on the elderly, we can't spend much on kids. Few if any members of Congress have made this argument publicly. I think that will have to change over the next few years as baby boomers retire in earnest.

Congressional staff members do not go out of their way to embrace deficit reduction or debt reduction as a children's issue. On the other hand, when asked, most agree that the national debt has substantial negative implications for children. A Democratic staff member puts it this way: "Yes, it's a children's issue. It's an issue for anyone under the age of forty. Our generation has inherited very large deficits from your generation. We will inherit even larger deficits from your generation as your generation gets older. What is sustainable? What kind of world will we be leaving our children? But there are obligations our country has made to your generation. Will we honor those obligations?" A Republican staff member agrees but fingers excessive spending as opposed to insufficient revenue as the culprit: "Is deficit reduction a children's issue? We say that all the time. Social Security, Medicare, and Medicaid are on track to overtake the entire budget. There will be no room for defense spending, for education spending, and especially for children's programs. If you care about children's programs, you should care about entitlement reform." Another Republican staff member expresses similar sentiments: "We have a demographic problem. If this continues, the consequences for children will be terrible."

Conclusion

More so than state legislatures, Congress suffers from acute party polarization, which makes it difficult for legislators to reach a consensus on children's issues and other issues as well. This is evident in the way Democratic and Republican congressional staff members respond to the same issue frames. Even congressional staff members who care about children's issues, read about children's issues, arrange hearings on children's issues, and draft legislation on children's issues exhibit sharp party differences in how they think about such issues.

On the other hand, some issue frames have excellent appeal to one congressional party and reasonably good appeal to the other. Both equal opportunity and investment frames fit this description. Children's advocates who use such frames have a reasonable chance to succeed in promoting a children's program, unless the program in question doesn't work or is unlikely to work or if broader economic and political forces militate against legislative action.

That said, children's advocates should not put all their eggs in the issue-framing basket. Compelling personal stories that link a policy proposal to a personal tragedy can play a key role in congressional debates. Personal experiences can motivate members of Congress to play a leadership role in support of a policy proposal. An evidence-based approach, promoted by President Obama and others, can also channel congressional support in favor of programs that really make a difference in people's lives.

CHAPTER EIGHT

Putting Frames
in Perspective

There is one group that we must protect at all costs—our children. We must sacrifice so that our children won't inherit a country that is less than the one our parents left us.
Geoffrey Canada, Harlem Children's Zone, 2011

In this book, I make several arguments:

—Public policies toward children in the United States have not gone far enough in helping children to escape poverty, disease, and ignorance.

—Strong policy arguments are needed in support of children's programs.

—Framing is of critical importance to policy arguments.

—Both moralistic and economic frames can promote and justify children's programs.

—Economic frames are more widely used by children's advocates today than they were in the 1960s, but they have not been well publicized by the mass media.

—Economic frames are more widely used in some issue areas (early childhood education, child health) than others (child welfare, special education).

—Economic frames are generally more effective than moralistic frames in shaping public opinion on children's issues.

—Economic frames are especially influential in shaping the thinking of independents and other swing voters.

—Economic frames appeal to political elites, but so too do equal opportunity frames.

—The political environment and the state of the economy can strengthen or weaken the appeal of particular frames in a particular place at a particular point in time.

While defending each of these assertions, I have tried not to overstate my claims about frames. In this final chapter, I confront some legitimate counterarguments. Are frames really that important? Are economic frames really more persuasive than moralistic frames? Have I unwittingly conjured up an imaginary policymaking process that is more evidence based than the real world?

Is Framing the Answer?

As a starting point, let's consider the broader political environment in which issue frames compete for attention and support. A leading study of the policymaking process contends that the rise and fall of issues depend on the confluence of problem, politics, and policy streams, which create windows of opportunity that policy entrepreneurs can exploit in pursuit of their preferred policy goals. Other studies of the policymaking process emphasize the role played by coalitions in advancing or resisting change. Studies of the legislative process stress the almost single-minded devotion of legislators to the goal of reelection. Studies of interest groups document a connection, albeit a modest one, between group resources and policy success.[1]

All of these studies attest to the importance of politics, which can easily eclipse or overwhelm rational argumentation. If politicians are dead set against raising taxes, can a clever issue frame really convince them to do otherwise? If the AARP—an organization so strong that it boasts its own zip code—presses vigorously to sustain or expand entitlement programs for the elderly, can advocates for children achieve a restructuring of intergovernmental transfers through the use of what Homer liked to call winged words?

In this book, I cite examples of powerful political and economic forces that conspire against the adoption of eloquently defended policies and programs that benefit children. In Utah, strong conservative values and the special status of the Mormon religion doom attempts by children's advocates to secure state-funded prekindergarten and other programs that would benefit children. In North Carolina, worsening economic conditions and the election of taxophobic Republican legislators rendered

---

1. Baumgartner and others (2009, pp. 215–38). Also see Kingdon (1995); Sabatier and Jenkins-Smith (1999); Hula (1999); Mayhew (1974).

futile an eloquent appeal by former governor Jim Hunt to protect the Smart Start and More at Four programs from sharp budget cuts.

In Congress children's programs have for many years fared worse than programs for the elderly, as manifested by a 7 to 1 spending ratio in favor of senior citizens' programs. An attempt to enact universal child care during the Nixon administration failed in Congress. Efforts to establish a child support assurance system, to fund children whose deadbeat dads fail to provide child support, have never gained traction. Proposals for an American war on child poverty, like one waged with some success in Great Britain by then prime minister Tony Blair, failed to win much support.[2]

If one thinks of framing and rational argumentation as alternatives to politics, then the deck is certainly stacked against framing. Perhaps we should hoist the white flag and concede the supremacy of politics. But framing is in fact a political act. When advocates, public officials, journalists, and researchers choose an issue frame, they are intentionally or not aligning themselves with a particular coalition in a contest for political support. Framing is not an alternative to politics but rather an effort to restructure political alliances through vigorous debate. To assert that frames matter a great deal is not to denigrate the importance of politics but to acknowledge that political combatants choose issue frames that may serve their cause either well or badly. In a given instance, a particular frame may be overwhelmed by an alternative frame, an alternative issue, or scarce resources. But the defeat of one issue frame is often accompanied by the victory of another. In short, it is best to think of frames as a way of engaging in the political process, not a doomed effort to evade or suppress politics.

But perhaps frames are not the best way to make headway in a political debate. Could it be that a compelling personal story is more effective? Recall the tragic case of Deamonte Driver, the young boy who died from complications from an untreated abscessed tooth. This story proved extremely useful to advocates of expanding the S-CHIP program in 2007. To cite another example, Pennsylvania State Representative Phyllis Mundy became a lifetime supporter of the Nurse-Family Partnership (NFP) program after meeting a young mother who conquered her drug addiction problem, found a new job, and raised a healthy daughter in part because of good advice and support from a registered nurse who visited her home on a regular basis for approximately two years.

2. Cohen (2001); Garfinkel (1992); Crowley (2003, pp. 194–99); Waldfogel (2010).

In addition to personal stories are personal experiences. Members of Congress who have served as foster parents or who have raised a son or daughter with disabilities find themselves drawn to legislation that benefits children facing these circumstances. More broadly, members of Congress who happen to be parents find it easy to relate to pleas for health insurance for children and for continued foster care for eighteen- to twenty-one-year-olds, who previously were ineligible for government support.

There is no denying the potency of personal stories and personal experiences in supplying motivation to public officials. But does this undermine the case for issue frames? In fact, citing a compelling personal story may simply be a good way to make the case for a particular issue frame. Thus the Deamonte Driver story helped members of Congress to advance a "vulnerable child" issue frame in the S-CHIP debate. Similarly, the Pennsylvania mother's story helped Representative Mundy to advance an economic frame, linking national studies documenting the long-term benefits of the NFP program to a concrete example right in her own backyard.

A good story, like a good picture, a good graph, or even a good joke, can be an excellent tactic for communicating and selling a frame. But it's important not to confuse the tail with the dog. It's the frame that matters and that endures. It's the frame that acts as a lens or prism to view the world. It's the frame that connects a specific policy proposal to a broader rationale for action. A good story is not really an alternative to issue framing. Instead, it is a way of selling an issue frame to a wider audience.

But is political debate nothing more than a spirited competition between competing issue frames? Traditionally, we think of frames as phrases pithy enough to be placed on a bumper sticker, as in Think Globally, Act Locally or Just Say No or Give Peace a Chance. Is it possible that the outcome of political debates depends on something more substantial and more robust than a clash of catch phrases? In short, if a good issue frame is grander and more important than a good story, is a good argument grander and more important than a good issue frame? If so, perhaps we should be thinking about how to craft a well-structured policy argument, not how to conjure up a clever phrase.

Someone who clearly subscribed to this viewpoint was Abraham Lincoln, arguably the most formidable orator ever to occupy the White House. A recent study demonstrates that Lincoln was a close, almost obsessive student of Euclid's *Elements* and that he systematically applied

Euclidean logic to many of his most famous speeches.[3] Lincoln's speech at the Cooper Union in 1860 is persuasive because it includes the classic elements of a Euclidean argument: enunciation, exposition, specification, construction, proof, and conclusion. The Gettysburg Address inspires us today not just because it includes some memorable phrases but because the author, Lincoln, built a Euclidean argument as masterfully as a master builder builds a magnificent home.

A careful analysis of policy arguments used by members of Congress suggests that some of the basics of good argumentation have been forgotten or ignored by many members of Congress.[4] Few congressional debates measure up to Lincoln's exacting standards. To cite one example, inaccurate assertions in congressional debates are seldom rebutted by the opposition. In this respect, congressional debates compare poorly to, let's say, your average high school forensic competition.

Congressional debates also sometimes take detours that distract members from the central issues at hand. For example, a House debate on the reauthorization of Head Start in 2007 slipped again and again from the central questions at hand—how to improve access to Head Start and enhance program quality—to the question of whether faith-based providers should be allowed to limit their hiring to members of their own faith. Republicans generally argued in favor of such discretion, while Democrats consistently argued that it constituted illegal discrimination.[5] This debate seems especially fruitless because the House Rules Committee had already decided that an amendment allowing faith-based hiring by Head Start programs would not come up for a vote.

Is Persuasion on the Decline?

A key assumption behind framing is that words, ideas, and arguments can persuade people to change their beliefs and their policy preferences. Throughout this book I offer many examples of that. But what if the conditions that facilitate persuasion are on the decline? For framing to work, people must be exposed to contrary sources of information and opinion, they must be receptive to such inputs, and they must be capable

---

3. Hirsch and Van Haften (2010).
4. Mucciaroni and Quirk (2006).
5. U.S. House of Representatives (2007).

of acting decisively in support of those new beliefs. Are these conditions less common than they used to be?

Consider first the way that ordinary Americans digest news about politics, economics, and public policy. Two generations ago, the overwhelming majority of adult Americans read a daily newspaper, which contained information and analysis from the community, the state, the nation, and the world.[6] One generation ago, most Americans watched the national nightly news on television, where they were exposed to jarring images and surprising facts that sometimes induced them to change their thinking about wars, social movements, and events. Walter Cronkite's coverage of the Vietnam War, for example, is said to have changed the thinking of many Americans and to have contributed to President Johnson's surprising decision not to seek a second term.[7]

Today, in contrast, Americans practice selective exposure to the mass media. Only 29 percent of all Americans watch the network news, down from 60 percent in 1993; only 52 percent watch the local news, down from 77 percent in 1993; only 34 percent read a daily newspaper, down from 58 percent in 1993.[8] Liberals and Democrats turn to CNN or NPR or the *New York Times,* while conservatives and Republicans turn to Fox News or conservative talk radio or the *Wall Street Journal.*

As Natalie Stroud demonstrates, with plenty of evidence, we live in an age of "partisan selective exposure." Thanks to media diversification and a technological revolution in communications technology, it is much easier today to build an electronic wall around yourself that insulates you from unwelcome mass media messages. As Cass Sunstein laments, "Technology has greatly increased people's ability to 'filter' what they want to read, see, and hear." Many Americans choose to ingest ideologically congenial news segments on their iPod, on the Internet, or elsewhere. Liberals and conservatives are especially likely to turn to the Internet to supplement their intake of political news. Sadly, most of us are more likely to be exposed to issue frames that reinforce our political views than to issue frames that challenge them. This undermines a

6. In 1965, 71 percent of all adult Americans reported reading a daily newspaper on an average day (Public Broadcasting System 2007).

7. On February 27, 1968, in a special report, Cronkite, CBS news anchor and the most trusted man in America, asserted that negotiation was the only way out of the Vietnam War; see Braestrup (1977, p. xxxvi). The following month, Johnson announced that he would not be a candidate for reelection.

8. Pew (2008).

key precondition for a well-functioning democracy. In Sunstein's words, "People should be exposed to materials that they would not have chosen in advance. Unplanned, unanticipated encounters are central to democracy itself. Such encounters often involve topics and points of view that people have not sought out and perhaps find quite irritating. They are important partly to ensure against fragmentation and extremism, which are predictable outcomes of any situation in which like-minded people speak only with themselves."[9]

Consider also the types of politicians who have come to dominate Congress, state legislatures, and other elected offices. A generation ago, the pivotal players in Congress were moderates who were often willing and able to form a political coalition that cut across political parties. Republicans like John Chafee, Bob Dole, and Mark Hatfield and Democrats like Bill Bradley, John Breaux, and Daniel Patrick Moynihan were sufficiently flexible in their thinking that they might embrace either a liberal or a conservative initiative, depending on its merits. In state legislatures, too, each party benefited from deal makers who were capable of working with colleagues across the aisle in support of major legislation that reflected a bipartisan consensus.

Regrettably, opportunities for bipartisan coalition building have shrunk, and shrunk dramatically. Beginning in the 1960s conservative Democrats began to disappear from the ranks of Congress. Later, moderate Republicans became practically an endangered species. And in November 2010 the ranks of moderate Blue Dog Democrats were thinned beyond recognition. Legislative gerrymandering helped to create congressional districts that were locks for either conservative Republicans or liberal Democrats. As swing districts diminished, the ability of voters to send a message diminished as well. Party voting has increased dramatically on Capitol Hill.

At the state level, a similar phenomenon has occurred. Gerrymandering has reduced the number of competitive legislative races, encouraging the election of liberal Democrats and conservative Republicans, as opposed to moderates. In Virginia, in the general election of 2011, only 27 of 100 races for the House of Delegates pitted a Democrat against a Republican. In the overwhelming majority of Virginia districts, the general election results were already predetermined. As Boris Shor documents, state legislatures are more polarized than ever before and are especially polarized in

9. See Stroud (2011, pp. 41–86); Sunstein (2001, pp. 3, 8–9); Nie and others (2010).

more rural states and in states characterized by greater income inequality. In many states, divisions between the two parties have become deeper and more striking in recent years. In Wisconsin, bitter interparty disputes led a band of Democratic senators to flee to a nearby state to prevent the Republicans from conducting business; in Minnesota, irreconcilable differences between Democrats and Republicans led to a three-week shutdown of the state government. As Alan Rosenthal puts it, "In most places, the bonds among members are becoming frayed."[10]

Framing depends on something else for its power: slack resources or, to be more precise, opportunities for discretionary spending. For frames to make a difference, public officials must have room to maneuver, to spend more here, less there, as public sentiment and elite preferences shift. Unfortunately, the rise of entitlement programs has made it increasingly difficult for Congress—and state legislatures—to reallocate resources in response to new information and ideas. In fiscal 1962, 68 percent of congressional spending was discretionary; in fiscal 2007, 38 percent of congressional spending was discretionary.[11] That constitutes a severe erosion of maneuverability and thus a threat to persuasion through framing.

Dramatic increases in the national debt during the first decade of the 2000s made a bleak situation even bleaker. The refusal of Republicans to consider tax increases made it hard to chip away at the national debt without deep cuts in vital social programs that help the poor, the sick, and the disabled.[12] The refusal of Democrats to consider a major overhaul of Medicare, Social Security, and other entitlements made it difficult to rein in runaway spending. At this point in time, with the national debt at an all-time high, with entitlement programs on track to grow dramatically (especially Medicare), and with discretionary spending under siege, it is difficult for legislative bodies to contemplate new social programs for children, substantial spending increases for children, or new

10. Rosenthal (2004, p. 94; also pp. 92–93). Also see "Two-Party System" (2011); Shor (2008); Williams (2011).

11. Congressional Budget Office (2007).

12. Republicans sometimes argue that the wealthiest Americans already pay more in taxes than the rest of us. For example, the top 10 percent of Americans pay 50 percent of federal taxes, including income taxes and payroll taxes. This sounds progressive, until one recognizes that the top 10 percent of Americans earn 42 percent of all income (Pfeiffer 2011), which is not much different from their tax burden. In other industrialized nations, the wealthy pay much higher tax rates than in the United States. Not surprisingly, the United States has a higher rate of income inequality, before and after taxes, than other wealthy nations (Smeeding 2004).

government regulations that could benefit children at some small expense to small businesses.[13] Under these circumstances, even the best of frames is unlikely to trigger a major shift in public policy direction.

It is impossible to deny the grim realities of partisan selective exposure, hyperpartisanship in Congress and state legislatures, and budget deficits so enormous that they threaten to extinguish discretionary spending. Yet despite all of these forces there remains a critical role for issue frames to play. Although liberals do gravitate toward liberal media outlets and conservatives gravitate toward conservative media outlets, plenty of conservatives watch CNN and plenty of liberals read newspapers that endorse Republican candidates for office. Both liberals and conservatives read *USA Today, Politico, The Economist,* and other publications whose ideological orientation would be very hard to pinpoint. Also, 37 percent of all Americans consider themselves independents. These voters determine the outcome of presidential elections and help to determine the outcome of other elections as well. They do not screen themselves from uncongenial media messages the way that strong partisan voters do.[14]

Although moderates are increasingly scarce in Congress and in state legislatures, one can imagine this changing before long. As voter frustration with partisan politicians boils over, we may see independent candidates faring better. We could even see a viable third-party movement, which would revolutionize American politics and send extreme partisans back to their home districts. Third Way, which sponsored a series of events on the national debt in late 2010, could pave the way for such a third-party movement. No Labels, which focuses more on local communities than on Washington, is another attempt to encourage moderate voices in the political process.

Even in the absence of a third-party movement, legislative party leaders do have ways of getting things done. The former Speaker of the house in Vermont, Ralph Wright, tried to accommodate as many special requests from legislators as possible so that, in a pinch, he could count on their votes: "My criteria to judge just how far I would go to help a member was simple and straightforward. As long as it wasn't against the law, didn't require that I go to confession, or wouldn't break up my marriage, I did

13. According to Tomasky (2011), the national debt is $15 trillion, or 72 percent of GDP.

14. See Stroud (2011, pp. 41–86); Pew (2010).

it."[15] Other legislative leaders have learned that building a consensus is easier if members are hungry (don't break for lunch) or looking ahead to a relaxing weekend (schedule big votes on Friday). In Rhode Island, it is said that the capitol building has not been air conditioned to make it more likely that legislators will reach a budget agreement before August! In short, clever coalition builders, especially party leaders, are not without resources.

Are Economic Frames Really Better?

Although I have extolled the virtues of economic frames, from a practical point of view, I have tried *not* to argue that moralistic frames have no place in our public discourse, on children's issues or other social issues. It has long been remarked that ours is a nation of joiners; the organizations we join with exceptional frequency are churches. By any measure (religious affiliation, church attendance, belief in God, agreement with the statement that religion is important in their lives), Americans are very religious and more so than their counterparts in other countries. And religion matters for public policy, too. As Michael Sandel notes, religious impulses are often linked to reform: "Secularists are wrong when they ask believers to leave their religion at the door before entering into the public square. . . . The majority of great reformers in American history . . . were not only motivated by faith, but repeatedly used religious language to argue for their cause."[16]

Religious sentiments continue to animate and motivate many Americans, and many moralistic arguments are similar to religious sentiments. For example, the Golden Rule (treat others as you would like to be treated yourself) is related to a classic Christian principle that also figures prominently in other religions: love thy neighbor as thyself. Admonitions to be generous and charitable echo New Testament passages such as the parable of the Good Samaritan from the Gospel of St. Luke (10: 25–37) or the parable of the Last Judgment from the Gospel of St. Matthew (25: 32–40) (I was hungry and you gave me food, I was thirsty and you gave me drink, I was a stranger and you welcomed me, I was naked and you gave me clothing, I was sick and you took care of me, I was in prison

15. Rosenthal (2004, p. 212; also see p. 223).
16. Sandel (2009, p. 246). Also see Tocqueville (1945); Lipset (1996); Campbell and Putnam (2010, pp. 7–10).

and you visited me). To the extent that moralistic arguments activate or reinforce deeply rooted religious convictions, they have the potential to galvanize true believers into action.

Moralistic frames also have the virtue of appealing to our better selves, to our common humanity rather than to our self-interest. As Ann Lewis notes, "We used to call for immunizing little children against disease. Now we call it an investment in human capital."[17] To some observers that change in language is a step in the wrong direction, because it substitutes accounting for empathy. Luckily, the smart thing to do is often also the right thing to do. But what if, in a particular instance, the smart answer and the right answer diverge? If we lose the ability to argue for policies on moralistic grounds alone, then we have lost something precious.

John Rawls makes a strong case for moralistic arguments in developing a theory of justice for the ages. Although he acknowledges utilitarianism (the wellspring of economic logic) as a legitimate and formidable ethical system, he nevertheless argues that a deontological theory of justice, rooted in a sense of duty or obligation, is more defensible. If you find yourself behind a "veil of ignorance," not knowing what assets you would possess in life, where you would live, or how productive you would be, Rawls believes that you would choose principles of justice (moralistic) rather than of utilitarianism (economic). He also believes that a strong predisposition to help the most disadvantaged members of society would be one of the pillars of such a theory of justice. Economic logic can justify such an emphasis on the poor, the sick, and the handicapped, but it does not do so consistently.[18]

Another advantage of moralistic arguments is that they do not wilt in the face of ambiguous evidence or no evidence at all. Because they direct our attention away from consequences and toward rights, obligations, and duties to our fellow citizens, moralistic arguments cannot be demolished by critics who question the evidence in support of a particular children's program or initiative. Many children's programs, such as Head Start, have been damaged by poor evidence.[19] Others have been stillborn because of missing evidence.

Of course, all moralistic arguments are not created equal. Of the many moralistic arguments that children's advocates have invoked in recent

17. Lewis is quoted in Dionne (2004, p. 105).
18. See Rawls (1971).
19. Zigler and Muenchow (1992).

decades, equal opportunity has a special appeal for both ordinary citizens and political elites. Americans seem largely indifferent to arguments against unequal outcomes, even when income disparities are astonishingly huge, as they are today. But Americans tend to respond sympathetically to arguments that everyone should have an equal chance to enjoy the fruits of the American dream, including a good education, a decent job, affordable housing, and affordable health care.[20]

The case for moralistic frames is especially strong in policy domains where legal issues must be resolved or where a strong consensus exists that government has an important role to play in meeting the needs of certain children. Both of these circumstances or conditions apply to issues involving special education, foster care, and child abuse and neglect. In all of these policy domains, both liberals and conservatives generally agree that the government must intervene, and public officials have determined that the courts have a special role to play in resolving any disputes that may arise. Such circumstances are ripe for strong moral arguments.

The Power of Economic Frames

Despite many good arguments in favor of moralistic frames, economic frames have become prominent in recent years. Economic frames are more frequently featured in congressional testimony by administration officials and in congressional testimony by the leading child advocate of her generation, Marian Wright Edelman. In addition, economic frames are now widely used by children's advocates at the state level. Although mass media coverage of children's issues has not adequately reflected this shift, references to "prevention" and "investment" are more common in newspaper stories on children and public policy, while references to "helping" children have declined since the mid-1990s.

Economic frames are invoked more often because they appeal to the general public and to relatively powerful subgroups within the general public. A cost-benefit argument is more potent than a helping-hand argument in convincing young voters to support the NFP program. The cost-benefit argument is especially effective in inducing independents (or swing voters) to change their thinking on this issue. A cost-benefit argument is also more effective than a helping-hand argument in persuading a representative cross-section of Americans to support increased spending for the

---

20. Haskins and Sawhill (2009).

Head Start program. Well-educated, relatively affluent Americans—the sorts of voters who are more likely to participate in elections and more likely to contribute money to campaigns—are especially receptive to a cost-benefit argument.

An economic frame evokes relatively positive reactions from both Democratic and Republican staff members on Capitol Hill. Staff members also cite the critical importance of the Congressional Budget Office, whose scoring exercises involve a rudimentary cost-benefit analysis. At the state level, Pennsylvania respondents cite evidence on long-term benefits and costs as a key reason for the adoption of the NFP program as well as strong support for that program, even in difficult budget cycles. Similarly, Connecticut respondents cite studies (by the Urban Institute and the Washington State Institute for Public Policy) on benefits and costs as key factors in convincing legislators to raise the age of adult jurisdiction in the courts from sixteen to eighteen.

A recent case in Virginia is also illustrative. For years, advocates for autistic children made conventional moralistic arguments, such as needing to help these children because it's the right thing to do. They got nowhere. Then they tried a different tack, supplying Virginia legislators with detailed benefit-cost analyses. A 2009 study projecting $1.4 billion of special education savings if autism is detected and treated early was particularly helpful. Teresa Champion, one of the activists and the mother of an autistic child, puts it this way: "We got smarter at trying to convey our issue. . . . It wasn't the crying mom saying, 'I need help'—and, you know, they're backing away." These tactics were successful. In May 2011 Governor Robert McDonnell signed into law a bill requiring state-regulated health plans to pay for diagnostic and treatment services for autistic children ages two through six.[21]

The rise of economic frames is attributable to both demand and supply factors. In general, economic frames became more popular with children's advocates during the Reagan administration—an era of sharp cutbacks in government-funded social programs, rising budget deficits, and growing concern over these deficits. Half-hearted congressional efforts to curb budget deficits—such as the Gramm-Rudman-Hollings Balanced Budget and Emergency Deficit Control Act of 1985 and the Balanced Budget and Emergency Deficit Control Reaffirmation Act of 1987, enacted to repair

---

21. See Saslaw (2011); Ursitti (2011); Kunkle and Kumar (2011); Autism Speaks (2011).

a constitutional flaw in the first law—proved ineffectual.[22] At the same time, state governments, facing sharp cutbacks in federal aid but constitutional requirements to balance their budgets (and in some instances new constraints on raising taxes), started scrutinizing state expenditures more closely.

Changes were also taking place on the supply side. The field of public policy analysis was maturing, and public policy programs at universities were growing. Existing think tanks were prospering, and new think tanks were sprouting up not only in Washington but also in the hinterlands.[23] State legislatures were strengthening their professional staffs, including both fiscal analysis (or budget) staffs and policy analysis shops.[24] The empirical research on which programs were more cost effective was growing, as demand for such information increased.

As economic conditions have worsened in recent years—since December 2007—the case for economic frames has grown even stronger. When programs must be cut, why not cut the less effective programs and spare the more effective programs? When the economy is on the ropes, why not adopt policies that strengthen the economy? Like Phyllis Mundy in Pennsylvania, children's advocates now distinguish between routine spending (dispensable in an era of fiscal austerity) and investments in our future (critical if our once-powerful economic engine is to roar again). President Obama has also drawn this distinction, though not always with success.

Frames for the Future

Public opinion changes over time, as do its components—its core values, belief systems, and policy preferences. Consider how far we have come since World War II on such issues as women's rights, racial equality, federal aid to education, child rearing, and environmental protection. Conceivably, the best frame for today will not turn out to be the best frame for tomorrow. Will other frames displace the economic frame? Are other frames worth considering for the future?

With so many of the world's economies, including the U.S. economy, on the brink of disaster, it is beginning to dawn on both citizens and

22. Joyce (2011, pp. 59–61).
23. Rich (2004).
24. Despite the professionalization of state legislative staffs, many states lack a critical mass of nonpartisan professional researchers. See Hird (2005).

public officials that some hard decisions will have to be made. The old illusion that we could enjoy good social services, low tax rates, and balanced budgets all at the same time has been exposed as a fraud. Difficult choices will have to be made. Some groups will benefit, while other groups will be harmed. Is it perhaps time for some zero-sum-game thinking?

An intergenerational equity frame explicitly acknowledges the need for difficult trade-offs across generations. In effect, it says that each generation should bequeath to its successor generation an economy, a society, and a planet that are in better shape than the ones they inherited. Admittedly, when I introduced an intergenerational equity frame in my interviews with congressional staff members, it did not fare very well. But maybe the timing of these interviews was bad. Given the tumultuous economic and political events of the past four years, perhaps we stand on the threshold of seismic shifts in public consciousness and equally profound shifts in elite thinking.

Also, perhaps a different label—*sustainability*—might help. The concept of sustainability, which has generated considerable interest in discussions about environmental protection, agriculture, and other areas, refers to our ability to bequeath to future generations a world at least as good as that which we inherited. In the context of social policy, that might mean a world characterized by less poverty, less inequality, better health, and better education. In the context of children's policy, that might mean a society in which tomorrow's children enjoy at least as many opportunities, at least as much security, and at least as much happiness as we ourselves did as children.

A different frame, one from the Rawlsian tradition, is redistribution. Instead of pitting seniors against children, perhaps we should contrast vulnerable populations of all ages with the rest of us. As Hubert Humphrey put it: "The moral test of a government is how it treats those who are at the dawn of life, the children; those who are at the twilight of life, the aged; and those who are in the shadow of life, the sick and the needy, and the handicapped."

At the moment, the word *redistribution* is anathema to many politicians—and not just to Republicans. When Bill O'Reilly asked President Obama whether he favored redistribution, Obama emphatically said no.[25]

25. Fox News (2011).

O'Reilly: Do you deny that you are a man who wants to redistribute wealth?

Obama: Absolutely.

O'Reilly: You deny that?

Obama: Absolutely. I didn't raise taxes once, I lowered taxes over the last two years.

O'Reilly: But the entitlements that you championed do redistribute wealth in the sense that they provide insurance coverage for 40 million people that don't have it.

Obama: What is absolutely true is I think in this country, there's no reason why, if you get sick you should go bankrupt. The notion that that's a radical principle, I don't think that the majority of people would agree with you.

Although political operatives might say that Obama dodged a bullet here, it could also be said that he missed a golden opportunity to educate the American people. Consider the exchange that *could* have taken place:

O'Reilly: Do you deny that you are a man who wants to redistribute wealth?

Obama: We already redistribute wealth through tax breaks to the rich, through subsidies to special interest groups, and through the rules that collectively constitute our market economy. The question is not whether we will redistribute wealth but to whom.

O'Reilly: But what gives the federal government the right to take money away from hard-working Americans and give it to people who don't work hard or at all?

Obama: I've met a lot of folks who are working as hard as they possibly can but still don't have enough to pay their grocery bills or to care for a sick child. The rest of us need to help them out.

O'Reilly: But isn't there a difference between voluntary contributions, through private charities, and coerced contributions, through higher taxes?

Obama: We need to do both. And if you look at the public opinion polls, the overwhelming majority of Americans are in favor of higher taxes on the richest Americans and opposed to deep cuts in social programs.

Of course, this second conversation never took place. President Obama, like most politicians, tries to avoid zero-sum thinking. Is he right? Instead of risking debilitating intergenerational conflicts or class conflicts, should we perhaps try to frame children's issues by emphasizing what we have in common or practical solutions to difficult problems?

Some Possibilities

Some advocates invoke common sense as a justification for policies that seemingly ought to be in place but are not. As Will Rogers noted years ago, "Common sense ain't common." Should we try to make it more common? Does a commonsense issue frame help to sell a policy proposal? Frank Luntz, the political consultant who has helped Republicans craft winning messages over the years, makes a strong case for a commonsense frame: "Ask Americans what one principle or value is most missing in Washington today and they'll say 'common sense' more than any other answer." Luntz goes on to say: "If you think back to every presidential election since the age of television, it can be argued that the candidate who best demonstrated 'common sense' always won."[26]

Children's advocates sometimes make explicit references to common sense. Richard Riley did so in congressional testimony on the Individuals with Disabilities Education Act (IDEA), though he invoked common sense to justify unilateral actions by the Department of Education rather than to justify proposed legislation. Marian Wright Edelman occasionally uses commonsense arguments and moralistic arguments in the same breath, as in congressional testimony on proposed child care legislation: "I think that the willingness of a nation to protect its children is a moral litmus test of any decent and compassionate society. It is also a test of the common sense of any nation seeking to preserve itself in the future."[27]

But common sense may be too ethereal and not concrete enough to be effective or even meaningful. Rhetorically, it is a way of saying, My

26. Luntz (2007, pp. 210, 211).
27. See Riley (1995, p. 4); Edelman (1988, p. 11).

argument is so obvious that I don't even need to make it. One alternative issue frame, which also stresses shared values, would be to label a policy proposal as *family friendly*. The family has considerable appeal to both liberals and conservatives. Every year *Working Mother* magazine publishes a list of the hundred most family-friendly corporations. The Partnership for Public Service publishes something similar for federal agencies. These gestures signal strong undercurrents of public support.

Family-friendly arguments may have helped to advance children's policies during the Clinton administration. Liberals saw child care subsidies as a way to support low-income working families, while conservatives saw a child tax credit as a way to support mothers who raised their children at home. Family-friendly arguments may also have been instrumental in generating support for child support enforcement policies. On the other hand, plenty of other arguments were used in both of these debates. For example, at different points in time, child development, family support, regulatory protection, and other arguments were used in support of national child care legislation. Also, family-friendly arguments seem to have done little to advance the cause of paid parental leave legislation in the United States.[28]

Some public officials, including President Obama, like to make cross-national comparisons that highlight the gap between our national aspirations and our national performance. For example, in a speech to the U.S. Chamber of Commerce, President Obama said: "In today's global, competitive economy, the best jobs and newest industries will take root in countries with the most skilled workers, the strongest commitment to research and technology, and the fastest ways to move people, goods and information." In the same speech, he argued that we have a responsibility as a nation to "invest in the skills and education of our young people." If artfully constructed, such arguments could appeal to conservatives, for whom patriotism is a core value. Our wounded pride as Americans might encourage us to invest more in children, to regain our footing in a global economy. On the other hand, cross-national comparisons sometimes encourage trade wars, justifications for inaction on the environment, and other public policy responses that do not advance the cause of children. Also, when making these arguments, politicians must walk a fine line between asserting that we can do better (arguably patriotic) and conceding that we're not doing a very good job (arguably unpatriotic).[29]

28. See Cohen (2001, pp. 174, 283); Crowley (2003).
29. Obama (2011); Haidt (2007).

Thus we face a quandary. Sustainability and redistribution frames, though tempting, run the risk of exacerbating conflicts among generations and among social classes. Similarly, commonsense and family-friendly frames have their own limitations. Common sense is an empty vessel into which advocates may pour almost any kind of message. Family friendliness is more substantive, and it does highlight a revered social institution—namely, the family. However, family friendliness begs the question of why we should adopt such policies: because families deserve it or because society benefits? Appeals to national pride might work, but they must be spun in such a way that they seem patriotic, optimistic, and yet also realistic.

In the final analysis, the best answer may be to take the best economic frame available (investment) and the best moralistic frame available (equal opportunity) and make them even more powerful. One way to strengthen the investment frame would be to gather more and better evidence on program effects, including long-term benefits and costs. Without such evidence, the investment frame is likely to be exposed and criticized as little more than speculation. With such evidence, the investment frame can be potent, as evidenced by growing support for nurse home visits and prekindergarten, both of which have been vindicated by strong empirical research.

Although moralistic arguments do not require empirical research as much as economic arguments, they too can benefit from relevant evidence. For example, a key problem with the equal opportunity frame is that most Americans believe that equal opportunity actually exists not just as an aspirational value but as reality. For example, 76 percent of all Americans believe that black children in their community have "as good a chance as white children . . . to get a good education."[30] Only 21 percent disagree. Surprisingly, even 49 percent of black Americans agree with this statement. The problem is obvious: If most Americans agree that equal opportunity has already been achieved, then why should we mobilize to adopt policies and practices that guarantee equal opportunity?

A Frame to Reduce Child Poverty

Investment and equal opportunity frames can stand alone, or they can be blended. It is important to link them to a specific problem, like child poverty. It is also important to acknowledge counterarguments, explicitly

30. Saad (2007).

or implicitly, and to rebut them if possible. Here, for example, is what an argument for a program to reduce child poverty might look like:

Nearly fifty years ago, our government declared war on poverty. We made great progress in reducing poverty for our oldest citizens, and we should be proud of that. But we made little progress in reducing poverty for our youngest citizens, and that should concern us greatly.

Nearly one-fourth of our children are poor, which means that they often lack food to eat, they seldom visit a doctor, they struggle to keep up with their schoolwork, and they are more prone to crime and substance abuse. Minority children face even tougher odds. One-third of Hispanic children and 40 percent of African American children are poor. For all too many of our youngest citizens, poverty is a curse that impairs their pursuit of happiness and prevents them from achieving their full potential.

Child poverty is a curse for the rest of us, too, because it has consequences for our communities and for our nation. Compared to other children, children who grow up poor are far less likely to graduate from high school, and they earn less as adults. Children who grow up poor are more likely to commit crimes and more likely to be in prison. Children who grow up poor are more likely to suffer from obesity and hypertension as adults. To ignore child poverty is to condemn our nation to a precarious future, with a shrinking number of productive citizens supporting a growing number of unproductive citizens.

Fortunately, we have the capacity to change all of that. If we invest in children's programs today, we can help to create a strong workforce that contributes to the treasury instead of depleting it. If we invest in children's programs today, we can help our country to compete vigorously in an increasingly global economy. If we invest in children's programs today, we can avoid expensive health care interventions down the road. Cost-effective public policies are available to us, and they have been shown to work. As taxpayers, we are better off paying a lower price today than a higher price tomorrow.

Child poverty has many causes, and government programs cannot cure all of them. Some families are too broken to be mended. Some individuals are too ill to be healed. Some economic and social trends are not easily reversed.

But the United States of America has met many challenges in the past. We overcame the Great Depression, we won two world wars, we put a man on the moon, we increased access to higher education, and we improved the quality of our lives through technological innovation. We can dramatically reduce child poverty if we resolve to do so. And if we do so, our children and our grandchildren will be far better off.

Conclusion

The case for children's programs is strong, but the arguments we make in support of them need to be stronger. Many other constituencies have made compelling arguments for their interests and their point of view. When rhetoric has failed, they have used cash, votes, or both. Children do not have these tools at their disposal. Therefore, children's advocates—inside and outside of government—need to think harder about what they will say and how they will say it. They also need to work more effectively to secure attention from the mass media.

All issue frames are not created equal. Economic frames are more widely used today than they were in the 1960s, and for good reason. These frames appeal to swing voters, to well-educated voters, and to wealthier voters—precisely the kinds of citizens whose political support is most valuable. As budget deficits and the size of the national debt dominate our discourse and impose constraints on what public officials can responsibly do, economic arguments are likely to become even more important. Economic frames appropriately recognize that we need to invest taxpayers' resources in programs that actually work. Neither children nor taxpayers are well served by programs that fail to meet this reasonable standard.

Although moralistic frames have become less prominent since the 1960s, they continue to be widely used, and they should be. Among moralistic frames, the equal opportunity frame is especially potent. It does reasonably well with the general public, and it does particularly well with political elites, such as congressional staff members. In contrast, the helping-hand frame fares worse. Although it has some appeal to some subgroups, such as Hispanics, it is less capable of persuading citizens to change their thinking.

Public policy choices depend on much more than rhetoric. In states with traditional views of the mother's role in the home (Utah) or with a rising Tea Party movement (North Carolina), pleas to launch new children's programs or to strengthen existing children's programs will face tough sledding. At the national level, our staggering national debt and our daunting annual budget deficits cast a pall over all social policy conversations. These obstacles are real, but they should not deter us from seeking a better future for our children. The language we use in our policy arguments is one important step in doing so.

Interviews:
State Case Studies

There follow, in the order presented in the text (Connecticut, Utah, North Carolina, and Pennsylvania) the names and positions of the persons interviewed for the study.

Connecticut

Christopher Donovan, Speaker, Connecticut House of Representatives. Personal interview, Hartford, October 7, 2010.

Robert Francis, executive director, Regional Youth Adult Social Action Partnership. Personal interview, Hartford, October 7, 2010.

Hector Glynn, vice president, Village for Families and Children (former executive director, Connecticut Juvenile Justice Alliance). Telephone interview, October 21, 2010.

Doug Hall, director, Economic Analysis and Research Network, Economic Policy Institute (former senior analyst, Connecticut Voices for Children). Telephone interview, September 23, 2010.

Jeanne Milstein, child advocate, Office of the Child Advocate, Connecticut. Personal interview, Hartford, October 7, 2010.

Toni Walker, state representative, Connecticut House of Representatives. Personal interview, Hartford, October 7, 2010.

Elaine Zimmerman, executive director, Connecticut Commission on Children. Personal interview, Hartford, October 7, 2010.

Utah

Karen Crompton, executive director, Voices for Utah Children. Personal interview, October 19, 2010.

Janis Dubno, senior policy analyst, Voices for Utah Children. Telephone interview, April 12, 2011.

Lyle Hillyard, senator, Utah state legislature. Telephone interview, April 13, 2011.

Kory Holdaway, government relations director, Utah Education Association (former representative, Utah state legislature). Telephone interview, October 25, 2010.

Patricia Jones, Senate minority leader, Utah state legislature. Personal interview, October 19, 2010.

Merlynn Newbold, representative, Utah state legislature. Telephone interview, April 29, 2011.

North Carolina

Stephanie Fanjul, president, North Carolina Partnership for Children. Telephone interview, August 26, 2011.

Joe Hackney, representative, North Carolina House of Representatives (former Speaker, North Carolina House of Representatives). Telephone interview, August 29, 2011.

Elaine Mejia, senior program associate, Demos (former director, North Carolina Budget and Tax Center). Telephone interview, January 14, 2011.

Gary Pearce, consultant (former staff member, Governor Hunt). Telephone interview, August 31, 2011.

Richard Stevens, chair, Appropriations Committee, North Carolina State Senate. Telephone interview, September 7, 2011.

Pennsylvania

Erika Bantz, director, program development, Nurse-Family Partnership program. Telephone interview, May 3, 2011.

Pat Browne, senator, Pennsylvania General Assembly. Telephone interview, August 9, 2011.

Jake Corman, senator, Pennsylvania General Assembly. Telephone interview, August 12, 2011.

Jay Costa, senator and minority leader, Pennsylvania General Assembly. Telephone interview, August 3, 2011.

Harriet Dichter, national director, First Five Years Fund (former secretary of public welfare under Governor Rendell). Telephone interview, June 14, 2011.

Lisa Fleming, staff member, House Appropriations Committee, Pennsylvania General Assembly. Telephone interview, July 5, 2011.

Karen Howard, director, policy and government affairs, Nurse-Family Partnership program. Telephone interview, April 22, 2011.

Feather Houstoun, president, William Penn Foundation (former secretary of public welfare under Governor Ridge). Telephone interview, June 21, 2011.

Phyllis Mundy, representative, Pennsylvania General Assembly. Telephone interview, July 11, 2011.

Deb Reeves, staff member, House Appropriations Committee, Pennsylvania General Assembly. Telephone interview, July 5, 2011.

Kathy Vranicar, staff member, House Appropriations Committee, Pennsylvania General Assembly. Telephone interview, August 4, 2011.

Interviews:
Congressional Staff

There follow the names and committee affiliations of the congressional staff interviewed for the study.

James Bergeron, Education and Labor Committee, U.S. House of Representatives. Interview, July 1, 2010.

Adam Carasso, Budget Committee, U.S. House of Representatives. Interview, July 8, 2010.

Chuck Clapton. Health, Education, Labor, and Pensions Committee, U.S. House of Representatives. Interview, July 16, 2010.

Kate Coler. Agriculture, Nutrition, and Forestry Committee, U.S. House of Representatives. Interview, July 15, 2010.

Indivar Dutta-Gupta. Ways and Means Committee, U.S. House of Representatives. Interview, June 11, 2010.

Denise Forte. Education and Labor Committee, U.S. House of Representatives. Interview, July 2, 2010.

Mike Friedberg. Appropriations Committee, U.S. House of Representatives. Interview, September 2, 2010.

Nick Gwyn. Ways and Means Committee, U.S. House of Representatives. Interview, July 23, 2010.

Deidra Henry-Spires. Finance Committee, U.S. Senate. Interview, August 20, 2010.

Kase Jabboori. Ways and Means Committee, U.S. House of Representatives. Interview, August 12, 2010.

Aruna Kalyanam. Ways and Means Committee, U.S. House of Representatives. Interview, August 12, 2010.

Bethany Little. Health, Education, Labor, and Pensions Committee, U.S. Senate. Interview, June 29, 2010.

Roger Mahan. Budget Committee, U.S. Senate. Interview, June 25, 2010.

Morna Miller. Budget Committee, U.S. House of Representatives. Interview, June 17, 2010.

Lisa Molyneux. Appropriations Committee, U.S. House of Representatives. Interview, August 27, 2010.

Sonja Nesbit. Ways and Means Committee, U.S. House of Representatives. Interview, June 11, 2010.

Courtney Reinhard. Budget Committee, U.S. House of Representatives. Interview, August 12, 2010.

Susan Ross. Education and Labor Committee, U.S. House of Representatives. Interview, August 24, 2010.

Laura Schifter. Education and Labor Committee, U.S. House of Representatives. Interview, July 16, 2010.

Andrew Schneider. Energy and Commerce Committee, U.S. House of Representatives. Interview, June 24, 2010.

David Schwartz. Finance Committee, U.S. Senate. Interview, June 25, 2010.

Naomi Seiler. Energy and Commerce Committee, U.S. House of Representatives. Interview, August 4, 2010.

Becky Shipp. Finance Committee, U.S. Senate. Interview, July 13, 2010.

Margo Smith. Ways and Means Committee, U.S. House of Representatives. Interview, June 17, 2010.

Austin Smythe. Budget Committee, U.S. House of Representatives. Interview, July 2, 2010.

Matt Weidinger. Ways and Means Committee, U.S. House of Representatives. Interview, June 17, 2010.

Rodney Whitlock. Finance Committee, U.S. Senate. Interview, July 8, 2010.

References

Aaron, Henry. 1978. *Politics and the Professors: The Great Society in Perspective*. Brookings.

Abramowitz, Alan. 2011. "Setting the Record Straight: Correcting Myths about Independent Voters." Charlottesville, Va.: Larry Sabato's Crystal Ball (www.centerforpolitics.org/crystalball/articles/aia2011070702).

Alberts, Bruce. 2011. "Getting Education Right." *Science* 333, no. 19: 919.

Alesina, Alberto, Edward Glaeser, and Bruce Sacerdote. 2001. "Why Doesn't the U.S. Have a European-Style Welfare System?" Working Paper 8524. Cambridge, Mass.: National Bureau of Economic Research.

Almond, Douglas, Hilary Hoynes, and Diane Schanzenbach. 2011. "Inside the War on Poverty: The Impact of Food Stamps on Birth Outcomes." *Review of Economics and Statistics* 93 (May): 387–403.

American National Election Studies. No date. "Guide to Public Opinion and Electoral Behavior." Ann Arbor: Center for Political Studies, University of Michigan.

Anderson, Abby. No date. "Small Targeted Investments Yielded Major Reform." Hartford: Connecticut Juvenile Justice Alliance (www.raisetheagect.org/anderson.html).

Annie E. Casey Foundation. 2011. "Child Welfare Permanence," p. 1 (www.aecf.org).

Aos, Steve, and others. 2004. "Benefits and Costs of Prevention and Early Intervention Programs for Youth." Olympia: Washington Institute for Public Policy.

Aron, Laudan, and Pam Loprest. 2012. "Disability and the Education System." *Future of Children* 22 (Spring): 97–122.

Associated Press. 2009. "Governor Signs Law on Big Budget." *Winston Salem Journal*, August 8.

———. 2011. "U.S. Tops Developed Nations in Children Raised by One Parent." *Washington Post*, April 28, p. 2.

Autism Speaks. 2011. "Virginia Becomes the 26th State to Enact Autism Insurance Reform Legislation." May 6 (autismspeaks.org).

Baesler, E. James, and Judee Burgoon. 1994. "The Temporal Effects of Story and Statistical Evidence on Belief Change." *Communication Research* 21: 582–602.

Bai, Matt. 2010. "Of Debts and Doubts," *New York Times,* December 5, "Week in Progress," p. 1.

Baird, Abigail. 2006. Connecticut Joint Committee on the Judiciary. Informational hearing, "Returning 16 and 17 Year Olds to Juvenile Court Jurisdiction." Hartford, February 21.

Baldassare, Mark. 2002. *A California State of Mind.* University of California Press.

Barnes, Robert. 2007. "Divided Court Limits Use of Race by School Districts." *Washington Post*, June 29, p. 1.

Barnett, W. Steven. 1996. "Lives in the Balance: Age-27 Benefit-Cost Analysis of the High/Scope Perry Preschool Program." Monograph 11. High/Scope Educational Research Foundation. Ypsilanti, Mich.: High/Scope Press.

———. 2011. "Effectiveness of Early Childhood Intervention." *Science* 333, no. 19: 975–78.

Barnett, W. Steven, and others. 2010. *The State of Preschool, 2010.* New Brunswick, N.J.: National Institute for Early Education Research.

Bartik, Timothy. 2011. *Investing in Kids: Early Childhood Programs and Local Economic Development.* Kalamazoo, Mich.: W. E. Upjohn Institute for Employment Research.

Baumgartner, Frank, Suzanna DeBoef, and Amber Boydstun. 2008. *The Decline of the Death Penalty and the Discovery of Innocence.* Cambridge University Press.

Baumgartner, Frank, and others. 2009. *Lobbying and Policy Change: Who Wins, Who Loses, and Why.* University of Chicago Press.

Bazemore, Gordon, and Mark Umbreit. 1997. "A Framework for Juvenile Justice in the 21st Century." Office of Juvenile Justice and Delinquency Prevention, U.S. Department of Justice.

Beckmann, David. 2010. Interview with Tavis Smiley, October 19. PBS online.

Bell, Terrel. 1975. Testimony. Hearings on extension of Education of the Handicapped Act before the Subcommittee on Select Education, House Committee on Education and Labor, June 9.

Berinsky, Adam, and Donald Kinder. 2006. "Making Sense of Issues through Media Frames: Understanding the Kosovo Crisis." *Journal of Politics* 68: 640–56.

Bitler, Marianne, and Janet Currie. 2005. "Does WIC Work? The Effects of WIC on Pregnancy and Birth Outcomes." *Journal of Policy Analysis and Management* 24, no. 1: 73–91.

Bogenschneider, Karen, and Thomas Corbett. 2010. *Evidence-Based Policymaking.* New York: Routledge.

Brademas, John. 1975. Remarks. Hearings on extension of Education of the Handicapped Act before the Subcommittee on Select Education, House Committee on Education and Labor, April 9, 10, June 9.

Braestrup, Peter. 1977. *Big Story: How the American Press and Television Reported and Interpreted the Crisis of Tet 1968 in Vietnam and Washington.* Boulder, Colo.: Westview Press.

Brewer, Paul, and Kimberley Gross. 2005. "Values Framing, and Citizens' Thoughts about Policy Issues: Effects on Content and Quantity." *Political Psychology* 22: 45–64.

Brown v. Board of Education of Topeka. 347 U.S. 483 (1954).

Brown, Sherrod. 2007. Remarks. *Congressional Record*, August 1, pp. S10587–88.

Brownback, Sam. 2008. Testimony. Hearings on Domestic Abstinence-Only Programs: Assessing the Evidence, before the House Committee on Oversight and Government Reform, April 23, pp. 27–34.

———. 2010. "Legislative Issues, Education, Abstinence Education" (http://brownback.senate.gov/public/legissues/education_abstinence.cfm).

Buckley, John, and Mark Schneider. 2007. *Charter Schools: Hope or Hype?* Princeton University Press.

Campbell, David, and J. Quin Monson. 2007. "Dry Kindling: A Political Profile of American Mormons." In *From Pews to Polling Places,* edited by Matt Wilson, pp. 105–29. Georgetown University Press.

Campbell, David, and Robert Putnam. 2010. *American Grace: How Religion Divides and Unites Us.* New York: Simon and Schuster.

Capps, Lois. 2008. Remarks. Hearing on Domestic Abstinence-Only Programs: Assessing the Evidence, before the House Committee on Oversight and Government Reform, April 23, pp. 15–18.

Cavanaugh, Sean. 2010. "Study Challenges States on 'Fairness' of Funding Models." *Education Week*, October 20, pp. 14–15.

Celebrezze, Anthony. 1965. Testimony. Hearings on the Elementary and Secondary Education Act before the Subcommittee on Education, Senate Committee on Labor and Public Welfare, January 26, pp. 77–81.

Center for Research on Educational Outcomes. 2009. "Multiple Choice: Charter School Performance in 16 States." Stanford University.

Children's Defense Fund. 2010 (www.childrensdefense.org).

Child Trends. 2010. "Violent Crime Victimization" (www.childtrendsdatabank.org?q=node/75).

Chong, Dennis, and James Druckman. 2007a. "Framing Theory." *Annual Review of Political Science* 10: 103–26.

———. 2007b. "A Theory of Framing and Opinion Formation in Competitive Elite Environment." *Journal of Communication* 57: 99–118.

Clark, David. 2010. Opening Remarks. Utah House of Representatives. Salt Lake City, January 28 (http://district74.blogspot.com/2010/01/opening-remarks.html).

Clotfelter, Charles, Helen Ladd, and Jacob Vigdor. 2008. "School Segregation under Color-Blind Jurisprudence: The Case of North Carolina." Working paper. Sanford Institute of Public Policy, Duke University.

Clymer, Adam. 1997. "Child-Support Collection Net Usually Fails." *New York Times*, July 17, p. 16.

Cohen, Sally. 2001. *Championing Child Care.* Columbia University Press.

Coleman, James, and others. 1966. *Equality of Educational Opportunity.* Office of Education, U.S. Department of Health, Education, and Welfare.

Committee for Economic Development. 2006. *The Economic Promise of Investing in High-Quality Preschool.* Washington.

Congressional Budget Office. 2007. "The Long-Term Budget Outlook." December.

Courtney, Mark, Amy Dworsky, and Harold Pollack. 2007. "When Should the State Cease Parenting? Evidence from the Midwest Study." Issue brief. Chapin Hall Center for Children, University of Chicago.

Cook, Fay Lomax, and Edith Barrett. 1992. *Support for the American Welfare State: The Views of Congress and the Public.* Columbia University Press.

Crain, Robert, and Rita Mahard. 1979. "Research on School Desegregation and Achievement: How to Combine Scholarship and Policy Relevance." *Educational Evaluation and Policy Analysis* 1 (July–August): 5–15.

Crowley, Jocelyn. 2003. *The Politics of Child Support in America.* Cambridge University Press.

Crutchfield, Leslie, John Kania, and Mark Kramer. 2011. *Do More than Give: The Six Practices of Donors Who Change the World.* San Francisco: Jossey-Bass.

Currie, Janet. 2009. "Healthy, Wealthy, and Wise: Socioeconomic Status, Poor Health in Childhood, and Human Capital Development." *Journal of Economic Literature* 47, no. 1: 87–122.

Currie, Janet, and Rosemary Hyson. 1999. "Is the Impact of Health Shocks Cushioned by Socioeconomic Status? The Case of Low Birthweight." *American Economic Review* 89, no. 2: 245–50.

Dalesio, Emery. 2011. "State Budget Passes; Perdue Must Decide on Veto." *Fayetteville Observer*, June 5, 2011.

Dallek, Robert. 1998. *Flawed Giant: Lyndon Johnson and His Times, 1961–1973.* Oxford University Press.

Davidson, Howard. 2010. "A U.S. National Ombudsman for Children." In *Big Ideas: Game-Changers for Children*, pp. 74–82. Washington: First Focus.

Davies, Gareth. 1996. *From Opportunity to Entitlement: The Transformation and Decline of Great Society Liberalism.* University Press of Kansas.

Dee, Thomas, and Brian Jacob. 2009. "The Impact of No Child Left Behind on Student Achievement." Working Paper 15531. Cambridge, Mass.: National Bureau of Economic Research.

DeParle, Jason, Robert Gebeloff, and Sabrina Tavernise. 2011. "Older, Suburban and Struggling, 'Near Poor' Startle the Census. *New York Times*, November 18.

Devaney, Barbara, L. Bilheimer, and J. Shore. 1992. "Medicaid Costs and Birth Outcomes." *Journal of Policy Analysis and Management* 11, no. 4: 573–92.

De Vise, Daniel. 2011. "U.S. Falls in Global Ranking of Young Adults Who Finish College." *Washington Post,* September 13, p. 4.

Dickson, Peter. 1982. "The Impact of Enriching Case and Statistical Information on Consumer Judgments." *Journal of Consumer Research* 8: 398–406.

DiIulio, John. 1995. "The Coming of the Super-Predators." *Weekly Standard,* November 27, p. 23.

Dillon, Erin. 2007. "Labeled: The Students behind NCLB's 'Disabilities' Designation." Washington: Education Sector (www.educationsector.org/publications/labeled-students-behind-nclbs-disabilities-designation).

Dionne, E. J. 2004. *Stand Up, Fight Back: Republican Toughs, Democratic Wimps, and the Politics of Revenge.* New York: Simon and Schuster.

Dodge, Kenneth, Helen Ladd, and Clara Muschkin. 2011. "N.C. Views—Cutting Smart Start and More at Four Doesn't Save Money." Durham, N.C. (www.starnewsonline.com/article/20110409/ARTICLES/110409604).

Dougherty, Conor. 2010. "U.S. Nears Racial Milestone." *Wall Street Journal,* June 11.

Druckman, James. 2001. "On the Limits of Framing Effects: Who Can Frame?" *Journal of Politics* 63, no. 4: 1041–66.

———. 2011. "What's It All About? Framing in Political Science." In *Perspectives on Framing,* edited by Gideon Keren, pp. 279–301. New York: Psychology Press.

Druckman, James, and Toby Bolsen. 2010. "Framing, Motivated Reasoning, and Opinions about Emergent Technologies." Department of Political Science, Northwestern University, January 14.

Druckman, James, and Kjersten Nelson. 2003. "Framing and Deliberation: How Citizens' Conversations Limit Elite Influence." *American Journal of Political Science* 47, no. 4: 729–45.

Duncan, Arne. 2008. Press release. "President-Elect Obama Announces Arne Duncan as Secretary of Education." White House. December 16 (http://change.gov/newsroom/entry/president_elect_obama_announces_arne_duncan_as_secretary_of_education)

———. 2009a. Testimony. Hearings on the Obama Administration's Education Agenda before the House Education and Labor Committee, May 20.

———. 2009b. Press release. "Secretary Arne Duncan Speaks at the 91st Annual Meeting of the American Council on Education." February 9 (www.ed.gov/news/speeches/secretary-arne-duncan-speaks-91st-annual-meeting-american-council).

———. 2010a. Press release. "The Quiet Revolution: Secretary Arne Duncan's Remarks at the National Press Club." July 27 (www.ed.gov/news/speeches/quiet-revolution-secretary-arne-duncans-remarks-national-press-club).

———. 2010b. "Secretary Arne Duncan's Remarks at OECD's Release of the Program for International Student Assessment (PISA) 2009 Results."

U.S. Department of Education, December 7 (www.ed.gov/news/speeches/secretary-arne-duncans-remarks-oecds-release-program-international).

———. 2010c. Press release. "Fulfilling the Promise of IDEA." Remarks on the 35th anniversary of the Individuals with Disabilities Education Act. November 18 (www.ed.gov/news/speeches/fulfilling-promsie-idea-remarks-35th-anniversary-individuals-disabilities-act).

Duncan, Greg, and Jeanne Brooks-Gunn. 1997. "Income Effects Across the Life Span: Integration and Interpretation." In *Consequences of Growing up Poor,* edited by Greg Duncan and Jeanne Brooks-Gunn, pp. 596–610. New York: Russell Sage.

Duncan, Greg, Kathleen Ziol-Guest, and Ariel Kalil. 2010. "Early Childhood Poverty and Adult Attainment, Behavior, and Health." Paper prepared for the annual meeting of the AAAS, San Diego, February 21.

Dworkin, Ronald. 1986. *Law's Empire.* Cambridge, Mass.: Belknap Press.

Edelman, Marian Wright. 1971. Testimony. Hearings on the Emergency School Aid Act before the General Subcommittee on Education, House Committee on Education and Labor, March 15, pp. 34–42.

———. 1973. Testimony. Hearings on the Juvenile Justice and Delinquency Prevention Act, S3148 and S821, before the Subcommittee to Investigate Juvenile Delinquency, Senate Judiciary Committee, March 27, pp. 522–27.

———. 1981. Testimony. Hearings on the first concurrent resolution on the budget, fiscal year 1982, Senate Budget Committee, April 6, pp. 218–21.

———. 1982. Testimony. Joint hearing on the impact of the administration's proposed budget cuts on children before the Subcommittee on Oversight, House Ways and Means Committee, and Subcommittee on Health and the Environment, House Energy and Commerce Committee, March 3, pp. 113–44.

———. 1983. Testimony. Overview of the administration's entitlement policies, Task Force on Entitlements, Uncontrollables and Indexing, House Budget Committee, March 10, pp. 98–103.

———. 1987a. *Families in Peril: An Agenda for Social Change.* Harvard University Press.

———. 1987b. Testimony. Hearings on the role of federal food assistance programs in strategies to reduce infant mortality before the House Select Committee on Hunger, April 29, pp. 5–9.

———. 1987c. Testimony. Hearings on welfare reform, HR 30, Fair Working Opportunities Act of 1987, and HR 1720, Family Welfare Reform Act of 1987 before the House Committee on Education and Labor, May 5, pp. 63–66.

———. 1988. Testimony. Hearing on HR 3660, the Act for Better Child Care Service, Subcommittee on Human Resources, House Committee on Education and Labor, February 25.

———. 1989. Testimony. Hearings on how to help the working poor and problems of the working poor before the House Ways and Means Committee, March 21, pp. 130–48.

————. 1993. Testimony. Joint hearings on keeping every child safe: curbing the epidemic of violence before the Subcommittee on Children, Family, Drugs, and Alcoholism, Senate Committee on Labor and Human Resources and House Select Committee on Children, Youth, and Families, March 10, pp. 61–63.

————. 2009. "Written Statement on the Comprehensive Health Reform Discussion Draft." Subcommittee on Health, House Committee on Energy and Commerce, June 23.

Elshtain, Jean Bethke. 2002. *Jane Addams and the Dream of American Democracy*. New York: Basic Books.

Epstein, Lee, and Joseph Kobylka. 1992. *The Supreme Court and Legal Change: Abortion and the Death Penalty*. University of North Carolina Press.

Erickson, Tiffany. 2006. "Kindergarten Bill Offering Full-Day Option Advances." *Deseret Morning News,* February 7.

Esterling, Kevin. 2004. *The Political Economy of Expertise*. University of Michigan Press.

Fagan, Jeffrey. 2008. "Juvenile Crime and Criminal Justice: Resolving Border Disputes." *Future of Children* 18, no. 2: 81–118.

Families USA. 2011. "Messaging Cheat Sheet: Mastering the 30-Second Sound Byte" (www.familiesusa.org).

Ferber, Thaddeus. 2010. "Big Idea: Youth Councils." In *Big Ideas: Game-Changers for Children*, pp. 42–49. Washington: First Focus.

Fight Crime: Invest in Kids. 2012. "Early Care and Education," p. 1 (www.fightcrime.org/page/early-care-and-education).

Finkelhor, David. 2009. "The Prevention of Childhood Sexual Abuse." *Future of Children* 19 (Fall): 169–94.

Fletcher, Michael. 2011. "Census Shows Impact of Recession." *Washington Post,* September 14, p. 1.

Flemming, Arthur. 1960. Address. White House Conference on Children and Youth, closing session. Washington, April 2.

Forest Grove School District v. *T.A.* 129 S. Ct. 2484 (2009) (www.supremecourt.gov/oral_arguments/argument_transcripts/08-305.pdf).

Fox News. 2011. "President Obama Sits Down with Bill O'Reilly ahead of Super Bowl." Interview transcript, February 6.

Frankena, William. 1973. *Ethics*. 2nd ed. Englewood Cliffs, N.J.: Prentice-Hall.

Franklin, Charles. 2008. "Age, Turnout, and Votes." August 11 (pollster.com/blogs/age-turnout-and-voteshtml.php?nr=1).

Gainsborough, Juliet. 2010. *Scandalous Politics: Child Welfare Policy in the United States*. Georgetown University Press.

Garfinkel, Irwin. 1992. *Assuring Child Support*. New York: Russell Sage.

Garrow, David. 1986. *Bearing the Cross: Martin Luther King Jr. and the Southern Christian Leadership Conference*. New York: William Morrow.

Gilens, Martin. 1999. *Why Americans Hate Welfare: Race, Media, and the Politics of Antipoverty Policy*. Princeton University Press.

Gilliam, Frank, and Shanto Iyengar. 1998. "The Superpredator Script." *Nieman Reports* 52 (Winter): 45–49.

Glendon, Mary Ann. 1991. *Rights Talk: An Impoverishment of Political Discourse.* New York: Free Press.

Golden, Olivia. 2011. "Children and Federal-State Budget Trade-Offs." Roundtable discussion. Washington: Urban Institute, March 17.

Goldsmith, Thomas, and T. Keung Hui. 2010. "Tumultuous Session Ends Diversity Policy." *Raleigh News and Observer*, March 24.

Gormley, William, Jr. 1989. *Taming the Bureaucracy: Muscles, Prayers, and Other Strategies.* Princeton University Press.

———. 2007. "Public Policy Analysis: Ideas and Impacts." *Annual Review of Political Science*, June: 297–313.

———. 2011. "From Science to Policy in Early Childhood Education." *Science* 333 (August): 978–81.

Gormley, William, Jr., and Helen Cymrot. 2006. "The Strategic Choices of Child Advocacy Groups." *Nonprofit and Voluntary Sector Quarterly* 35 (March): 102–22.

Goss, Kristin. 2006. *Disarmed: The Missing Movement for Gun Control in America.* Princeton University Press.

Graetz, Michael, and Ian Shapiro. 2005. *Death by a Thousand Cuts: The Fight over Taxing Inherited Wealth.* Princeton University Press.

Graham v. *Florida.* 2010. U.S. Supreme Court, slip opinion, May 17.

Green, Frank. 2005. "Execution of Juvenile Offenders Opposed." *Richmond Times Dispatch.* January 18, p. 8.

Greenwald, Rob, Larry Hedges, and Richard Laine. 1996. "The Effect of School Resources on Student Achievement." *Review of Educational Research* 66 (Autumn): 361–96.

Gregg, Judd. 2010. Press release. "Gregg: Fiscal Commission's Final Proposal Represents a Step Forward." December 1. Office of U.S. Senator Judd Gregg.

Haider, Aliya. 2006. "*Roper* v. *Simmons:* The Role of the Science Brief." *Ohio State Journal of Criminal Law* 3: 369–77.

Haider-Markel, Donald, and Mark Joslyn. 2001. "Gun Policy, Opinion, Tragedy, and Blame Attribution: The Conditional Influence of Issue Frames." *Journal of Politics* 63: 520–43.

Haidt, Jonathan. 2007. "The New Synthesis in Moral Psychology." *Science* 316 (May): 998–1002.

Hamington, Maurice. 2009. *The Social Philosophy of Jane Addams.* University of Illinois Press.

Hammond, Sarah. 2008. "States Debate What the Best Response is to Teenagers Who Commit Crimes." *State Legislatures* 34, no. 4: 31.

Hanushek, Eric. 1981. "Throwing Money at Schools." *Journal of Policy Analysis and Management* 1, no. 1: 19–41.

———. 1986. "The Economics of Schooling: Production and Efficiency in Public Schools." *Journal of Economic Literature* 24: 1141–77.

Hanushek, Eric, John Kain, and Steven Rivkin. 2002. "Inferring Program Effects for Special Populations: Does Special Education Raise Achievement for Students with Disabilities?" *Review of Economics and Statistics* 84 (November): 584–99.

Hanushek, Eric, and Alfred Lindseth. 2009. *Schoolhouses, Courthouses, and Statehouses: Solving the Funding-Achievement Puzzle in America's Public Schools*. Princeton University Press.

Harkin, Tom. 2007. Remarks. *Congressional Record*, August 1, pp. S10551–52.

Harrington, Michael. 1962. *The Other America: Poverty in the United States*. New York: Macmillan.

Haskins, Ron. 2006. *Work over Welfare: The Inside Story of the 1996 Welfare Reform Law*. Brookings.

Haskins, Ron, and Isabel Sawhill. 2009. *Creating an Opportunity Society*. Brookings.

Haveman, Robert, Barbara Wolfe, and Kathryn Wilson. 1997. "Childhood Poverty and Adolescent Schooling and Fertility Outcomes." In *Consequences of Growing up Poor*, edited by Greg Duncan and Jeanne Brooks-Gunn, pp. 419–60. New York: Russell Sage.

Hayward, Mark, and Bridget Gorman. 2004. "The Long Arm of Childhood: The Influence of Early-Life Social Conditions on Men's Mortality." *Demography* 41 (February): 87–107.

Heckman, James. 2000. "Policies to Foster Human Capital." *Research in Economics* 54: 3–56.

———. 2010. "A Research Agenda for Understanding the Dynamics of Skill Formation." American Economics Association White Paper, October 4 (www.aeaweb.org/econwhitepapers/white_papers/Jim_Heckman).

Hedges, Larry, Richard Laine, and Rob Greenwald. 1994. "An Exchange: Part I: Does Money Matter? A Meta-Analysis of Studies of the Effects of Differential School Inputs on Student Outcomes." *Educational Researcher* 23 (April): 5–14.

Heller, Walter. 1964. Testimony. Hearings on the Economic Opportunity Act of 1964 before the Subcommittee on the War on Poverty Program, House Education and Labor Committee, March 17, pp. 25–30.

Hellmich, Nancy. 2011. "New Report Urges Parents to Invest Early in Childhood Obesity Prevention." *USA Today*, June 24.

Hinrichs, Peter. 2010. "The Effects of the National School Lunch Program on Education and Health." *Journal of Policy Analysis and Management* 29, no. 3: 479–505.

Hird, John. 2005. *Power, Knowledge, and Politics: Policy Analysis in the States*. Georgetown University Press.

Hirsch, David, and Dan Van Haften. 2010. *Abraham Lincoln and the Structure of Reason.* New York: Savas Beatie.

Hodges, Luther. 1964. Testimony. Hearings on the Economic Opportunity Act of 1964 before the Subcommittee on the War on Poverty Program, House Education and Labor Committee, March 19, pp. 231–38.

Howell, William, and others. 2002. "School Vouchers and Academic Performance: Results from Three Randomized Field Trials." *Journal of Policy Analysis and Management* 21, no. 2: 191–217.

Hoxby, Caroline, Sumali Murarka, and Jenny Kang. 2009. "How New York City's Charter Schools Affect Achievement." Cambridge, Mass.: New York City Charter Schools Evaluation Project.

Hui, T. Keung. 2010. "Wake School Board Passes Neighborhood School Resolution." *Raleigh News and Observer*, March 2.

———. 2011. "Wake School Board Could Tweak Assignment Plan." *Raleigh News and Observer,* December 20.

Hui, T. Keung, and Thomas Goldsmith. 2010. "Diversity Policy Voted Down in Tense Meeting." *Raleigh News and Observer*, March 3.

Hula, Kevin. 1999. *Lobbying Together: Interest Group Coalitions in Legislative Politics.* Georgetown University Press.

Hunt, Jim. 2011. "Governor Jim Hunt Discusses the Importance of Smart Start." Raleigh, N.C., March 23 (www.youtube.com/watch?v=0_995_Kx91Q).

Hurwitz, Jon, and Mark Peffley. 2005. "Playing the Race Card in the Post-Willie Horton Era: The Impact of Racialized Code Words on Support for Punitive Crime Policy." *Public Opinion Quarterly* 69: 99–112.

Isaacs, Julia. 2009. "Spending on Children and the Elderly: An Issue Brief." Brookings.

Iyengar, Shanto. 1991. *Is Anyone Responsible? How Television Frames Political Issues.* University of Chicago Press.

Iyengar, Shanto, and Kyu Hahn. 2009. "Red Media, Blue Media: Evidence of Ideological Selectivity in Media Use." *Journal of Communication* 59: 19–39.

Iyengar, Shanto, and Nicholas Valentino. 1999. "Who Says What: Source Credibility as a Mediator of Campaign Advertising." In *Elements of Reason*, edited by A. Lupia, M. McCubbins, and S. Pokin, pp. 108–29. Cambridge University Press.

Jacobson, Louis. 2010. "Looking at Unemployment, Education, Obama's Approval Rating." *Politifact*, August 17.

Jacoby, William. 2000. "Issue Framing and Public Opinion on Government Spending." *American Journal of Political Science* 44: 750–67.

Johnson, Haynes, and David Broder. 1997. *The System: The American Way of Politics at the Breaking Point.* Boston: Little-Brown.

Johnson, Lyndon. 1964. "Remarks upon Signing the Economic Opportunity Act." *Public Papers of the Presidents of the United States: Lyndon B. Johnson, 1963–64.* August 20, pp. 988–89.

———. 1965a. "Commencement Address at Howard University." *Public Papers of the Presidents of the United States: Lyndon B. Johnson, 1965.* June 4, pp. 635–40.

———. 1965b. Special Message to the Congress. "Toward Full Educational Opportunity." *Public Papers of the Presidents of the United States: Lyndon B. Johnson, 1965.* January 12, pp. 25–33.

Joyce, Philip. 2011. *The Congressional Budget Office: Honest Numbers, Power, and Policymaking.* Georgetown University Press.

Kaiser Health Tracking Poll. 2011. Henry J. Kaiser Family Foundation, March (www.kff.org/Kaiserpolls/upload/8166-f.pdf).

Kahneman, Daniel, and Amos Tversky. 1973. "On the Psychology of Prediction." *Psychological Review* 80: 237–51.

———. 1979. "Prospect Theory: An Analysis of Decision under Risk." *Econometrica* 47: 263–91.

———. 1984. "Choices, Values, and Frames." *American Psychologist* 39: 341–50.

Kamerman, Sheila. 2004. "Maternity and Parental Leaves." New York: Clearinghouse on International Developments in Child, Youth and Family Policies at Columbia University (www.childpolicyintl.org/maternity.html).

Keppel, Francis. 1965. Testimony. Hearings on the Elementary and Secondary Education Act of 1965 before the Subcommittee on Education, Senate Labor and Public Welfare Committee, January 26, pp. 629–35.

Kerry, John. 2007. Remarks. *Congressional Record*, August 1, p. S10558.

Kids Count. 2010. "Kids Count Data Book, 2010." Baltimore: Annie E. Casey Foundation.

Kingdon, John. 1995. *Agendas, Alternatives, and Public Policies.* 2nd ed. New York: Holt.

Kirp, David. 2007. *The Sandbox Investment: The Preschool Movement and Kids-First Politics.* Harvard University Press.

Krueger, Alan, and Pei Zhu. 2003. "Another Look at the New York City School Voucher Experiment." Working Paper 9418. Cambridge, Mass.: National Bureau of Economic Research.

Kunkle, Fredrick, and Anita Kumar. 2011. "Autism Bill Advances in Virginia." *Washington Post,* February 6, p. C1.

Labaree, Leonard, ed. 1960. *The Papers of Benjamin Franklin,* vol. 2. Yale University Press.

Ladd, Helen. 2010. "Wake County BOE Meeting on April 23rd—A Summary of My Comments during the Meeting." Duke University, April 27 (http://dialog. econ.duke.edu/schoolchoice/2010/04/27/wake-county-boe-meeting-on-april-23rd-a-summary-of-my-comments-during-the-meeting).

Lasch, Christopher, ed. 1965. *The Social Thought of Jane Addams.* Indianapolis: Bobbs-Merrill.

Lav, Iris, and Dylan Grundman. 2011. "A Balanced Approach to Closing State Deficits." Washington: Center on Budget and Policy Priorities.

Lavy, Victor. 2007. "Using Performance-Based Pay to Improve the Quality of Teachers." *Future of Children* 17, no. 1: 87–110.

Lee, Stephanie, Steve Aos, and Marna Miller. 2008. "Evidence-Based Programs to Prevent Children from Entering and Remaining in the Child Welfare System: Benefits and Costs for Washington." Olympia: Washington State Institute for Public Policy.

Lindblom, C. Edward. 1959. "The Science of Muddling Through." *Public Administration Review* 19 (Spring): 79–88.

————. 1977. *Politics and Markets: The World's Political and Economic Systems*. New York: Basic Books.

Lipset, Seymour Martin. 1996. *American Exceptionalism: A Double-Edged Sword*. New York: Norton.

Lucchese, Lauren. 2010. "Children's Dental Campaign Issues First Report." *Trust* 12, no. 3: 4.

Luntz, Frank. 2007. *Words that Work: It's Not What You Say, It's What People Hear*. New York: Hyperion.

Lupia, Arthur, and Mathew McCubbins. 1998. *The Democratic Dilemma: Can Citizens Learn What They Need to Know?* Cambridge University Press.

Lynch, Julia. 2006. *Age in the Welfare State: The Origins of Social Spending on Pensioners, Workers, and Children*. Cambridge University Press.

Mahoney, Christine. 2008. *Brussels versus the Beltway: Advocacy in the United States and the European Union*. Georgetown University Press.

Majone, Giandomenico. 1989. *Evidence, Argument, and Persuasion in the Policy Process*. Yale University Press.

Mak, Tim. 2011. "Jackson, Sebelius Tout Health Efforts." *Politico*, October 17.

Manna, Paul. 2006. *School's In: Federalism and the National Education Agenda*. Georgetown University Press.

Manuel, Tiffany. 2009. "Refining the Core Story of Early Childhood Development: The Effects of Science and Health Frames." Washington: FrameWorks Institute, April.

Marks, James. 2010. "Does CBO Need a Nudge to Invest in our Children?" In *Big Ideas: Game-Changers for Children*, pp. 126–30. Washington: First Focus.

Mayer, Jane. 2011. "State for Sale: A Conservative Multimillionaire Has Taken Control in North Carolina, One of 2012's Top Battlegrounds." *New Yorker*, October 10.

Mayhew, David. 1974. *Congress: The Electoral Connection*. Yale University Press.

McCartney, Kathleen, and Robert Rosenthal. 2000. "Effect Size, Practical Importance, and Social Policy for Children." *Child Development* 71, no. 1: 173–80.

McCarty, Nolan, Keith Poole, and Howard Rosenthal. 2006. *Polarized America: The Dance of Ideology and Unequal Riches*. MIT Press.

McCrummen, Stephanie. 2010. "In N.C., a New Battle on School Integration." *Washington Post*, January 12, p. 1.

McKee, Guian. 2010. "'This Government Is with Us': Lyndon Johnson and the Grassroots War on Poverty." In *The War on Poverty and Grassroots Struggles for Racial and Economic Justice,* edited by Annelise Orleck and Lisa Hazirjian, pp. 31–62. University of Georgia Press.

McLanahan, Sara. 1997. "Parent Absence or Poverty: Which Matters More?" In *Consequences of Growing up Poor,* edited by Greg Duncan and Jeanne Brooks-Gunn, pp. 35–48. New York: Russell Sage.

Mead, Lawrence. 1986. *Beyond Entitlement: The Social Obligations of Citizenship.* New York: Free Press.

Mejia, Elaine. 2009. "Between a Rock and a Hard Place: North Carolina's Worsening Budget Gap Calls for Spending Cuts and Tax Increases." BTC brief. Raleigh: Business and Technology Center (www.nc justice.org/?q=node/294).

Mendelberg, Tali. 2001. *The Race Card: Campaign Strategy, Implicit Messages, and the Norm of Equality.* Princeton University Press.

Miller, Joanne, and Jon Krosnick. 2000. "News Media Impact on the Ingredients of Presidential Evaluations: Politically Knowledgeable Citizens are Guided by a Trusted Source." *American Journal of Political Science* 44 (April): 295–309.

Morse, Wayne. 1965. Remarks. Hearings on the Elementary and Secondary Education Act of 1965 before the Subcommittee on Education, Senate Committee on Labor and Public Welfare, January 26.

Mucciarioni, Gary. 2011. "Are Debates about 'Morality Policy' Really about Morality? Framing Opposition to Gay and Lesbian Rights." *Policy Studies Journal* 39 (May): 187–216.

Mucciaroni, Gary, and Paul Quirk. 2006. *Deliberative Choices: Debating Public Policy in Congress.* University of Chicago Press.

Murray, Patty. 2007. Remarks. *Congressional Record,* August 1, p. S10570.

Myrdal, Gunnar. 1944. *An American Dilemma: The Negro Problem and American Democracy.* New York: Harper and Brothers.

National Commission on Fiscal Responsibility and Reform. 2010. "The Moment of Truth: Report of the National Commission on Fiscal Responsibility and Reform." White House.

National Governors Association, Center for Best Practices. 2004. "A Governor's Guide to Children's Cabinets." Washington.

National Long-Term Care, Ombudsman Resource Center. No date. "About Ombudsmen" (www.ltombudsman.org/about-ombudsmen).

Nelson, Thomas, Rosalee Clawson, and Zoe Oxley. 1997. "Media Framing of a Civil Liberties Conflict and Its Effect on Tolerance." *American Political Science Review* 91: 567–83.

Newport, Frank. 2009a. "Americans Doubt Effectiveness of 'No Child Left Behind.'" *Gallup Monthly Report,* August 19 (www.gallup.com/poll/122375/americans-doubt-effectiveness-no-child-left-behind.aspx).

————. 2009b. "Religious Identity: States Differ Widely." Gallup report, August 7.

————. 2010. "In U.S. Increasing Number Have No Religious Identity." *Gallup Monthly Report*, May 21 (www.gallup.com/poll/128276/increasing-number-no-religious-identity.aspx).

Nie, Norman, and others. 2010. "The World Wide Web and the U.S. Political News Market." *American Journal of Political Science* 54 (April): 428–39.

Nisbett, Richard, and Eugene Borgida. 1975. "Attribution and the Psychology of Prediction." *Journal of Personality and Social Psychology* 32: 932–43.

North Carolina Department of Public Instruction. 2010. "More at Four Helps Level Academic Playing Field for Disadvantaged Students" (www.dpi.state.nc.us/newsroom/news/2010-11/20101104-01).

North Carolina General Assembly, Fiscal Research Division. 2011. "Summary of Fiscal Year 2011–2012 General Fund Appropriations" (www.ncga.state.nc.us/fiscalresearch).

North Carolina Justice Center. 2009. "Together NC: New Advertisements Running across North Carolina."

Obama, Barack. 2011. "Obama's Remarks at the Chamber of Commerce." *New York Times*, February 7.

Okun, Arthur. 1975. *Equality and Efficiency: The Big Tradeoff.* Brookings.

Olds, David. 2007. "From Trials to Practice." Power Point presentation, Minneapolis, December 7.

————. 2010. Remarks. Workshop on Preventing Child Abuse in an Age of Budget Deficits. Brookings, July 20.

Olds, David, and others. 1997. "Long-Term Effects of Home Visitation on Maternal Life Course and Child Abuse and Neglect: Fifteen-Year Follow-Up of a Randomized Trial." *Journal of the American Medical Association* 278, no. 8: 637–43.

————. 1998. "Long-Term Effects of Nurse Home Visitation on Children's Criminal and Antisocial Behavior: 15-Year Follow-Up of a Randomized Control Trial." *Journal of the American Medical Association* 280, no. 14: 1238–44.

————. 2004. "Effects of Home Visits by Paraprofessionals and by Nurses: Age 4 Follow-Up Results of a Randomized Trial." *Pediatrics* 144, no. 6: 1560–68.

———— 2007. "Effects of Nurse Home Visiting on Maternal and Child Functioning: Age-9 Follow-Up of a Randomized Trial." *Pediatrics* 120, no. 4: 832–45.

————. 2010. "Enduring Effects of Prenatal and Infancy Home Visiting by Nurses on Maternal Life Course and Government Spending: Follow-Up of a Randomized Trial among Children at Age 12 Years." *Archives of Pediatrics and Adolescent Medicine* 164, no. 5: 419–24.

Olson, Ilene. 2004. "Juvenile Death Penalty Examined." *Wyoming Tribune-Eagle*, January 5, p. 1.

Orszag, Peter. 2009. "Building Rigorous Evidence to Drive Policy." Office of Management and Budget blog, June 8 (www.whitehouse.gov/omb/blog/09/06/08/BuildingRigorousEvidencetoDrivePolicy).

Otto, Mary. 2007. "For Want of a Dentist." *Washington Post*, February 28, p. B1.

Parents Involved in Community Schools v. *Seattle*, 551 U.S. 701 (2007).

Paris, Michael. 2010. *Framing Equal Opportunity: Law and the Politics of School Finance Reform*. Stanford University Press.

Parker, Kim. 2009. "The Harried Life of the Working Mother." Washington: Pew Research Center (www.pewsocialtrends.org/2009/10/01/the-harried-life-of-the-working-mother).

Paulsell, Diane, and others. 2010. *Home Visiting Evidence of Effectiveness Review: Executive Summary*. Office of Planning, Research and Evaluation, Administration for Children and Families, U.S. Department of Health and Human Services.

Pear, Robert. 1997. "President Moves to Protect Half of Uninsured Children." *New York Times*, February 7, p. 25.

Pershing, Ben. 2010. "Retiring Rep. Obey not Going Out with a Whimper." *Washington Post*, November 30, p. 19.

Peterson, Paul. 1995. "A Critique of the Witte Evaluation of Milwaukee's School Choice Program." Occasional Paper 95-2. Cambridge, Mass.: Center for American Political Studies, Harvard University.

Pew Research Center for the People and the Press. 2008. "Key News Audiences Now Blend Online and Traditional Sources." August 17. Washington.

———. 2010. "Independents Oppose Party in Power Again." September 23. Washington.

Pfeiffer, Dan. 2011. "Getting the Facts Straight on America's Tax Burden." White House blog, September 26 (www.whitehouse.gov/blog/2011/09/26/getting-facts-straight-americas-tax-burden).

Poppendieck, Janet. 2010. *Free for All: Fixing School Food in America*. University of California Press.

Pre-K Now. 2011. "Transforming Public Education: Pathway to a Pre-K-12 Future," September, p. 3 (www.preknow.org).

Pressman, Matt. 2008. "The Incredible Shrinking *New York Times*?" *Vanity Fair*, June 4 (www.vanityfair.com/online/daily/2008/06/the-incredible.html).

Public Broadcasting System. 2007. "Where Do We Get Our News?" Washington, February 27 (www.pbs.org/wgbh/pages/frontline/newswar/part3/stats.html).

Quie, Albert. 1975. Remarks. Hearings on the extension of Education of the Handicapped Act before the Subcommittee on Select Education, House Committee on Education and Labor, June 9.

Rather, Dan. 2004. "Ronald Reagan, Master Story Teller." *CBS News Special Report*. June 7.

Ravitch, Diane. 2010. *The Death and Life of the Great American School System*. New York: Basic Books.

Rawls, John. 1971. *A Theory of Justice*. Cambridge, Mass.: Belknap Press.

Reed, Douglas. 2001. *On Equal Terms: The Constitutional Politics of Educational Opportunity.* Princeton University Press.

Renwick, Trudi. 2011. Power point presentation on poverty. U.S. Census Bureau, September (www.census.gov/newsroom/releases/pdf/2010_Report.pdf).

Reynolds, Arthur, and others. 2011. "School-Based Early Childhood Education and Age-28 Well-Being: Effects by Timing, Dosage, and Subgroups." *Science* 333, no. 6040 (July 15): 360–64.

Ribicoff, Abraham. 1962. Testimony during hearings on intensive immunization programs before the House Committee on Interstate and Foreign Commerce, May 15, pp. 43–50.

Rich, Andrew. 2004. *Think Tanks, Public Policy, and the Politics of Expertise.* Cambridge University Press.

Riley, Richard. 1993. Testimony. Hearings on H.R. 1804, Goals 2000: Educate America Act, before the Subcommittee on Elementary, Secondary, and Vocational Education, House Education and Labor Committee, April 22.

————. 1995. Testimony. Hearings, Individuals with Disabilities in Education Act, before the Subcommittee on Early Childhood, Youth, and Families, House Committee on Economic and Educational Opportunities, June 20.

Roche, Lisa. 2010. "Tobacco Tax Increase: Quit or Buy out of State?" *Deseret News,* July 1.

Rolnick, Arthur, and Rob Grunewald. 2003. "Early Childhood Development: Economic Development with a High Public Return," p. 1. Minneapolis: Federal Reserve Board (www.minneapolisfed.org/publications_papers/studies/earlychild/abc-part2.pdf).

Roman, John. 2006. Notes prepared for testimony before the Connecticut Joint Committee on the Judiciary. Hartford, February 21.

Roper v. *Simmons.* 543 U.S. 551 (2005).

Rosenthal, Alan. 2004. *Heavy Lifting: The Job of the American Legislature.* Washington, D.C.: CQ Press.

Rothstein, Jesse. 2008. "Teacher Quality in Education Production: Tracking, Decay, and Student Achievement." Working Paper 14442. Cambridge, Mass.: National Bureau of Economic Research.

Rouse, Cecilia. 2005. "The Labor Market Consequences of an Inadequate Education." Paper prepared for symposium, Teachers' College, Columbia University, September.

Rubin, David, and others. 2010. "Variation in Pregnancy Outcomes Following Statewide Implementation of a Prenatal Home Visitation Program." *Archives of Pediatric and Adolescent Medicine,* November 1 (www.archpediatrics.com).

Rumberger, Russell. 2011. "Solving the Nation's Dropout Crisis." *Education Week,* October 26, pp. 28–24.

Saad, Lydia. 2007. "Black-White Educational Opportunities Widely Seen as Equal." *Gallup Monthly Reports,* July 2, pp. 1–3.

Sabatier, Paul, and Hank Jenkins-Smith. 1999. "The Advocacy Coalition Framework: An Assessment." In *Theories of the Policy Process,* edited by Paul Sabatier, pp. 117–66. Boulder, Colo.: Westview Press.

Samuels, Christina. 2011. "Cooling Signs in Wake Debate." *Education Week,* February 23, p 1.

Sandel, Michael. 2009. *Justice.* New York: Farrar, Strauss and Giroux.

Sardell, Alice. 1990. "Child Health Policy in the U.S.: The Paradox of Consensus." *Journal of Health Politics, Policy and Law* 15, no. 2: 271–304.

Saslaw, Richard. 2011. "Virginia Autism Reform." January 14 (www.dicksaslaw.com).

Schattschneider, E. E. 1960. *The Semi-Sovereign People.* New York: Holt, Rinehart, and Winston.

Schneider, Anne, and Helen Ingram. 1993. "Social Construction of Target Populations: Implications for Politics and Policy." *American Political Science Review* 87, no. 2: 334–47.

Schuldt, Jonathan, Sara Konrath, and Norbert Schwarz. 2011. "'Global Warming' or 'Climate Change'? Whether the Planet Is Warming Depends on Question Wording." *Public Opinion Quarterly* 75 (Spring): 115–24.

Schultz, Theodore. 1963. *The Economic Value of Education.* New York: Columbia University Press.

Schuman, Howard, Charlotte Steeh, and Lawrence Bobo. 1985. *Racial Attitudes in America: Trends and Interpretations.* Harvard University Press.

Schweinhart, Lawrence, and others. 2005. "Lifetime Effects: The High/Scope Perry Preschool Study through Age 40." Ypsilanti, Mich.: High/Scope Educational Research Foundation.

Sebelius, Kathleen. 2009. Testimony. Hearings on health reform in the twenty-first century before the House Committee on Energy and Commerce, June 24.

Secret, Mosi. 2011. "States Prosecute Fewer Teenagers in Adult Courts." *New York Times,* March 6, p. 1.

Serafini, Marilyn. 2011. "Rebranding 'Obamacare.'" *Kaiser Health News,* January 3 (www.kaiserhealthnews.org/Stories/2010/December/27/rebranding obamacare.aspx).

Shaddox, Colleen. 2008. "Juvenile Justice and the Theater of the Absurd." Santa Barbara: Miller-McCune Center for Research.

Shalala, Donna. 1993a. Testimony. Hearings on appropriations for fiscal year 1998 for Departments of Labor, Health, and Human Services and Education and Related Agencies before a subcommittee of the Senate Appropriations Committee, April 21, pp. 2–8.

———. 1993b. Testimony. Joint hearings on the health status of children before the Senate Labor and Human Resources Committee and the Subcommittee on Health and the Environment, House Energy and Commerce Committee, April 21, pp. 39–44.

Shor, Boris. 2008. "Stronger Bridges: Putting Congress and State Legislatures in Common Ideological Space." Working Paper 08.14. Harris School, University of Chicago.

Shor, Boris, and Nolan McCarty. 2010. "The Ideological Mapping of American Legislatures." Working paper. Harris School of Public Policy Studies, University of Chicago.

Shriver, R. Sargent. 1964. Testimony. Hearings on the Economic Opportunity Act of 1964 before the Subcommittee on the War on Poverty Program, House Education and Labor Committee, March 17, pp. 20–25.

Skocpol, Theda. 1992. *Protecting Soldiers and Mothers: The Political Origins of Social Policy in the United States.* Harvard University Press.

Smeeding, Timothy. 2004. "Public Policy and Economic Inequality: The United States in Comparative Perspective." Maxwell School, Syracuse University.

Smith, Daniel. 2004. "Peeling away the Populist Rhetoric: Toward a Taxonomy of Anti-Tax Ballot Initiatives." *Public Budgeting and Finance* 24, no. 4: 88–110.

Smith, James. 1991. *The Idea Brokers: Think Tanks and the Rise of the New Policy Elite.* New York: Free Press.

Smith, Mark. 2007. *The Right Talk: How Conservatives Transformed the Great Society into the Economic Society.* Princeton University Press.

Sniderman, Paul, and Sean Theriault. 2004. "The Structure of Political Argument and the Logic of Issue Framing." In *Studies in Public Opinion*, edited by William Saris and Paul Sniderman, pp. 133–65. Princeton University Press.

Sparks, Sarah. 2011. "New Measure Yields a Subtler Portrait of Child Poverty." *Education Week*, November 16, p. 10.

Spellings, Margaret. 2007. Press release. "U.S. Secretary of Education Margaret Spellings Delivers Remarks at the 2007 Special Olympics Global Policy Summit in Shanghai." U.S. Department of Education, October 3 (www2.ed./gov/news/presreleases/2007/10/10032007.html).

Springer, Matthew, and others. 2010. "Teacher Pay for Performance: Experimental Evidence from the Project on Incentives in Teaching." National Center on Performance Incentives, Vanderbilt University.

Stabenow, Deborah. 2007. Remarks. *Congressional Record*, August 1, pp. S10555–56.

Stagner, Matthew, and Jiffy Lansing. 2009. "Progress toward a Prevention Perspective." *Future of Children* 19 (Fall): 19–38.

Stanford v. *Kentucky*. 1989. 492 U.S. 361.

Stein, Rob. 2007. "Abstinence Programs Face Rejection." *Washington Post*, December 16, p. 3.

Steinberg, Lawrence, and Elizabeth Scott. 2003. "Less Guilty by Reason of Adolescence: Developmental Immaturity, Diminished Responsibility, and the Juvenile Death Penalty." *American Psychologist* 58: 1009–18.

Stepp, Laura. 2007. "Study Casts Doubt on Abstinence-Only Programs." *Washington Post*, April 14, p. 2.

Stimson, James. 2004. *Tides of Consent: How Public Opinion Shapes American Politics*. Cambridge University Press.

Stroud, Natalie Jomini. 2011. *Niche News: The Politics of News Choice*. Oxford University Press.

Sunstein, Cass. 2001. *Republic.com*. Princeton University Press.

Szabo, Liz. 2010. "More than 1 in 5 Kids Live in Poverty." *USA Today*, June 8.

Tanenbaum, Sandra. 1995. "Medicaid Eligibility Policy in the 1980s: Medical Utilitarianism and the Deserving Poor." *Journal of Health Politics, Policy and Law* 20, no. 4: 933–54.

Teferra, Ezana. 2012. Personal correspondence, January 18.

Theriault, Sean. 2008. *Party Polarization in Congress*. Cambridge University Press.

Tocqueville, Alexis de. 1945. *Democracy in America*. New York: Knopf.

Tomasky, Michael. 2011. "The Budget Battles on Which His Reelection Depends." *New York Review of Books*, May 26, pp. 12–14.

Turque, Bill. 2010. "Fenty Outlines Plans to Cut Special-Ed Costs and Return Students to Public Schools." *Washington Post*, July 2, p. B5.

Tversky, Amos, and Daniel Kahneman. 1981. "The Framings of Decisions and the Psychology of Choice." *Science* 211: 453–58.

"Two-Party System on the Ropes in Virginia Races." 2011. Editorial. *Washington Post*, October 25

Underhill, Kristen, Paul Montgomery, and Don Operario. 2007. "Sexual Abstinence Only Programmes to Prevent HIV Infection in High-Income Countries: Systematic Review." *British Medical Journal* 335 (August 4): 248.

UNICEF. 2007. "Child Poverty in Perspective: An Overview of Child Well-Being in Rich Countries." Florence, Italy: UNICEF, Innocenti Research Centre.

Urbina, Ian. 2009. "2 Years after 4 Deaths, D.C. Welfare System Remains under Scrutiny." *New York Times*, October 21, p. 22.

Ursitti, Judith. 2011. "Virginia's Miracle Season." May 11 (www.blog. autismspeaks.org).

U.S. Census Bureau. 2010. Statistical Abstract of the United States. "Public Elementary and Secondary Estimated Finances, 1980 to 2007, and by State, 2007."

———. 2011. "Poverty Status of People, by Age, Race, and Hispanic Origin: 1959 to 2010." *Historical Poverty Tables*, table 3.

———. 2012. Statistical Abstract of the United States. "State Rankings" (www. census.gov/compendia/statab/2012/ranks/rank03.html).

U.S. House of Representatives. 1995. Hearings on the Individuals with Disabilities Education Act before the Subcommittee on Early Childhood, Youth and Families, Committee on Economic and Educational Opportunities, June 20.

———. 2007. "Improving Head Start Act of 2007." *Congressional Record*, May 2.

Wagner, Mary, and Serena Clayton. 1999. "The Parents as Teachers Program: Results from Two Demonstrations." *Future of Children* 9, no. 1: 91–115.

Waldfogel, Jane. 1998. *The Future of Child Protection: How to Break the Cycle of Abuse and Neglect.* Harvard University Press.

———. 2010. *Britain's War on Poverty.* New York: Russell Sage.

Watson, Sara, and Robert Dugger. 2010. "Mobilizing Business Champions for Smart Investments in Young Children." In *Big Ideas: Game-Changers for Children*, pp. 131–41. Washington: First Focus.

Waxman, Henry. 1989. "Kids and Medicaid: Progress but Continuing Problems." *American Journal of Public Health* 79, no. 9: 1217–18.

———. 2008. Remarks. "Domestic Abstinence-Only Programs: Assessing the Evidence." Hearing, House Committee on Oversight and Government Reform, April 23.

Webb Yackee, Jason, and Susan Webb Yackee. 2006. "A Bias toward Business? Assessing Interest Group Influence on the Bureaucracy." *Journal of Politics* 68: 128–39.

Wedeking, Justin. 2010. "Supreme Court Litigants and Strategic Framing." *American Journal of Political Science* 54 (July): 617–31.

Weill, Jim. 2011. "Memo to Members of Congress." June 3. Washington: Food Research and Action Center.

Wilcox, W. Clyde. 1992. *God's Warriors: The Christian Right in Twentieth-Century America.* Johns Hopkins University Press.

Williams, Juliet. 2011. "As in Washington, States Face Deep Partisan Rifts." *Washington Post,* August 8, p. 13.

Wirtz, Willard. 1964. Testimony. Hearing on the Economic Opportunity Act of 1964 before the Subcommittee on the War on Poverty Program, House Committee on Education and Labor, March 19, pp. 184–88.

Witte, John. 2001. *The Market Approach to Education: An Analysis of America's First Voucher Program.* Princeton University Press.

Wolf, Richard. 2007. "Poll: Mixed Feelings on Children's Health Insurance." *USA Today,* October 15 (www.usatoday.com/news/washington/2007-10-15-poll-schip_N.htm).

Zigler, Edward, and Susan Muenchow. 1992. *Head Start: The Inside Story of America's Most Successful Educational Experiment.* New York: Basic Books.

Index